Farmingdale State College

CAYUGA COMMUNITY COLLEGE

S·C·H·E·N·E·C·T·A·D·Y COUNTY COMMUNITY COLLEGE S·U·N·Y

JCC JAMESTOWN COMMUNITY COLLEGE S U N Y

RCC Rockland Community College
STATE UNIVERSITY OF NEW YORK

STATE UNIVERSITY OF NEW YORK JEFFERSON

The College at BROCKPORT STATE UNIVERSITY OF NEW YORK

FIT Fashion Institute of Technology State University of New York

UPSTATE MEDICAL UNIVERSITY

GENESEO

EMPIRE STATE COLLEGE
STATE UNIVERSITY OF NEW YORK

MVCC MOHAWK VALLEY COMMUNITY COLLEGE

ESF
State University of New York College of Environmental Science and Forestry

SUNY DOWNSTATE Medical Center

HERKIMER COUNTY COMMUNITY COLLEGE

FM Fulton-Montgomery Community College

DUTCHESS COMMUNITY COLLEGE

UB University at Buffalo The State University of New York

SUNY Cobleskill

SUNY Ulster Start Here. Go Far.

COLUMBIA GREENE COMMUNITY COLLEGE

SUNY GCC Genesee Community College

NORTH COUNTRY

Purchase College
STATE UNIVERSITY OF NEW YORK

FingerLakes COMMUNITY COLLEGE

MORRISVILLE STATE COLLEGE

Alfred University

Westchester Community College
State University of New York

THE COLLEGE AT OLD WESTBURY STATE UNIVERSITY OF NEW YORK

OSWEGO STATE UNIVERSITY OF NEW YORK

For my brother
dearest brother
and his family!
Julie, Nathaniel &
Seth

With love
Ken

SIXTY-FOUR CAMPUSES— ONE UNIVERSITY

THE STORY OF
SUNY

Long Island

Farmingdale State College

Nassau County Community College

State University College at Old Westbury

Stony Brook University

Suffolk County Community College

New York City

Downstate Medical Center

Fashion Institute of Technology

Maritime College

College of Optometry

Mid-Hudson

Dutchess Community College

State University College at New Paltz

Orange County Community College

State University College at Purchase

Rockland Community College

Sullivan County Community College

Ulster County Community College

Westchester Community College

Capital Region

Adirondack Community College

University at Albany

Columbia-Greene Community College

Empire State College

Hudson Valley Community College

SUNY Polytechnic Institute

Schenectady County Community College

SUNY The State University of **New York**

North Country

College of Technology at Canton

Clinton Community College

Jefferson Community College

North Country Community College

State University College at Plattsburgh

State University College at Potsdam

Mohawk Valley

College of Agriculture and Technology at Cobleskill

Fulton-Montgomery Community College

Herkimer County Community College

Mohawk Valley Community College

Morrisville State College

State University College at Oneonta

Central New York

Cayuga Community College

State University College at Cortland

College of Environmental Science and Forestry

Onondaga Community College

State University College at Oswego

Tompkins Cortland Community College

State University of New York Health Science Center at Syracuse

Finger Lakes and Genesee Valley

State University College at Brockport

Finger Lakes Community College

Genesee Community College

State University College at Geneseo

Monroe Community College

Southern Tier

Binghamton University

Broome Community College

New York State College of Agriculture and Life Sciences at Cornell University

New York State College of Human Ecology at Cornell

New York State School of Industrial and Labor Relations at Cornell

New York State College of Veterinary Medicine at Cornell University

Corning Community College

College of Technology at Delhi

Western New York

New York State College of Ceramics at Alfred

Alfred State College

State University College at Buffalo

University at Buffalo

Erie Community College

State University College at Fredonia

Jamestown Community College

Niagara County Community College

SIXTY-FOUR CAMPUSES— ONE UNIVERSITY

THE STORY OF

SUNY

W. BRUCE LESLIE AND KENNETH P. O'BRIEN

with Kimberly Schutte

Foreword by Nancy L. Zimpher

State University of New York Press

Published by

STATE UNIVERSITY OF NEW YORK PRESS, ALBANY

© 2016 State University of New York

All rights reserved

Printed in the United States of America

For information, contact
State University of New York Press, Albany, NY
www.sunypress.edu

Title: Sixty-four campuses—one university : the story of SUNY
Library of Congress Control Number: 2016957638
ISBN 9781438461731 (hardcover : alk. paper)

10 9 8 7 6 5 4 3 2 1

CONTENTS

vii   Foreword, Chancellor Nancy L. Zimpher

1   Introduction

9   Long Island

33   New York City

53   Mid-Hudson

89   Capital Region

121   North Country

149   Mohawk Valley

177   Central New York

209   Genesee Valley

233   Southern Tier

257   Western New York

293   Concluding Thoughts

299   Acknowledgments

FOREWORD

Nancy L. Zimpher, Chancellor

New York is on the verge of a historic new standard. For the first time, by 2020, a full seventy percent of jobs in the Empire State will require a college degree.

Such has the world changed in less than a half century. In 1970 about three-quarters of middle-class workers in the United States had no education beyond high school. Simply put, most people didn't go to college because they didn't need to. Most jobs—in manufacturing, service, agriculture—didn't require a college degree, and the skills needed to earn a living could be learned on the job. But increasingly, lower- and even some middle-skilled jobs have been shipped overseas or are being replaced by advanced mechanization, by computers, by artificial intelligence. And the bulk of "new jobs"—those of the twenty-first-century knowledge economy—require education beyond high school.

In 2016, at the time of this writing and as we fast approach that seventy-percent need, only forty-seven percent of adult New Yorkers have a college degree or credential. So there's a gap—and we need to fill it. And the State University of New York has taken up that challenge.

It only makes sense. When SUNY was founded in 1948, its mission—its commitment to quality, to inclusiveness, to expansiveness, to diversity—was made clear and expressed in state education law. The SUNY system would

> provide to the people of New York educational services of the highest quality, with the broadest possible access, fully representative of all segments of the population in a complete range of academic, professional, and vocational postsecondary programs. . . . offered through a geographically distributed comprehensive system of diverse campuses . . . to meet the needs of both traditional and non-traditional students and to address local, regional and state needs and goals.

Though times have changed, and though workforce and education needs have changed, these words hold fast as SUNY's guide more than sixty years after our system's founding.

Since I came to SUNY in 2009 as its twelfth chancellor, we have done a few things we had not done before. You could say we've cultivated a holistic view of our system, and this has changed not only how we work but also how we see ourselves, and our responsibility to the state, as an institution. Considering the individuality and independence of our campuses, I quickly became convinced that we had a capability, a power, beyond that which even the largest, or most competitive, or hardest working of our individual campuses could exercise on their own, if we could only come to see ourselves as a whole that is greater, stronger, and smarter than the sum of its many parts.

As I've said so many times before, to look at a map of New York State is to look at a map of SUNY. We are everywhere, in every region. In many communities, a SUNY campus is the largest employer. No New Yorker is further than thirty miles from a SUNY campus, and our online learning consortium, Open SUNY, is now the largest in the world. All this is to say that we have tremendous reach, and since 2009 we have been exercising that reach like never before, in the most concerted way, to tear down any barriers to educational access and completion—to the gateways to success—that any New Yorker might encounter.

Contained in the pages to come are chapters that each, in its turn, tells the story of a SUNY institution—how it came to be, how it serves a region, how it makes good on SUNY's core mission and on our newest commitment to close the achievement gap.

I would be remiss, considering the historical nature of this book, if I did not mention that our System Administration headquarters in Albany is now in the midst of celebrating its centennial. Built between 1914 and 1918, the building—locally known as "the castle"—was designed by architect Marcus T. Reynolds and was built to house the headquarters of the Delaware and Hudson Railroad and a local newspaper, the *Albany Evening Journal*. SUNY took over the space in the early 1970s, renovated it, and consolidated its System Administration offices there in 1978. Since that time, the university has been the steward of this landmark building, which strikes a commanding presence on the west bank of the Hudson River in historic downtown Albany.

In addition to SUNY Plaza, the SUNY Research Foundation, SUNY Press, and the SUNY-run Small Business Development Council are headquartered in downtown Albany. SUNY also has an office in New York City—SUNY Global—which is housed in a 1927 Georgian-style building originally constructed as a private residence.

The publication of this book is timely. It captures the moments, the right now, of the State University of New York's sixty-four campuses at a pivotal time in the university's history, a critical time in higher education, and at a complex time in American, and even human, history. Arguably, changes to the way we live our lives have been more profound and sweeping over the last few decades than they have been in the whole of human history. The continuum of education—from early childhood through high school and into college and a career—is longer, more necessary, and costlier than ever before, and some might say there is more at stake than ever before as global boundaries are subsumed by technology and cultures and ideologies clash and mingle.

As the largest comprehensive public university system in the nation, SUNY sees it as its responsibility not only to New York but to the nation and the world to prepare students to succeed in work and life today and for generations to come. We are plugged into the world like never before—flexible, focused, with an eye toward continuous improvement, and fully committed to meet any changes and challenges that come our way, forever guided by our mission and in service to the people of New York.

SUNY System Administration, Albany, 2016.

INTRODUCTION

The Unlikely Tale of an Educational Giant

On April 3, 1948, Governor Thomas E. Dewey interrupted his Wisconsin presidential primary campaign to fly back to Albany. On the election path leading ultimately to his famous upset by Harry S. Truman and despite trailing Republican rival Senator Robert Taft, Dewey returned to New York's capital to sign legislation destined to transform the state's public higher education. The next day, with a stroke of his pen, Dewey created the State University of New York (SUNY), incorporating thirty-two state-supported institutions of higher education outside New York City and envisaging future medical schools and community colleges.

Who could have imagined that this fledgling university of 32,000 students and 2,500 faculty was destined to become the nation's largest comprehensive system of higher education? But over the following nearly seven decades, New Yorkers

have made an extraordinary investment in the future. With sixty-four campuses, nearly half a million students, and over three million alumni, SUNY demonstrates an enduring commitment to New York State's youth and to the state's and the nation's future.

SUNY campuses span New York State from eastern Long Island into Manhattan, up the Hudson Valley into the Adirondack Mountains to the Canadian border, along the St. Lawrence River to the Great Lakes and Niagara Falls, and along the Southern Tier and back to the Catskills. As America's largest comprehensive university system, SUNY incorporates community colleges, colleges of technology, university colleges, research universities, medical schools, health science centers, and specialized campuses in fields as diverse as optometry, ceramics, horticulture, fashion, forestry, and maritime training.

In the twenty-first century, higher education auto-

New York State Capitol, Albany.

matically commands attention. If nations once judged their strength in terms of battleships, and then bombers, and later missiles, today they place their higher education systems' reputations among their highest national priorities, seen as inextricably connected to economic progress, quality of life, and national prestige. And SUNY, along with other American state systems, is expected to play a central role in the world's leading system of higher education. But it wasn't always so. Public higher education in New York had long been only a minor part of legislative debate and budgetary provision. Powerful forces opposed its expansion; the mere act of creating SUNY was highly controversial.

SUNY's story is inextricably tied to the dramatic expansion of public higher education, one of post–WWII America's most striking developments. New York came late to the party. By the end of World War II, only New York State lacked either a state university or a system of public higher education. New York's tardiness was ironic, as all of its educational institutions are overseen by the oldest educational umbrella organization in the country and possibly the world, the University of the State of New York, better known as the "Board of Regents." Founded in 1784 to administer Kings College (quickly renamed the more patriotic "Columbia"), the Board of Regents often made New York a national leader in elementary and secondary public education. Its record in public higher education, however, was unimpressive. The Regents championed New York's notable array of private colleges and universities while dampening discussions of public higher education. New York City created public colleges, most notably founding the City College of New York in 1847. But

When President Roosevelt signed the GI bill, it transformed American higher education.

the only publicly supported "upstate" institutions of higher education were small "normal schools" and agricultural and technical institutes with enrollments rarely exceeding one thousand. On the eve of the attack on Pearl Harbor, the normal schools were upgraded to baccalaureate degree–granting state teachers' colleges. But the Regents' 1944 postwar plan proposed only very modest expansion.

Before World War II, the Regents deflected concerns that private institutions could not satisfy New Yorkers' rising demand for postsecondary education. They successfully opposed a proposal at the 1938 Constitutional Convention that could have led to a public university. The same year, the board closed three Depression-inspired Emergency Collegiate Centers, rejecting pleas to turn them into publicly supported junior colleges. Also in 1938, a Regents-sponsored inquiry into New York's higher education future concluded that all additional resources should go into existing institutions and that there was no need to create state-supported junior colleges or a state university.

But World War II and the veterans' unexpected enthusiasm for the GI Bill's higher education benefits revived the specter of a state system. In order to head that off, the private colleges, with the support of the Board of Regents, created temporary state-aided institutions that were designed to close after the flood of veterans ebbed. As Syracuse University's chancellor William P. Tolley frankly warned Commissioner of Education George D. Stoddard, "We ought to guard against the danger of temporary agencies becoming permanent institutions. We do not want an embryo of a state university . . . which would be difficult to liquidate."

Tolley's fears might not have become reality had several forces in postwar New York not intersected with the veterans' return. Worries about the postwar economy, Dewey's national ambitions, and New York's intense ethno-religious political tensions combined with the returning GIs' unpredicted desire for postsecondary education to frame the debates that shaped the founding of the State University of New York.

The revelations of the Holocaust made discrimination, particularly anti-Semitism, a burning issue, especially in New York. Studies documenting religious discrimination in New York's elite private colleges and universities, especially the professional schools, set off a political firestorm and touched Governor Dewey's commitment to civil rights. Meanwhile, as he contemplated another presidential run, Dewey needed an achievement to match the ambitious proposals of President Truman's Commission on Higher Education.

In 1946, the New York State Legislature approved Governor Dewey's request to create the Temporary Commission on the Need for a State University. Although chaired by Owen D. Young, founder of Radio Corporation of America (RCA) and *Time* magazine's "Man of the Year" in 1929, the commission progressed slowly and the proceedings were contentious. Finally, in January 1948, the commission issued its report, which recommended placing all state-supported institutions under a new umbrella, a state university. In addition, it proposed community colleges, two medical schools, and new colleges in underserved areas of the state.

But the plans to reform the Empire State's postsecondary education aroused vigorous opposition from powerful players on the New York political scene. The Board of Regents opposed Dewey's proposals for SUNY on the grounds that it would create unwelcome competition for New York's 138 private colleges. The Regents were particularly upset that SUNY would be autonomous, beyond the board's control on most matters. And the Catholic Church fought especially hard to protect its colleges. Finally, after bitter conflicts and painful compromises, the legislation passed and Dewey's signature launched SUNY.

After the high drama surrounding SUNY's birth, its first decade was surprisingly quiet. The compromises necessary to get legislative approval inevitably restricted the infant enterprise. The obstacles thrown into its path are even reflected in an anomaly

SUNY's first President and thirty-two campus leaders finally get to know each other in April 1949.

in SUNY's seal. The "1948" inscription hides the reality that the legislation Dewey signed contained a poison pill that prohibited the system from operating for a year. Therein lies a telling tale. Over the next year, opponents tried to stuff the genie back in the bottle by giving the unfriendly Regents control of SUNY. The Regents-backed Condon-Barrett bill was finally defeated in March 1949 after another bitter legislative fight. On April 5, 1949, SUNY's first president, Alvin Eurich (1948–1952), could summon the leaders of New York's thirty-two state-operated campuses to Albany. A system was born.

The new system was modest, enrolling a mere thirty-two thousand students in its first year, an average of only one thousand per campus. Eleven state teachers' colleges and six agricultural and technical institutes formed the core. Six colleges were administered under state contract by three private universities, Alfred, Cornell, and Syracuse. One, the Maritime Academy, was on Federal land. The five Institutes of Applied Arts and Sciences (in Binghamton, Buffalo, Brooklyn, Utica, and White Plains) had been hastily created after the war as temporary institutions and were only authorized for five years. All five occupied rented quarters and faced uncertain futures. Champlain College, Sampson College, and Middletown College, the three "GI colleges," were slated for eventual closure. So it looked as though SUNY might lose one-quarter of its original institutions when postwar enrollment pressures abated, although the proposed community colleges and medical schools offered hopes of expansion.

The guiding principle was that SUNY would only "supplement" the private colleges and universities. Dewey's primary motivation to create SUNY had been his concern over the record of religious and racial discrimination, especially in private medi-

The Founder and the Builder

cal programs. Beyond that, however, his vision for SUNY was limited. When SUNY sought to mark its entry onto the higher education stage with an elaborate academic symposium in 1950 on the "Functions of a Modern University," naturally Dewey was the featured speaker. But his message was clear: "The State University shall work in cooperation with our priceless private colleges and universities. There must be no competition between them. They must supplement each other with neither weakening the other." He further dampened educational ambitions with his claim that machinists and taxi drivers earned more than lawyers. "To regard a college degree as a guaranteed ticket to security in earnings, is an illusion which I think all of us should join together in shattering."

The compromises accepted in order to secure passage of the legislation creating SUNY in 1948, and then to defeat the Condon-Barrett bill in 1949, also constrained SUNY. Opponents of SUNY's independence from the Regents prevented the creation of a permanent Board of Trustees until 1954, still hoping to bring SUNY under the Board of Regents' control. Informal bans on teaching liberal arts and on training secondary teachers in academic subjects (except at Albany), on engineering programs (except at the Maritime Academy), and on raising private funds had been exacted. In addition, doctoral programs and scholarly research were prohibited, reserved for the private sector.

SUNY's second president, William S. Carlson (1952–1958), chafed at these limitations and campaigned to create a flagship university. He covertly commissioned the "Blegen Report," which opened with the observation that the "State University is an academic animal without a head" and predictably called for a flagship. Public disclosure of the report incurred the wrath of Frank C. Moore, chairman of the

SUNY Board of Trustees, and of Governor W. Averell Harriman. Carlson was summarily dismissed.

SUNY seemed destined to remain a modest collection of institutions with limited missions leaving most areas of higher education to private institutions. But then the stars aligned for SUNY with *Sputnik*'s launch (and the moral panic that followed), Nelson A. Rockefeller's election as governor, the approaching waves of baby boomers, and the lapse of the curricular bans combined to liberate SUNY from the mandate to "only supplement the private colleges."

Rockefeller promptly appointed the blue-ribbon Heald Commission to draw up a blueprint for expansion. Its 1960 "Report on Meeting the Increasing Demand for Higher Education in New York State" and the resulting 1961 Master Plan outlined a very different kind of university. Former state teachers' colleges would become liberal arts colleges, community colleges would rapidly expand, and students would bear some of the burden by beginning to pay tuition. Most dramatically, SUNY faculty would now participate in scholarly research, not centered in Blegen's single flagship but led by four university centers offering doctoral programs, spread across the state in Albany, Binghamton, Buffalo, and Stony Brook. Finally, SUNY would become fully independent, freed from the restrictions of the earlier compromises and from the Regents' interference.

Carlson's successor, Thomas Hamilton (1959–1962), did not fit the go-go Rockefeller mold and left for the more relaxed demands of the University of Hawai'i. The following nearly two-year interregnum

Ground was being broken all over New York State in the Rockefeller years.

permitted unique gubernatorial influence. Rockefeller was passionately committed to making SUNY a distinguished university, and he threw his legendary energy and influence into procuring the funding to make it so. In particular, he created the Construction Fund to make an end run around the existing roadblocks and fund dramatic expansion. Across New York State, new campuses were created and existing ones looked as though giant moles had attacked. Incredibly, SUNY's enrollment, which began the 1960s at about 65,000, leapt to over 150,000 by 1964 and more than doubled again to over 320,000 at the end of the decade.

And Rockefeller found his chancellor. Samuel B. Gould (1964–1970) had been chancellor of the Santa Barbara campus in the University of California system. California had become the gold standard in public higher education as it implemented its widely admired 1960 Master Plan, authored by University of California president Clark Kerr. Upon Gould's arrival in Albany, he immediately rewrote SUNY's pending 1964 Master Plan, proposing to dramatically expand its mission as well as its student enrollments, faculties, and facilities. The dynamic Rockefeller-Gould partnership launched SUNY into what many remember as a "golden age."

As baby boomers swelled enrollment and public and private support for research grew, SUNY rapidly expanded. In addition to developing the four research centers and diversifying the missions of the former teachers' colleges and "ag and techs," SUNY created several new four-year colleges, while its community colleges ballooned and intercampus programs were launched. Gould's picture on the cover of the January 12, 1968, *Time* magazine accompanied by a laudatory story on SUNY confirmed the transformation and recognized SUNY's growing national reputation.

Almost as quickly as the "golden years" began, however, they ended. Ironically, some of the beneficiaries of the growth helped end it. The combination of many students adopting leftist politics or embracing countercultural lifestyles, "Black Power" supplanting the civil rights movement, and protests against the Vietnam War ended business as usual on campuses. Across SUNY, and across the country, massive protests and campus closures followed the shooting of Kent State students in the spring of 1970. Chancellor Gould resigned for his health. Although calm slowly returned to campus life, much of the public and many in the legislature resented students' seeming ingratitude. Finally, a disenchanted Governor Rockefeller resigned in 1973.

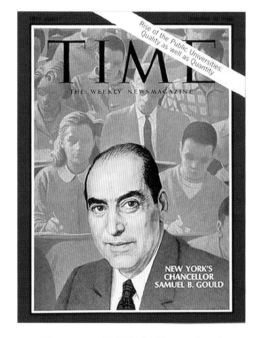

Time honors SUNY's "golden age" and Rockefeller's favorite Chancellor, Samuel Gould.

Gould's talented successor, Ernest L. Boyer (1970–1977), grasped what proved to be a poisoned chalice. A decline in public, gubernatorial, and legislative support, as well as a state and regional economy spiraling downward, destroyed both budgets and hopes. New York City nearly went bankrupt, "Rockefeller Republicans" were discredited, and New York's image as a Rust Belt state seemingly condemned it to permanent decline. As Governor Hugh Carey (1975–1983) famously pronounced, "The days of wine and roses are over." Soon the scary term "retrenchment" entered the SUNY lexicon. Chancellor Boyer was no doubt relieved when President Jimmy Carter invited him to become commissioner of education in 1977.

Even without wine and roses, SUNY remained a prodigious educational engine of approximately one-third of a million students on sixty-four campuses that had awarded 650,000 degrees by Boyer's departure. But, the mood was anything but expansive. The number of students plateaued as the baby boomers graduated and the proportion of youth entering higher education temporarily dipped. Higher education and the nation's youth, the darlings of the postwar era, no longer commanded ever-increasing financial support.

Not surprisingly, SUNY's priorities shifted from growth to efficiently managing existing or even shrinking resources. Boyer's successor, Clifton R. Wharton, Jr. (1978–1987), brought stability during the longest chancellorship in SUNY's history. *The Challenge and the Choice*, a report commissioned by Wharton, became a blueprint for reducing bureaucratic inefficiency, and when adopted it freed campuses from many of the central administration's restrictive budgetary rules. Under his successor, D. Bruce Johnstone (1988–1994), budgets began to recover and relative tranquility returned.

But Johnstone's resignation due to illness along with the defeat of Governor Mario Cuomo (1983–1994) tossed SUNY into controversy once again. Governor George Pataki (1995–2007) appointed new members to the Board of Trustees who believed SUNY needed major reform to make it both more efficient and educationally effective. The board's 1995 report, "Rethinking SUNY," recommended cost efficiencies, even cuts. Some vocal trustees publicly criticized SUNY. The Board of Trustees later imposed a systemwide General Education curriculum that sparked heated debate on SUNY campuses over this unprecedented intrusion into what had

Governor Hugh L. Carey and and SUNY Chancellor Clifton R. Wharton, Jr. at the dedication of the SUNY Plaza in 1978. Clifton Wharton guided SUNY after the days of wine and roses.

previously been a faculty domain. The sense of a system at war with itself undercut legislative support and lowered morale across campuses.

The problems were compounded by a lack of stable leadership. Seven individuals led SUNY on permanent or temporary bases in the fifteen years preceding the appointment of Nancy L. Zimpher as chancellor in June 2009. Although her tenure began in the midst of the most severe financial crisis since the Great Depression of the 1930s, SUNY has weath-

ered the storm remarkably well and has regained its position as a national leader.

The preceding Albany-centric discussion is intended to contextualize the central focus of this book, the important historical sketches of SUNY's sixty-four campuses. Their collective achievements can easily elude our grasp. Through periods of feast and famine, SUNY's campuses have awarded over three million degrees, trained a highly skilled workforce, raised our quality of life, and educated a more informed citizenry for New York State and beyond.

SUNY institutions are bound together in a system while at the same time being intricately tied to their local environments and regions. They occupy a physical world and have developed specific built environments within their own historical and ecological realities. They are shaped by the economy, geography, and society in which they are placed. And in turn, SUNY's institutions play an increasing role in shaping the world around them. In recognition of this interaction of the parts and the whole,

and of SUNY's critical role in shaping New York State's future, the book is organized by region—or, more formally, into the state's ten Regional Economic Development Council regions.

As we look back across nearly seven decades, we can see that some of SUNY's characteristics were imprinted at birth. But in other ways the founders would have trouble recognizing their creation in its maturity. This pictorial history of SUNY depicts the many parts that yield a greater whole. And it is a story that should give New Yorkers great satisfaction in our collective accomplishment.

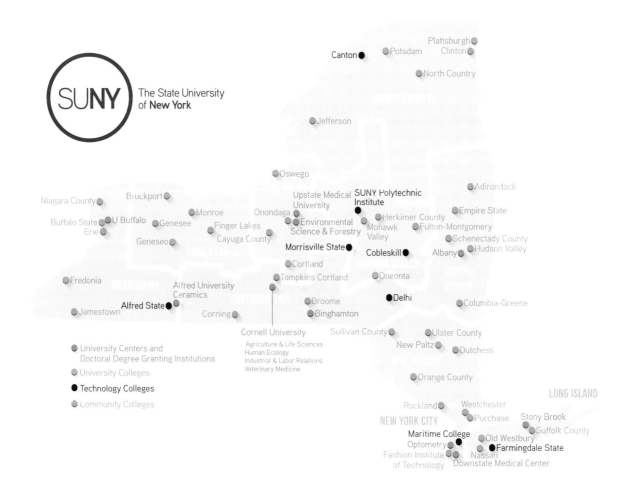

New York State's Economic Development Council Regions.

LONG ISLAND

Farmingdale State College

Nassau Community College

State University College at Old Westbury

Stony Brook University

Suffolk County Community College

Long Island, a twenty-mile-wide sand spit stretching from New York harbor to Montauk Point, 118 miles to the east, is the largest and most heavily populated island of the continental United States. It has long been a place of imagined opportunity, and it is fitting that F. Scott Fitzgerald located his fictional protagonist, Jay Gatsby, that most opportunistic of literary characters, in the town of West Egg on "the Island." Like the 1920s Long Island portrayed in *The Great Gatsby*, Long Island today remains a study in contrasts. Whereas Brooklyn, Queens, and Nassau counties have emerged as leading centers of technology, further east, Suffolk County retains its agricultural heritage with vineyards that stretch toward the ocean. The island of stark contrasts is home to those grand mansions along its south shore in the Hamptons, classic suburbs like Levittown, and areas nearby in genuine economic distress.

Prior to European settlement, Long Island was home to several Native American groups, and it remained so well into the twentieth century. The Dutch first settled the western side of the island but lost control to the British in 1664. A century later, the British forces held the island after the defeat of revolutionary forces at the Battle of Brooklyn Heights during the American Revolution. Through the nineteenth century, Long Island remained largely rural, but after regular ferry service and then the Brooklyn Bridge connected it to Manhattan and the rest of New York City, the western region developed an increasingly suburban character.

Improved transportation prompted population growth and the development of Long Island as an accessible holiday destination, with summer homes of New York's elite families dotting its shores. In the twentieth century further transportation improvements, many the creation of Robert Moses, allowed more workers from the city to make their homes on western Long Island, creating ethnic enclaves, especially those of Italian Americans, Jewish Americans, and Irish Americans.

In the first half of the twentieth century, Long Island emerged as a center for the burgeoning aviation industry. Charles Lindbergh took off on his historic trans-Atlantic flight from Roosevelt Field near Mineola. Important aerospace companies were locating on the island, and the first commercial airfield, Floyd Bennett Field, was located in Brooklyn near Rockaway. Today, New York City's two primary airports, LaGuardia and JFK, are on Long Island.

World War II disrupted the pattern of slow and steady growth, as war industries, especially aircraft industries, built huge factories on the island that employed tens of thousands of workers. At their peak in 1943, Grumman and Republic Aircraft, two major aircraft producers, employed almost fifty thousand workers between them. After a brief postwar slump, the Long Island aerospace industry survived, even prospered, during the Cold War. Grumman, for example, built thirteen lunar landing modules for NASA's space program, and it still employed twenty-three thousand workers as late as 1986 before it was bought out and manufacturing moved elsewhere.

Population growth accelerated following the end of the Second World War; the island's population doubled between 1940 and 1960, putting pressure on all public services, especially affordable housing

Early Grumman aircraft.

and schools. A Long Island firm, Levitt & Sons, that had built homes for the upper middle class before the war, provided one answer to the housing shortage by applying modern mass production techniques to housing construction. With the economies offered by these techniques, Levitt offered veterans and their families thousands of small, inexpensive homes, first as rentals in 1947, and then for sale. Financed by FHA and Veterans Administration loans, "Levittown" grew beyond town and village lines, becoming the prototype of the mass suburban development of the period. For many hundreds of thousands of New Yorkers, this was the beginning of life on the highways and rail lines that knit these residential communities to their distant working sites, all made possible through funding and legal arrangements provided by federal, state, and local governments.

To secure the future, Long Island's leaders understood the importance of providing educational opportunities for the young, especially affordable public higher education. The creation and maintenance of an educated and skilled workforce has been and remains a challenge for the region as it moves from the agricultural/industrial economy of mid-century to a high-tech service future. To help provide the intellectual and human capital needed for the modern economy, Long Island's five SUNY schools have grown dramatically in both size and importance.

When SUNY was created in 1948, it only included one campus on the island, originally called the New York State School of Agriculture on Long Island when chartered in 1912. Today's Farmingdale State College has moved far beyond its rural roots, offering a number of bachelor's degrees in technical and technological fields, including one in Aviation, leading to a professional pilot's license, and another in Aviation Administration.

Two of the SUNY schools on Long Island have strong ties to the same Gold Coast mansion, Planting Fields at Oyster Bay. Stony Brook University and the State University College at Old Westbury were both housed there for a time. William Robertson Coe was an insurance and railroad executive married to Mary, the daughter of Henry H. Rogers, who made his fortune in Standard Oil. The name Planting Fields came from the Matinecock Indians who cultivated the area. After Stony Brook moved in 1962 to its current location, the space provided a temporary home for Old Westbury when it began in 1965.

"Planting Fields" William Robertson Coe house, Oyster Bay, 1926, view to Blue Pool Garden and tea house by Frances Benjamin Johnston, 1864-1952, hand-colored glass lantern slide.

Stony Brook University opened in 1957 with a special mission: to develop programs in the sciences, mathematics, and engineering. It has evolved into one of the larger and more important public universities in the East. Reflecting its original role, Stony Brook maintains its excellence at every degree level in the natural, physical, and medical sciences, which is symbolized by its association with the Brookhaven National Laboratory. Old Westbury, on the other hand, has remained small, serving as a symbolic bridge between New York City and Long Island, providing programs that have been characterized by "community engagement and global citizenship."

Nassau Community College and Suffolk County Community College were founded in 1959 in order to provide affordable education to the population of Long Island, one in the western, the other in the eastern half of the island. These large, geographically dispersed and populous counties are served by very large community colleges. Nassau, for example, awards more associate degrees than does any other campus in the state of New York and the third largest number among American public colleges. Suffolk County, housed originally in a former tuberculosis sanatorium, is the largest community college in the SUNY system with over twenty-six thousand students and offers the lowest tuition on Long Island at its three campuses.

Exacerbated by the economic collapse of 2008, which devastated the financial sector, and by Hurricane Sandy, which wrought physical havoc, deep pockets of poverty remain across Long Island. Many workers are not equipped to participate meaningfully in the economy of the twenty-first century, while many of those who have needed skills choose to leave the region. Long Island's leadership—economic, political, social, and academic—is working to remedy that, and SUNY universities and colleges are playing critical roles in this effort. Long Island is a place where the past and the future come together to create vibrant communities. Fitzgerald's characters saw Long Island as a path to the good life in the early twentieth century, and the educators and community leaders of the region in the twenty-first century are hard at work to recreate that sense of possibility.

Throgs Neck Bridge, Long Island in background, 1991.

FARMINGDALE STATE COLLEGE

SUNY's oldest institution on Long Island, Farmingdale State College rose out of Long Island's farming heritage. While some hints of that origin remain, over its first century Farmingdale has evolved dramatically, reflecting the transformation of Long Island's economy and society.

Owing its creation to the spirit of the "Back to the Soil" and the "Country Life" movements, Farmingdale has roots extending back to April 1912 when the New York State School of Agriculture on Long Island received its charter. Local business leaders and political figures lobbied the state to create an agricultural school on Long Island to complement and compete with the state's four upstate "ag" schools. Despite their opposition, the New York State Legislature chartered Farmingdale and appropriated start-up funding. The college drew up plans to provide students from Long Island, New York City, and the surrounding counties with cutting-edge agricultural education and to preserve a lifestyle that seemed to be fading away.

Construction soon began on classrooms, a dormitory, and water and power systems on land the state purchased near the Nassau-Suffolk border in the heart of Long Island. The founders proposed a course of study that emphasized fieldwork, a practical approach that was to be supplemented by classroom instruction in the theory of agriculture and its underlying sciences. This curriculum was designed to give students a thorough grounding in both the practical and scientific aspects of farming. In addition to the agriculture courses, students would study mathematics, citizenship, English, and economics. The practical emphasis pleased *The Long Islander*, which noted in 1914, with the typical

Agriculture remained the core mission until World War II. When these students brought in the milk, the surrounding area was still largely rural.

populist ambivalence about applying higher learning to agriculture, that Farmingdale "is going to be the real thing. It won't be an emporium for the distribution of fancy initials for the attachment to the end of somebody's name. It will be a practical, vitally necessary institution for the turning out of competent, capable, self-supporting, outdoor men and women."

Students practice on an inanimate "patient" before they provide care to the community through the Dental Hygiene Care Center.

In March 1916, the first sixty male students began their studies, and women joined them that summer. By the time of American involvement in World War I, 170 acres were under cultivation, and the students were managing hogs and cows and other barnyard animals. Observing from nearby Oyster Bay, Theodore Roosevelt gushed that Farmingdale stood out among agriculture schools "because it not only teaches farming, but to an extent equaled nowhere else, it creates farmers."

Between the wars enrollment grew to nearly five hundred students and the campus matured. Sedate Georgian horticulture and agronomy buildings graced the campus as well as a poultry plant, greenhouses, and barns. Students pursued specialties in horticulture, poultry husbandry, animal husbandry, and dairy farming. And Country Life programs promoted the school's work and the lifestyle the school embodied. Products such as Farmingdale grass seed demonstrated the benefits of scientific agriculture.

The post-WWII years brought dramatic changes to Long Island's economy and to Farmingdale's mission as the curriculum began shifting. In 1946 dental hygiene entered the curriculum and has remained a favorite. Technical programs soon followed. Thus Farmingdale joined the SUNY system in 1953 as the SUNY Long Island Agricultural and Technical Institute. Continuing name changes reflected the growing emphasis on technological education. In 1966 it became the Agricultural and Technical College at Farmingdale; two decades later it was renamed the SUNY College of Technology at Farmingdale; and since 2006, simply, Farmingdale State College. Reflecting the dense suburban developments and high-tech industries now surrounding Farmingdale, most of the agricultural program was phased out in the 1980s. Only the Urban Horticultural and Design program echoes the agricultural curricular heritage.

Today, the college strongly emphasizes technology in its academic programs. Most notably, as the largest college of technology in the SUNY system, Farmingdale has blazed a trail as a pioneer in the field of renewable energy. The Solar Energy Center was the fourth to be accredited in the nation and the first in the Northeast. The Renewable Energy & Sustainability Center focuses on applied research and workforce training in order to enhance public awareness of renewable energy resources.

Farmingdale's students can literally soar. At the Aviation Center at nearby Republic Airport, Farmingdale's pioneering Aviation Department offers BS degrees in Aeronautical Science with either a Professional Pilot or Aviation Administration focus. It is the largest collegiate flight school in the Northeast preparing its graduates either to become pilots or take technical, managerial, and governmental positions in the industry.

The college also reaches out to the region's advanced high school students. Every summer, students participating in the K–12 STEM and Energy Summer Camp are introduced to technology, engineering, energy, science, and leadership through modules created by the School of Engineering Technology faculty. The Future Stars Summer Camp offers sports and specialty camps including baseball, basketball, and magic. During the school year, the college's University in the High School permits high school juniors and seniors to earn college credit for courses taught in their own schools.

Urban Horticultural and Design students tend their gardens in the last remnant of the agricultural curriculum.

With more than thirty buildings set on a four-hundred-acre campus, Farmingdale State College now serves more than nine thousand residential and commuting students. Its students pursue thirty-nine baccalaureate and associate degree programs in four schools—Engineering Technology, Business, Health Sciences, and Arts and Sciences—with a strong emphasis on experiential learning. And Farmingdale has been approved to offer its first master's degree, in Technology Management, in 2017.

Among the many new buildings that have enabled Farmingdale to fulfill the changing educational needs of Long Island, one of the most important is the recently opened Campus Center, which welcomes campus visitors while facilitating faculty-student interactions and serving as a center of student life on the campus.

Throughout its history the college has responded to the current and anticipated needs of Long Island's economy. Founded to serve a rural agrarian society, Farmingdale State College has evolved to serve the suburban high-tech world of modern central Long Island. This flexible heritage should serve both Farmingdale and the region well in the decades ahead.

Appropriately for Farmingdale's pioneering work in energy conservation, the campus's autos are powered by electricity.

Farmingdale's students fly high.

The silos and solar panels unite Farmingdale's historical tradition and modern role.

NASSAU COMMUNITY COLLEGE

Nassau Community College's name—and the orange and blue colors carried by its athletes—derive from the Dutch House of Nassau's William III, who is better known to Americans for ascending the English throne after the "Glorious Revolution" and ruling with his wife as "William and Mary." The reference to the dual monarchy reflects Nassau County's origins as a Dutch settlement that was later subjected to English rule. Western Long Island boasts a rich historical heritage from the earliest European settlement to the most recent decades.

Post–World War II prosperity and GI Bill housing loans fueled a mass migration from New York City to the suburbs, and the baby boom ignited a school construction boom across the country. By the 1950s, a generation of parents—many of whom had experienced college education via the GI Bill—wanted their children to go to college as well. A grassroots campaign lobbied Nassau County and New York State for affordable higher education on central Long Island. After study by the Nassau County Temporary Commission for Collegiate Education and a series of public hearings, SUNY chartered Nassau Community College in 1959. The college opened in February 1960, in a wing of the old County Courthouse in Mineola, with 632 students and thirty faculty members.

At the first graduation only forty-two degrees were awarded to the Class of 1962. But dramatic growth loomed. The boastful sign on the Long Island Expressway reading "Welcome to Nassau County: The Fastest Growing Community in the United States" foreshadowed dramatic growth at NCC. Classes and offices were moved to more spacious facilities at the

Mitchel Air Force Base in 1959, shortly before it was given to Nassau County to house Nassau Community College.

George Gallup, Daniel Ellsberg, and Edmund Muskie, drew three thousand people at the height of the Watergate scandal. The college increasingly became a cultural center for Nassau County, and its outstanding athletic facilities have hosted national and international events.

The 1980s and 1990s brought further expansion and change. As the student body became more racially diverse, mirroring the changing population of Long Island, campus life reflected increasingly multicultural interests. Degree programs grew in number and size. Once again, the needs of a growing student body outstripped the college's facilities, and modern social science and visual arts

former US Air Force base at Mitchel Field—wooden barracks and brick buildings became classrooms, an airplane hangar the gym, the airplane runway the parking lots. The chapel was transformed into the theater and the firehouse into the art gallery, while the social club became the student center and the Air Force administration building housed the college's library.

SUNY's seemingly wildly optimistic 1963 forecast that Nassau Community College would enroll eight thousand full-time students by 1970 was soon an historical artifact. As the 1970s dawned, enrollment more than doubled the prediction, making the college the largest of SUNY's twenty-eight community colleges. To accommodate such rapid growth, buildings providing new classrooms, laboratories, and offices transformed the campus. Little by little, the charming but antiquated Mitchel Field buildings began disappearing, although the Cradle of Aviation Museum on the edge of the campus provides an enduring reminder of the campus's heritage.

Life on the growing campus thrived as well. Students joined clubs and sports teams, many of which won regional and national championships. A memorable 1973 panel, including national figures such as

Office Technology students enjoy their classroom experience.

buildings and a College Center Building were completed.

Today, Nassau is the largest single-campus community college in the state of New York. More than twenty-three thousand students are enrolled in credit-bearing courses in the thirty academic departments. Among them are individuals from eighty-eight countries who speak over thirty-five different languages. The college has instituted a multifaceted First-Year Experience program in order to increase the sense of community on campus and encourage academic achievement.

Over 120 academic, athletic, cultural, religious, political, and social clubs are available to students, including male and female championship athletic teams and the national- and international-award-winning Speech and Debate Team. The college has fifty buildings on a 225-acre campus, with more on the way, including the recent $40 million Life Sciences Building, housing the Nurs-

The award-winning Life Science Building opened in 2012.

ing and Chemistry departments. A performing arts center is on the drawing board.

Nassau Community College continues to adapt and grow in order to best serve its sponsoring

Class meets by the historical Gazebo.

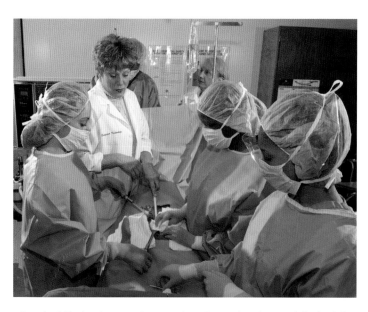
Surgical Technology students and professor hard at work in the lab.

Greenhouse, founded in 1979, has "graduated" an estimated six thousand children ages two months to five years old. The many theatrical and musical programs, art exhibits, concerts, and faculty and guest speakers inspire the public and campus community while serving as educational resources for students.

For over fifty-five years, Nassau Community College's mission of high-quality education, small classes, excellent teaching, and affordable tuition has had a tremendous impact on the residents of Nassau County as well as on its students. The college has been an ever-increasing economic stimulus for Nassau County as a major employer and purchaser of local goods and services, giving a superb return on the tax dollars invested in the college. The over 136,000 alumni and the nearly eight hundred thousand residents who have taken advantage of NCC's programs and resources have benefited from that 1950s dream of affordable higher education in Nassau County. In turn, they have contributed to Nassau County's remarkable maturation.

county. New career-oriented programs in Fire Science, Emergency Management, Human Services, and Health Information Technology complement the traditional strengths of the Liberal Arts, Business, and Health Sciences degrees. Evening and weekend course offerings have been expanded, along with online courses and programs such as the new Certificate in Financial Markets. Fully twenty programs are now offered as "hybrids," with instruction in both online and in-person classrooms.

Workforce training continues to expand, as well as new noncredit programs such as Emergency Medical Technician and Pharmacy Management. The college serves the community with such offerings as its Senior Observer Program, GED and CLEP progams, Drinking/Driving classes, and Lifelong Learning. More than nine thousand enroll annually in noncredit Lifelong Learning and Workforce Development classes. The Children's

NCC's alumni serve throughout Nassau County, New York State, and beyond.

STATE UNIVERSITY COLLEGE AT OLD WESTBURY

Situated on six hundred acres of woodland and rolling meadows in one of Long Island's most affluent suburbs is a surprising and unique SUNY campus. Begun as an explicitly experimental college in response to the educational ferment in the mid-1960s, Old Westbury has continued to chart its own path.

The SUNY Master Plan Revision of 1966 specified a daring mission for a college to be founded in Nassau County. Students would be admitted regardless of whether they had graduated from high school and would receive their bachelor's degree based on competencies rather than time spent enrolled or credits. Students were to be partners in the academic enterprise with considerable influence over the curriculum, and faculty were instructed to teach largely outside of traditional classrooms. It bravely began

in a temporary site, the Planting Fields mansion in Oyster Bay, welcoming its first class of eighty-five students. Unfortunately, administrative and curricular problems bedeviled the noble experiment and the temporary campus closed after two years.

But a seed had sprouted that would be transplanted in more fertile soil. SUNY purchased the six-hundred-acre former estate of F. Ambrose Clark on the North Shore of Long Island as a permanent site for the new college. The campus was readied, and "Old Westbury II" opened in the fall of 1971 with 570 students and a broader mission as a regional college for Long Island, including serving the graduates of Long Island's booming community colleges. Responding to a change in the SUNY Master Plan calling for more attention to career outcomes at Old Westbury, a business program was established in 1975.

Despite the reorganization, Old Westbury continued to be innovative. The curriculum is anchored in the critical analysis of important issues in American society. This emphasis on understanding their cultural context remains a cornerstone of the education offered to Old Westbury College students. College government continued to involve reciprocal responsibility among students, faculty, and staff.

Students in an exuberant moment.

The broader mission attracted a rapidly increasing enrollment, reaching nearly four thousand by the early 1980s. A building program matched it with construction of the Academic Village, residential halls, the Campus Center, a library, a theater, and natural science and physical education buildings.

Designed to offer an exceptional educational experience, the college seeks to provide students with both the skills and knowledge they need to fol-low their chosen career path and to give them a broader understanding of the cultural global context in which they will live. General Education is the crucial vehicle for conveying that broad perspective as the foundation for their upper-class courses and career preparation.

The college's two-semester First-Year Curriculum sets the tone for students' time at the college. In the fall freshmen take a course focused on *The Ethics of Engagement: Educating Leaders for a Just World*, a seven-hundred-plus-page textbook composed of great writings from Plato to the present, edited by the faculty as a tool to facilitate conveying the intellectual tools and sensibilities of the liberal arts. The goal of the first semester is to sensitize students to national and global issues. In the spring the Learning and Action course brings them back to local conditions by combining classroom

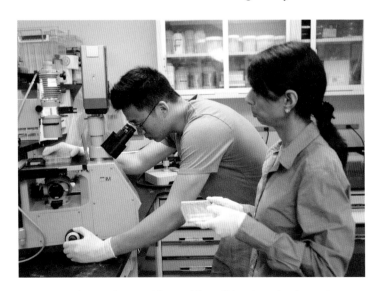

Innovation combines with traditional academic study.

The essence of a liberal arts education is instilled in the First-Year Curriculum.

study with fifty hours of service learning.

As SUNY's only University College on Long Island, Old Westbury serves over 4,500 students, one of the most ethnically and racially diverse in SUNY, with an emphasis on excellence and individual attention. It offers more than sixty undergraduate and graduate degrees housed in three schools: The School of Arts and Sciences, the School of Business, and the School of Education. Each of the three schools has as a part of its mission the emphasis on innovation that characterizes the college as a whole. The School of Arts and Sciences offers the upper-

The arts enhance campus life.

class years of a "liberal education" with every major promoting "life-long learning; global citizenship; and social justice." The School of Business emphasizes teaching effectiveness, encouraging its faculty to experiment with pedagogical methodology and to be open and accessible to students. The School of Education faculty are particularly encouraged to undertake game-changing research and to bring that into their classrooms. Its Regional Center for Autism Spectrum Disorders has emerged as a leader in the quest to enable children on the autism spectrum to have more successful outcomes.

A vibrant student life characterizes Old Westbury.

The Panthers field thirteen Division III teams.

As is apparent in the renovation of the library, SUNY Old Westbury has embraced the possibilities inherent in the technology revolution. For instance, the Collaborative Media Center reaches across the disciplines to support the use of emerging media tools and increasing digital literacy.

Creativity is found in all aspects of the Old Westbury experience. One unusual tradition is celebrating Halloween with the "Rise of the Jack O' Lanterns," a festival that features jack o' lanterns carved by professional artists from across the nation. The more than five thousand pumpkins are arranged according to theme along a quarter-mile path through Old Westbury Gardens. Students also enjoy more traditional campus activities, including an active athletics program.

Throughout its history, Old Westbury has remained committed to some core values. It continues to stress close interaction among students, faculty, and staff while weaving critical thinking, integrity, community engagement, and an international perspective into its curriculum and campus life. As a public liberal arts college, Old Westbury seeks to stimulate a passion for learning and a commitment to building a more just and sustainable world. Over twenty-four thousand alumni, most living in the Greater New York metropolitan area, bring those values to the service of the region and beyond.

As befits its beautiful location, the college has recently made great strides toward creating a greener campus. In 2012, the new 147,000-square-foot Academic Building opened, which received LEED Gold Certification by the US Green Building Council on the basis of its highly efficient heating, ventilation, and cooling systems; efficient lighting fixtures; maximum use of natural light; and effective filtration of rainwater.

The overriding characteristic of Old Westbury has always been innovation. Recently, it became clear that the library, built in the 1980s, no longer met students' needs. In response, the college undertook an intensive study that led to a revamped library with collaborative study rooms, analog and digital media labs, individual research spaces, and an expanded range of seating. The reimagined library has become a centerpiece of the campus, housing a growing collection and providing adaptable technology-rich spaces across the library.

STONY BROOK UNIVERSITY

In only six decades Stony Brook University has followed a dramatic trajectory from a small teacher preparation college to an internationally recognized research institution. Its membership in the prestigious, invitation-only Association of American Universities marks Stony Brook as one of the sixty-two leading research institutions in North America. As part of the management team of Brookhaven National Laboratory and with a faculty that includes Nobel laureates, Guggenheim fellows, and MacArthur grant winners, Stony Brook's reputation extends far beyond its Long Island home.

Stony Brook's 1,040-acre campus on Long Island's North Shore encompasses not only the main academic areas of the university but also Stony Brook Medicine, which includes six schools in the health sciences, as well as Stony Brook University Hospital, Stony Brook Children's Hospital, and the Long Island State Veterans Home. The university's reach also extends to a Research and Development Park; five business incubator locations; and to a Southampton campus on Long Island's East End, home to the Southampton Arts graduate programs in creative writing, theater, and film, graduate programs in the health sciences, and the School of Marine and Atmospheric Sciences' new Marine Sciences Center. Songdo-based SUNY Korea, a partnership between Stony Brook University, SUNY, and the South Korean government, opened its doors in March 2012 as the first American university established on Korean soil.

Stony Brook's origins date from a 1955 SUNY Trustees' decision to establish a college on Long Island. After two years of intensive planning, classes commenced in September 1957, with 148 students

Coe Hall, a grand site for the first classes on September 17, 1957, and Stony Brook's home for the first five years.

enrolled at the tuition-free State University College on Long Island at Oyster Bay. The college's administrators were mandated to "prepare teachers of science and mathematics for secondary schools and community colleges." Course offerings were initially limited to humanities, English, social sciences, education, mathematics, and the natural sciences. Less than three weeks later a small metal ball named "Sputnik" arched across the sky, creating a panic that pushed science education to the top of national priorities.

SUNY quickly expanded the college's scope to include degree programs in the fields of science, mathematics, and engineering. William Robertson Coe's exquisite 350-acre former arboretum estate, Planting Fields, provided a temporary campus, while a new campus was being constructed in historic Stony Brook on land donated by philanthropist Ward Melville. The permanent Stony Brook campus opened in September, 1962, serving 780 students.

The school grew steadily from the early 1960s, as it matured from a science and engineering college into a full-scale university offering a wide range of liberal arts and sciences for undergraduates as well as master's and doctoral programs. The 1960s were

a decade of growth and development at SUNY Stony Brook as the school recruited world-class researchers and scholars, including Nobel Prize recipient C. N. Yang, to take faculty positions.

The Muir Report of 1963 added a new dimension. It recommended to Governor Rockefeller and the SUNY Board of Trustees that a new medical center, including schools of medicine, dentistry, and allied health professions, be established at Stony Brook by 1970. The university's administrators began planning for a comprehensive Health Sciences Center on Stony Brook's East Campus. The towers of the Health Sciences Center were completed by 1980. Stony Brook's scientific mission and reputation expanded further when it embarked on a joint venture with Brookhaven National Laboratory, Cold Spring Harbor Laboratory, and North Shore Hospital to create the Long Island Research Institute in 1992.

Stony Brook Medicine is Long Island's premier academic medical center and serves as the region's only tertiary care center and Regional Trauma Center. It also has the only Level 4 Regional Perinatal Center in Suffolk County and is home to the Stony Brook University Cancer Center, Heart Institute, Stony Brook Children's Hospital and Neurosciences Institute. A Medical and Research Translation (MART)

The heart of Stony Brook's 1,040-acre campus in autumnal colors.

building, dedicated to imaging, neurosciences, cancer care, and research, and a new Hospital Pavilion and Children's Hospital will open in 2018.

In 2011, a transformational $150 million gift to the university from James and Marilyn Simons was announced, the largest bequest ever to public higher education in the state of New York and among the ten largest gifts to any public college or university in America. A former professor of mathematics at Stony Brook who went on to found a highly successful hedge fund, James Simons's gift is the largest ever given by an academic. As Simons's mathematical modeling had a profound impact on physics, fittingly the Simons Center for Geometry and Physics enables researchers to explore synergies between theoretical physics and math.

The university's twelve schools and colleges offer more than two hundred undergraduate programs, one hundred master's programs, and forty doctoral programs to more than twenty-five thousand students from nearly all fifty states and more than one hundred countries. Innovative programs include the award-winning Undergraduate Research and Creative Activities program, which involves undergraduates in research in nearly every discipline and has produced Beckman, Gates, Goldwater, Marshall,

The Simons Center for Geometry and Physics draws researchers from around the world to explore the physical universe.

The Medical and Research Translation Building (MART) is dedicated to imaging, neurosciences, cancer care, and research.

and Truman scholars. Its programs offering extensive academic and other support for its large number of students from racial minorities have achieved national distinction by the Education Trust.

The arts continue to thrive at Stony Brook. In the 1980s the Stony Brook Foundation acquired the Pollock-Krasner House, the former home and studio of artists Jackson Pollock and Lee Krasner. The Staller Center for the Arts offers a rich program of theater, dance, classical music, and popular entertainment to both the campus and broader community throughout the year. Each summer, the Stony Brook Film Festival brings leading and emerging filmmakers and fans to campus.

The Student Activities Center is the heart of student life. Stony Brook's twenty NCAA Division I varsity intercollegiate athletic programs range from football to women's lacrosse. The student-athletes compete in modern facilities, such as Kenneth P. LaValle Stadium and the newly renovated Island Federal Credit Union Arena, the home for men's and women's basketball teams.

The name of the renovated arena speaks to a major effort by Stony Brook to reach out to regional,

Umbilic Torus, a sculpture at one of the gateways to the Academic Mall, celebrates the fusion of mathematics and art.

New York State industry and university research. In addition, the Advanced Energy Research and Technology Center brings together academic and research institutions, energy providers, and industry to focus on innovative energy solutions.

With these programs, Stony Brook provides leadership for the SUNY system in realizing goals of both *The Power of SUNY*, the system's strategic plan, and START-UP NY, the state's tax-free opportunity to locate new businesses on or near SUNY campuses. As they develop, these companies provide tangible supports for the academic programs through direct research funding, student internships, and other employment.

In a little less than sixty years, then, Stony Brook University has risen from a small, unknown campus with its classes meeting in a mansion to a world-class research university, one recognized as one of the top ten in the nation by the National Science Foundation for combining research and undergraduate education and as one of the top one percent of the world's higher education institutions by the Center for World University Rankings. The Stony Brook University community looks to the future to build on this extraordinary record.

national, and international businesses for new private-public partnerships. For example, Stony Brook's Center of Excellence in Wireless and Information Technology and three state-designated Centers for Advanced Technology—in diagnostic tools and sensor systems, in biotechnology, and in integrated electric energy systems—facilitate partnerships between

The 8,300-seat LaValle Stadium, which hosts the Stony Brook Seawolves, is Suffolk County's largest outdoor sports facility.

SUFFOLK COUNTY COMMUNITY COLLEGE

When a college was first proposed for Suffolk County in the 1950s, many doubted that enough students would enroll to sustain it. Situated in what was still a very rural county, its prospects were uncertain. But a little over a half-century later, both the County and the College have changed. Population started spreading out from New York City and its inner suburbs and began to flow over the Nassau County line into Suffolk. Today Suffolk County Community College, with its three campuses, is the largest community college in the SUNY system, an economic development catalyst for the region serving more than twenty-five thousand students.

The College was chartered in 1959, largely due to the efforts of Dr. Albert M. Ammerman, who spearheaded the efforts to found an affordable college on Long Island and served as its first president. When the temporary site at Sachem High School opened its doors in 1960, barely five hundred students enrolled to be taught by thirteen faculty. Construction at today's Ammerman Campus was already underway, but the former tuberculosis sanitarium at Selden provided the spaces needed for the college. In August 1961 six renovated buildings on 156 wooded acres were readied for a student population that tripled in the first year. The following June forty-two graduates received their associate degrees at Suffolk's first graduation.

Two of the original buildings, both built by the New Deal's Works Project Administration, are still used today. The county added more buildings so that by 1970 a central plaza was surrounded by a new library, theater, and classroom buildings.

Suffolk's first student government already shows school spirit.

Residents in western Suffolk have the convenience of the Michael J. Grant Campus.

Even as the Ammerman campus was expanding, plans were being laid to bring education closer to residents in the eastern and western ends of Suffolk County. In 1974 a new campus, now known as the Michael J. Grant Campus, was opened in the town of Brentwood at the edge of the Pilgrim Psychiatric Center on land made available by the state. Then, in 1977, the Eastern Campus in Riverhead was opened, making college available for potential students living on the north and south forks of Long Island.

The suburban population of Long Island and SCCC grew in parallel. By the time President Ammerman retired in 1983, the staff had grown to two thousand, teaching twenty-three thousand students on the three campuses with thirteen satellite locations,

offering accessible education to every county resident. Currently nearly twenty-seven thousand students choose from more than one hundred degree and certificate programs and enjoy a low 22:1 student/faculty ratio.

Consistent with its community college mission, Suffolk County Community College aims to prepare its students for many different post-graduate possibilities, ranging from transferring to a baccalaureate program in almost any discipline to taking a place within the local and regional workforce. For those seeking transfer, the college's curriculum offers a myriad of programs in the liberal arts and sciences that provide for seamless transfer to many colleges, public and private, local and in other states. The "Stay on Long Island Initiative" enables SCCC's

Students in eastern Suffolk benefit from a well-designed, growing campus on Long Island Sound.

highest achieving students to transfer to one of Long Island's four-year colleges by offering full and partial scholarships. The College's transfer programs include the liberal arts, science and engineering, fine arts, computer science, performing arts, and business education, which prepare thousands of SCCC students to transfer successfully to baccalaureate programs each year.

For those seeking immediate employment, the college offers programs designed to match regional employment needs and student occupational goals. The nursing program, including the satellite education center in Sayville, is one of the largest two-year RN programs in the nation. In addition, the Culinary Arts and Hospitality Center opened in Riverhead in 2008. The college also offers welding, CNC Machining, and IPC Soldering classes with industry certifications, all of which are needed by local businesses and industries.

The college is currently developing a new Renewable Energy STEM Center on its Michael J. Grant Campus. This facility will be the cornerstone of new academic initiatives (both credit and non-credit) being developed in Energy Management, Alternative Energy Technologies, and Sustainability Studies, as well as Cybersecurity and other STEM disciplines. The building will house laboratories and classrooms where solar photovoltaics, wind power, geothermal, and other renewable energy and energy conservation technologies can be taught. And, SCCC has received three consecutive National Science Foundation Scholarships Science, Technology, Engineering, and Mathematics (NSF S-STEM) grants.

A student and instructor in the Veterinary Tech program care for "man's best friend."

Training students to give the young a good start is vital to Long Island's future.

Because many SCCC students have work and family responsibilities, the college accommodates their challenging schedules with a large number of evening, weekend, and early morning classes. In addition, a growing number of courses are being offered online. Currently, more than 275 distance education courses are offered and there is a fully online AAS degree in Business Administration. Suffolk County Community College also offers a large number of professional development and continuing education courses.

For more than a half century, Suffolk County Community College, which today has more than 125,000 alumni, has contributed immeasurably to the growth and vibrancy of Long Island. What began as a vision in a largely rural Suffolk County in the late 1950s has grown into a critical component in the continuing economic growth of Long Island, ever evolving to meet the changing post-secondary educational needs of the region.

The arts and sciences courses offered at Suffolk prepare students to transfer to baccalaureate colleges.

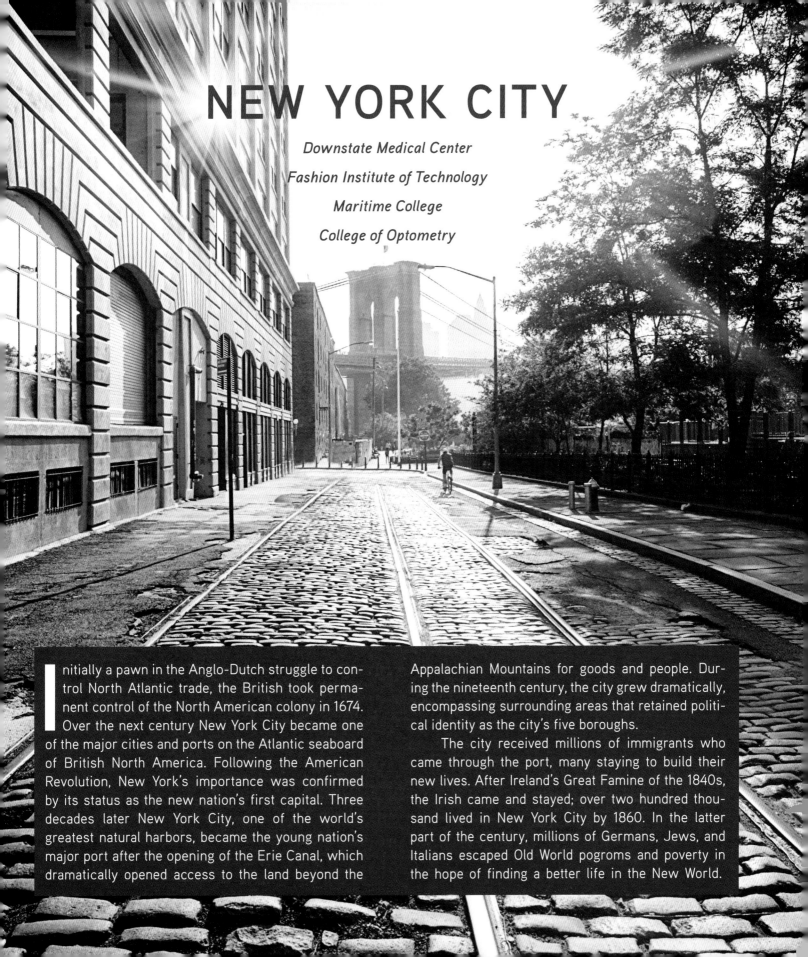

NEW YORK CITY

Downstate Medical Center

Fashion Institute of Technology

Maritime College

College of Optometry

nitially a pawn in the Anglo-Dutch struggle to control North Atlantic trade, the British took permanent control of the North American colony in 1674. Over the next century New York City became one of the major cities and ports on the Atlantic seaboard of British North America. Following the American Revolution, New York's importance was confirmed by its status as the new nation's first capital. Three decades later New York City, one of the world's greatest natural harbors, became the young nation's major port after the opening of the Erie Canal, which dramatically opened access to the land beyond the Appalachian Mountains for goods and people. During the nineteenth century, the city grew dramatically, encompassing surrounding areas that retained political identity as the city's five boroughs.

The city received millions of immigrants who came through the port, many staying to build their new lives. After Ireland's Great Famine of the 1840s, the Irish came and stayed; over two hundred thousand lived in New York City by 1860. In the latter part of the century, millions of Germans, Jews, and Italians escaped Old World pogroms and poverty in the hope of finding a better life in the New World.

In fact, more than twelve million immigrants passed through Ellis Island between 1892 and 1924, many of whom remained in the city, as described in Israel Zangwill's popular play, *The Melting Pot*. In the twentieth century, the city became home to hundreds of thousands of African Americans who left the agricultural South for possible employment in the North and who, in the last half of the century, were joined by many more Hispanics, Asians, and Middle Easterners who today make ethnic and racial minorities a majority in the city.

New York City has been the home to many of America's most iconic urban scenes, bridges, and buildings, from Frederick Law Olmsted's masterpiece, Central Park, to the George Washington Bridge, which Le Corbusier called "the most beautiful in the world," from the glaring, alluring lights of Times Square to Wall Street; from the Empire State Building, which in 1933 served as the monumental setting

George Washington Bridge, from New York City.

Central Park, New York City.

for the cultural clash between brute natural force and the modern city in *King Kong*, to the World Trade Center, which five decades later served the same function in the 1976 remake, from the art deco Chrysler Building to the Seagram Building built two decades later, an example of the international style.

In recent decades, the city's post–World War II dominance in international finance has been challenged, but not surpassed. And New York City remains a major center for the arts, particularly theater and dance, transportation, tourism, media, and advertising. Today, it attracts the artists, intellectuals, and business people who help maintain its prominence in every industry and cultural movement. Throughout its history, New York has been a symbol of "Yankee" power in many forms, which is one reason that terrorists, funded by al Qaeda's Osama bin Laden, targeted the twin towers of the World Trade Center at the turn of the twenty-first century.

The four SUNY schools in New York City are as unique and vibrant as the city itself; yet, each differs from the traditional college model. It makes sense that each SUNY school in the "Big Apple" focuses on a different area of the working world, providing educations for the twenty-first century in the health and medical, maritime, and fashion industries.

The oldest and youngest SUNY schools in New York City focus on medical care and health. SUNY Downstate Medical Center opened its doors to students in 1860 after receiving its charter as the teaching division of Long Island College Hospital. It was the first medical school in the nation to bring medical education to patients' bedsides and one of eleven medical schools at that time to admit African American students. In the decades since it joined SUNY (1950), Downstate has provided education and training to its students through its four colleges and nineteen clinical training programs as well as superb medical services to the extraordinarily diverse Brooklyn community. True to its tradition, its student body, professional staff, and faculty mirror the rich diversity of the borough. Downstate is also a major center of research, one of whose faculty members was awarded the 1998 Nobel Prize in Physiology or Medicine.

Bryant Park, New York City.

The youngest member of SUNY, the College of Optometry was established in 1971 and sits on the north side of Manhattan's 42nd Street, just across from Bryant Park and the New York Public Library. It is the only school of optometry in New York State, and it has become a center for vision research. Despite enrolling fewer than 350 students, its impact on New York State is immense—more than sixty percent of its practicing optometrists were educated at the College of Optometry.

Established in 1874, Maritime College, located in Fort Schuyler on the Bronx's Throgs Neck Peninsula, was the first federally approved college to offer commercial maritime instruction, and it remains one of only seven such schools today. While the school, which was administered by the city's Board of Education, provided needed nautical training, it frequently faced closure due to repeated financial crises, a situation that did not appreciably improve even after its transfer to state authority in 1913. But, World War I renewed interest in maritime education, and the col-

lege moved to its present site at Fort Schuyler in 1938. A decade later it was one of the initial institutions to comprise the SUNY system.

The Fashion Institute of Technology was founded in 1944 and today is ranked among the top five fashion schools in the world. Located on Seventh Avenue in the midst of New York's Garment District, the school offers students a unique range of programs, from associate degrees to graduate programs that provide entry into the fashion industry. Famed designers Calvin Klein and Michael Kors are among the school's many graduates who are currently working in New York City.

New York City has never adhered to the example set by the rest of the world; similarly, the SUNY schools there are also outside the collegiate norm. Because of their specialized characters, they play unique roles in creating the educated citizenry and workforce necessary to ensure the economic well-being of the city and state in the decades ahead.

New York Harbor.

SUNY DOWNSTATE MEDICAL CENTER

For over a century and a half the SUNY Health Science Center at Brooklyn, better known as "SUNY Downstate," has provided excellent education for medical professionals, advanced scientific research in numerous disciplines, and delivered the highest-quality patient care to an urban community that for more than a century has been the arrival point for immigrants. Today, SUNY Downstate's faculty, staff and student body reflect Brooklyn's rich ethnic and cultural diversity, and its campus includes five health and science-focused colleges and schools (Medicine, Nursing, Health Related Professions, Graduate Studies, and Pub-

In 1873, Long Island College Hospital launched Brooklyn's first ambulance service, with a horse-drawn vehicle donated by New York City.

lic Health) and a major research complex, as well as its own on-site teaching hospital.

Downstate's history dates to 1860, when on the eve of the Civil War, the Long Island College Hospital (LICH), founded a teaching division. It was the first medical school in America to combine with a hospital and to use the wards and clinics for teaching purposes providing hands-on experience for students. The inclusion of bedside experience was a revolutionary European import that foreshadowed future American medical education reform.

The elements and length of medical education were significantly different in 1860. When the

Downstate's 1888 College of Medicine graduating class, reflecting the long heritage of diversity.

first class of 57 students began their medical careers at LICH, the science of medicine was very different from that practiced today. There were no antibiotics for infection, no vaccines to mitigate pandemic illnesses, and few effective treatments beyond surgical excision. And the Civil War placed unique demands on medical practice, with wounded soldiers filling the wards, for which the hospital received 37 cents per day for each soldier treated.

After the war, the evolution of the medical school reflected the evolution of American medical education in general, with professionalization and standardization steadily increasing. In 1869, daily class examinations were established; in 1879, the curriculum expanded from sixteen weeks to five months. To facilitate these reforms, new buildings were constructed, equipped with the best technology of the day. The Hoagland Laboratory was one of the most advanced in the country when it opened in 1888.

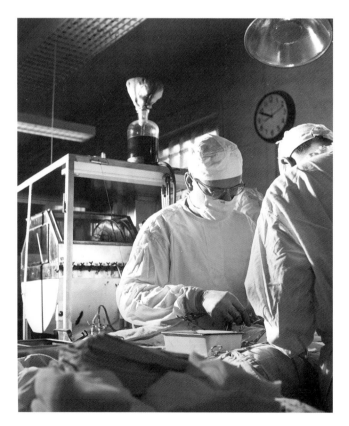

Dr. Clarence Dennis, chairman of Downstate's Department of Surgery from 1951 to 1972, developed the heart-lung machine in 1951, and performed the first successful open-heart operation in New York State on June 30, 1955.

President Dwight D. Eisenhower delivered the keynote address at the cornerstone-laying ceremony of Downstate's Basic Sciences Building (BSB) on October 21, 1954.

The Polhemus Memorial Clinic Building, completed in 1898, provided dramatically improved facilities for patient care, research, and teaching. It was not until 1897 that the entering class of medical students was subject to a four-year course of graded instruction. The student body changed over time as well; by World War I the college was admitting women and offering postgraduate training.

In 1930, the medical school officially separated from LICH and was chartered as the Long Island College of Medicine. During the 1930s the new Polak Memorial Laboratory improved facilities for histology, pathology, bacteriology, physiology, gynecology, and surgery. The medical school merged with SUNY in 1950, and the campus was relocated to its current site in Central Brooklyn. President Dwight D. Eisenhower spoke at the cornerstone-laying ceremony for the new campus's first building in 1954. In 1966, the campus added a College of Nursing, College of Health Related Professions, and a School of Graduate Studies. That same year, Governor Nelson A. Rockefeller dedicated University Hospital of Brooklyn, Downstate's own on-site teaching hospital. The School of Public Health was launched in 2008, and a new academic building to house it is slated for completion in 2017.

With an annual enrollment of over 1,800 students, the campus is a significant contributor to the healthcare workforce—locally, regionally, and nationally. Downstate is fourth among the nation's 145 allopathic medical schools in the number of graduates (8,613) having an active license to practice medicine in the U.S. An estimated one of every nine physicians practicing in New York City and one of every three practicing in Brooklyn graduated or trained at Downstate. Downstate ranks twelfth in the number of graduates who hold faculty positions at U.S. medical schools and twenty-third in the number who are department chairs.

Downstate takes pride in its many research achievements. Dr. Robert Furchgott, who served on the faculty from 1956 until his death in 2009, was awarded the 1998 Nobel Prize in Physiology or Medi-

Downstate faculty member Dr. Robert F. Furchgott was awarded the 1998 Nobel Prize in Physiology or Medicine for his discovery of the role that nitric oxide plays as a signaling molecule in the cardiovascular system. Dr. Furchgott was the first Nobel Laureate within the SUNY system to have conducted Nobel Prize-winning research on a SUNY campus.

cine for his identification of nitric oxide as a signaling molecule important in vascular health, which revolutionized treatment for heart disease, stroke, and other conditions. The first MRI machine capable of taking full-torso human images was built at Downstate; its inventor, Dr. Raymond Damadian, was awarded the National Medal of Technology by President Ronald Reagan. More recently, Dr. Todd Sacktor discovered a molecule in the brain that is vital for memory retention; the journal Science identified this as one of the top ten scientific discoveries of 2006.

Downstate faculty members were the first to perform open-heart surgery in New York State, establish a federally funded dialysis clinic in the United States, conduct a federal study of perinatal transmission of HIV disease; and establish a gynecologic oncology division. In addition to bedside teaching, academic "firsts" include offering a direct-entry degree in Midwifery in the College of Health Related Professions, and being among the first to offer an accelerated nursing program funded by the U.S. Department of Health and Human Services.

As part of StartUP New York, a tax-free initiative launched by New York State to promote entrepreneurship and encourage companies to work in partnership with universities, Downstate recently launched two initiatives to foster the growth of biotechnology in Brooklyn and New York City: a Biotechnology Incubator for new start-ups, and BioBAT, a site on the Brooklyn waterfront for mature companies requiring larger space. The school also partners with other SUNY campuses on research and academic projects, such as the SUNY Eye Institute, a consortium of vision researchers from all four academic medical universities in the SUNY system and the SUNY College of Optometry. Downstate offers a combined MD/PhD degree in Medicine and Nanoscale Science or Engineering with SUNY Polytechnic Institute.

Through its clinical care and community outreach programs, Downstate has had, and continues to have, an immediate impact on the health and well-being of Brooklyn's diverse communities. University Hospital, for example, is a safety net teaching hospital that serves some of the most vulnerable populations in New York State. Minorities comprise nearly ninety percent of its service-area population; nearly half of the residents are foreign born; and almost two-thirds of inpatient discharges are Medicare or Medicaid patients. Downstate also has strong involvement with churches, senior citizen centers, local schools, and community groups, and broad-based service-learning projects such as the student-run Brooklyn Free Clinic, which provides care to the uninsured. The School of Graduate Studies has teamed with SUNY and the National Academy of Sciences to mentor children in local middle schools in science and math, while the School of Public Health sponsors a 200-hour field experience project focusing on community issues as well as a global health elective in developing countries through which some 400 medical students have participated in projects in forty-one resource-poor countries. The NIH-funded Center for Health Disparities is a collaborative effort between Downstate, the Arthur Ashe Institute for Urban Health, and the Brooklyn Borough President's Office.

The Downstate community today remains as committed to its mission—excellence in education, research, and clinical care—as it has for the past century and a half, and looks forward to continuing its service to Brooklyn, to New York State, and to the nation.

Downstate College of Medicine students on "Match Day," the ritual that occurs annually on the third Friday of March, at which medical students across the nation learn where they will do their graduate medical training program.

FASHION INSTITUTE OF TECHNOLOGY

From its origins in New York City's dynamic fashion industry of the 1940s, the Fashion Institute of Technology has evolved into a globally renowned college, offering almost fifty undergraduate and graduate degree programs to prepare students for entry into the creative industry.

New York City has long been renowned as a leader in the needle trades, an industry that offered a critical source of employment for generations of aspiring immigrants. But in the post–World War II era, management and labor worried about the industry's ability to continue to attract talent and maintain a cre-

The Central High School of Needle Trades, FIT's first home, reflected its origins in the garment industry.

ative edge. Both sides of the negotiating table agreed on the necessity of higher-level formal education in the garment industry. Working together, they procured a charter from the Regents of the State of New York for what has become this premier educational institution.

The project was launched modestly on the top two floors of the Central High School of Needle Trades. In September 1944 classes began with one hundred students, ten faculty, and equipment provided by the Board of Education. Students could pursue programs in either apparel design or "scientific management"—the business side of fashion. In addition to technical training, from the beginning liberal arts played an important role in educating the future practitioners of a creative industry that needed to simultaneously reflect and lead society's fashion consciousness.

In 1951, FIT became SUNY's second community college and the first community college in New York City. As such, it was empowered to grant the Associate in Applied Science degree. After fifteen years in the confines of the former high school, FIT moved to a new purpose-built nine-story building on Seventh Avenue in the heart of the garment district designed for 1,200 students. To accommodate an enrollment that soon swelled to over four thousand, six more buildings were constructed by the early 1970s.

As the fashion industry grew in scope and complexity, FIT added programs and adapted its curriculum to address rapid changes. To reflect FIT's growing educational mission, SUNY granted it the authority to confer bachelor's and master's degrees in the 1970s—a rare distinction within SUNY for a community college. The curriculum grew beyond traditional notions of fashion to include related areas in the creative industries, such as advertising, interior design, photography, communications, cosmetics, marketing, jewelry, and even toy design.

Today, the college offers nearly fifty undergraduate and graduate degree programs through its schools of Art and Design, Business and Technology, Graduate Studies, and Liberal Arts. Some of these programs, such as Packaging Design and Cosmetics/Fragrance Marketing, are unique to FIT; others—Accessories Design, Fashion Business Management, Toy Design, and Visual Presentation and Exhibition Design—were the first of their kind in the country, or even the world. The newest additions to the curriculum are bachelor's degree programs in Entrepreneurship and in Film and Media.

FIT serves the creative industries through its wide variety of design, fine and applied arts, and business and technology programs, all grounded on a strong foundation of liberal arts. Students pursue

The curriculum has grown in directions the founders could not have imagined.

The Marvin Feldman Center is the heart of the campus.

experiential learning made possible by the college's many industry partners. Faculty members bring invaluable industry expertise into their classrooms, and FIT helps define New York City's culture and supports its economic growth.

While FIT continues to grow and change in sometimes surprising ways, the college retains a focus on the industries that provide its essential character. As vital today as it was to the institution's founders, this close connection to New York's industries is critical to every aspect of the college, from program development to faculty recruitment to the student experience to job placement after graduation. In the classroom and beyond, students are immersed in the real-world practice of the industries they will soon enter as professionals. Most students explore their fields through internships at a wide variety of leading organizations—retailers, e/digital media companies, advertising agencies, museums and galleries, packaging and branding firms, trend forecasters, and more. The blend of high-level practical skills with creativity, inspiration, and a broad liberal arts perspective remains the hallmark of an FIT education.

FIT offers unique resources such as state-of-the-art apparel production equipment, a computerized knitting lab, and the only professional-level fragrance studio on an American college campus. Specialized facilities include laboratories for computer-aided design, textile testing, gemology, lighting, film production, toy design, and interactive media. The Gladys Marcus Library provides extensive print and electronic resources as well as in-depth research materials for FIT's specialized programs, such as fashion and trend forecasting services, sketch collections, clipping files, and fashion show DVDs.

Each year, FIT welcomes nearly ten thousand undergraduate, graduate, and continuing education students to its campus in Manhattan's Chelsea neighborhood. They come from across New York State, all over the country, and around the world, drawn by the college's groundbreaking curricula, its outstanding faculty of working professionals, its industry connections, and its extraordinary location in the heart of New York City, an international center of art, design, fashion, and commerce.

The Museum at FIT, New York's only museum dedicated to fashion, is one of the city's cultural

FIT's fragrance studio, where students learn to evaluate scents.

The annual runway show, the capstone of the Fashion Design Curriculum.

The Museum at FIT showcases the world of fashion through its exhibitions, programs, and publications.

treasures. It houses one of the world's most important collections of costume and textiles, including works by influential designers such as Adrian, Balenciaga, Chanel, and Dior. Its holdings, including some fifty thousand garments and accessories dating from the eighteenth century to the present, emphasize contemporary avant-garde fashion and provide a resource for both research and inspiration for students, designers, and historians. Each year, it welcomes one hundred thousand visitors to its exhibitions, symposia, talks, and tours.

Every college's greatest legacy is its alumni, and FIT claims a growing list of notable successes in a variety of fields. Alumni include fashion designers such as Calvin Klein, Michael Kors, Norma Kamali, Dennis Basso, Francisco Costa, Ralph Rucci, Isabel Toledo, and Nanette Lepore; *Marie Claire* creative director Nina Garcia; global restaurant and interior designer Tony Chii; Ivy Ross, Google vice president of design and user experience for hardware products; Lisa Versaicio, chief creative and merchandising officer of Restoration Hardware; cosmetics entrepreneur Leslie Blodgett, creator of bareMinerals; and Emmy Award–winning animator William Frake.

At the same time that FIT proudly celebrates its past and current achievements, it remains firmly focused on its future as an institution where students, scholars, and teachers cross traditional disciplinary boundaries to stimulate innovation, partner with creative industries worldwide, and develop design and business solutions. And it does this while contributing to New York City's vibrant economy.

MARITIME COLLEGE

Within the SUNY system, Maritime College rightfully claims "unique" as its descriptor. One reason is the college's magnificent campus located on a peninsula in the east Bronx where the East River meets Long Island Sound. Ships and pleasure boats sail these waters, while automobile traffic hums across the Throgs Neck Bridge above and jets descend toward nearby JFK or LaGuardia airports.

Besides its unique setting, Maritime College also has an unusual history. Begun in 1874 aboard the USS *St. Mary's*, what was once known as the New York

The war sloop *St. Mary's*, lent as the first training ship of the New York Nautical School in 1874.

Nautical School joined the SUNY system in 1949. Like the tide's ebb and flow, waves of inadequate funding, uncertain enrollment, and attempts to abolish the school seemed never ending. However, committed alumni and New York City merchants fought untiringly to enlist state support and keep the school, literally, afloat. Two key factors facilitated their eventual success: the federal government's creation of the US Maritime Commission in 1936 to revitalize the shipping industry and the choice of Fort Schuyler—a location close to the heart of New York City, seaport par excellence and center of global trade—as the school's permanent home.

Built during Andrew Jackson's presidency and commandeered as a Union hospital during the Civil War, historic Fort Schuyler needed major repair and required a new pier. Thanks to the Works Progress Administration, and President Franklin D. Roosevelt's personal intervention, both projects were realized. In 1938, Fort Schuyler was dedicated as the New York State Merchant Marine Academy. Steadily, this academy increased its enrollment, added academic rigor to its curriculum, updated classrooms, and added modern training ships. As a result, its postwar faculty comprised both credentialed academicians and licensed merchant mariners. With relative ease, the New York State Merchant Marine Academy obtained permission to award a Bachelor of Maritime Science degree. By 1949, New York's Maritime Academy, with its unique meshing of vocational and academic curriculum strands, made the school a logical choice for inclusion in SUNY. Now a college, Maritime added four additional Bachelor of Science degrees, augmented the curriculum in marine transportation and marine engineering, and strengthened its offerings in the sciences and humanities.

The mid-1950s saw three more programs initiated and approved: Marine Operations, Marine Engineering Design and Construction, and Marine Business Administration. Maritime College also developed

Fort Schuyler, the Throgs Neck Bridge, and the campus with the training ship *Empire State VI* at the pier in the background.

one of the few Naval Architecture programs in the country. In 1968 a graduate program leading to a master's degree in Marine Transportation Management—the first of its kind in the United States—met with SUNY approval. This curricular expansion required adding new facilities, building new dorms, and renovating Fort Schuyler so that today it is home to both the Maritime Industry Museum (formerly the Museum of the Brooklyn Navy Yard) and the architectural prize–winning Stephen B. Luce Library.

Today, Maritime College continues to evolve. Academic programs continue to expand, and a newly completed, state-of-the-art academic building—its classrooms and labs fitted with current and emerging technology—now overlooks the East River. The south façade, made entirely of glass, provides a magnificent view of Manhattan's skyline, while faculty and students enjoy the latest simulators in up-to-the minute laboratory, lecture, and class meeting sites.

Maritime College's enrollment has grown from 600 to over 1,800 in recent years. Many factors are responsible: welcoming "civilian" students to the campus to study alongside the traditional regimental cadets; recruiting more women into traditionally male-dominated career paths; and developing international programs in conjunction with overseas universities in the Bahamas, Brazil, China, and Norway. The curriculum has grown to include a variety of new

Students of the New York Nautical School were trained in traditional seamanship. The students are learning to handle sails, circa 1900.

Cadets also master smaller craft.

Cadets in formation at Maritime College during Homecoming 2010.

writer and lecturer on Turkish politics, was awarded a SUNY Levin Fellowship to teach at a Turkish university, while Professor Richard Burke was recently invited to Italy, to observe and report on the *Costa Concordia*'s restoration. Professor Maryellen V. Keefe's biography *Casual Affairs: The Life and Fiction of Sally Benson* (a prolific short story and Hollywood screenplay writer) was released by State University of New York Press on the 110th anniversary of the St. Louis World's Fair commemorated in Benson's *Meet Me in St. Louis.*

As academics have grown in importance, arts and sciences faculty have tapped Maritime College's proximity to the cultural wonders of New York City— museums, theater, botanical and zoological sites—by immersing students in this cultural wealth via related projects and onsite visits. Maritime College's athletics has gained greater prominence with both men's and women's teams taking first place within their divisions. Finally, a Navy NROTC unit housed at Maritime has welcomed students from nearby Fordham and Columbia Universities, while Maritime students can join either the Army ROTC at Fordham University or the Air Force ROTC at nearby Manhattan College in the Bronx.

Maritime graduates have served with distinction on vessels around the globe and in many other capacities of the maritime industry. Yet, more surprising has been the range of their achievements, as illustrated by Edward Villella, world-renowned star of the ballet, and Commander Scott Kelly, famous for his achievements in space. Both claim Maritime College as their alma mater.

And tomorrow? Maritime will matter. The dedication, pride, and commitment to learning and service that have characterized Maritime College for over 140 years will continue to flourish and bear fruit for our city, state, country, and global community. May there be nothing but "Fair winds and following seas."

electives in areas such as Irish literature and Constitutional law. Graduate programs in Maritime Studies and International Transportation Management add to Maritime College's attraction, while remaining true to its mission.

At sea, Maritime College has doubled the length of its traditional summer term voyage from forty-five to ninety days. For each of three summers, cadets studying for the Coast Guard license gain not only valuable experience at sea but also the privilege of sampling European and other cultures during visits to ports such as Dublin and Cobh, Ireland; Liverpool, England; Ostia, Trieste, and Naples, Italy; Valletta, Malta; Gibraltar; St John's, Newfoundland; New Orleans, Louisiana; San Miguel, Azores; Reykjavik, Iceland; Palma and Mallorca, Spain; Piraeus and Andros, Greece. On campus, the presence of international students affords American-born students an introduction to other cultures.

Maritime College faculty continue to develop and refine expertise in very diverse areas of scholarship and inquiry. For example: Professor Mark Meirowitz,

COLLEGE OF OPTOMETRY

Facing the New York Public Library and Bryant Park in vibrant Midtown Manhattan, the College of Optometry and its predecessors have been pioneers and national leaders in vision care for over a century. In 1910, Columbia University opened the first university-based school of optometry in the United States. But when the college closed its doors in 1956, the Metropolitan area was left without a school or college of optometry.

Later that year a committed group of optometrists and philanthropists from New York City and the surrounding region formed the Optometric Center of New York (OCNY), a nonprofit health and education resource, to partially fill the void left by the closing of the school at Columbia. The OCNY conducted vision and eye research, provided postgraduate coursework, and established a much-needed clinic as well as satellite clinics in underserved areas of the city. But New York still lacked a college of optometry.

After more than a decade of lobbying by the OCNY, as well as the New York State Optometric Association, the New York City Health Commissioner, and others who recognized a desperate and growing need for more optometrists in the New York City metropolitan region, the New York State Legislature unanimously voted to establish a new college of optometry in 1970. After modifications added during the next legislative session, Governor Nelson A. Rockefeller signed the bill on April 14, 1971, officially establishing the State University of New York College of Optometry. Dr. Alden N. Haffner, the OCNY's executive director, became the founding president. The first students entered the college in September 1971, and in 1975, for the first time in fourteen years,

Governor Nelson A. Rockefeller signing the bill
that established the college.

The college grew steadily. Between 1972 and 1982, enrollment jumped from 50 to over 250 students. Today the College of Optometry enrolls well over four hundred students. In 1974 the college launched its first year-long residency programs, including the first vision therapy residency program in the nation.

In 1999, SUNY approved the college's plan to move from 24th Street to its current home, a historic, eighteen-story building on West 42nd Street. Built in 1912 for the Aeolian Piano Company, the building originally housed the renowned Aeolian Hall, which hosted numerous, highly regarded performances in

students graduated with a Doctor of Optometry (OD) degree in New York State.

In addition to its educational and clinical responsibilities, the college also took over the OCNY's research program, helping to quickly establish the College of Optometry's reputation as a major hub for vision science research that has continued to this day. Research activities have steadily grown at the college over the years. Today, the College of Optometry secures over $3.5 million dollars in research grant funding annually, a sixfold increase since the turn of the twenty-first century.

The College of Optometry initially operated in an eight-story building on East 24th Street near Lexington Avenue in Manhattan, where the OCNY had operated a clinic for many years. Shortly after opening, however, the college rented space in a second building on East 23rd Street and, in 1976, it consolidated its facilities into a 130,000-square-foot space within a twenty-story building at East 24th Street and Park Avenue South, which was the College of Optometry's home for the next quarter century.

The college's first building, on Manhattan's East 24th Street.

the 1910s and 1920s, including the world debut of George Gershwin's *Rhapsody in Blue* in 1924. After a series of renovations to accommodate the college's clinic, the move was completed in May 2000.

In 2008, under new leadership, the college adopted a comprehensive strategic plan titled *A Shared Vision*, with the goal of putting the institution on the appropriate track toward providing the most innovative education and patient care possible, as well as helping advance vision science through significant and bold research. In spite of the challenging economic environment in which it was implemented, *A Shared Vision* led to the establishment of several key programs at the college, including the Graduate Center for Vision Research, the Center for International Programs, the Career Development Center, the MBA certificate program, and the Clinical Vision Research Center.

In 2009, the OCNY launched The Vision and the Promise, a five-year, ten-million-dollar fundraising campaign designed to support the growing and ambitious educational, research, and patient care activities of the institution and to help support its increased philanthropic work in the community. The first such campaign in the college's history, it was successfully completed in 2014.

That same year, the college's clinic, the University Optometric Center, was renamed the University Eye Center (UEC) and its referral service was established. The UEC is one of the largest optometric outpatient facilities in the nation, offering both primary and specialized vision care services. Since 2009 the number of patients referred to the UEC each year has increased nearly threefold. The clinic receives about seventy thousand patient visits per year. Its community outreach includes the Indigent Patient Fund, the Homebound Program, Bowery Mission, and numerous other partnerships with hospitals and diagnostic and treatment centers affiliated with the NYC Health and Hospitals Corporation and other institutions in North America and beyond.

After more than five years of planning and design—and two years of construction—the three-floor, twenty-thousand-square-foot Center for Student Life and Learning opened in 2013. The dynamic new space includes a large preclinical procedures laboratory, classroom and study space, a large seminar room, lounges, event space, and a fitness cen-

The College of Optometry's mission combines advanced research and community care.

Students raise money for community projects.

ter. The new center vastly improved both the learning and recreational facilities of the college, while other enhancements upgraded the college's research facilities.

Having produced more than sixty percent of New York State's practicing optometrists, as well as PhD and MS students, the College of Optometry has more than lived up to the promise made over four decades ago to provide the region and state with much-needed health care practitioners. Indeed, the college is a thriving and innovative institution that is dedicated to meeting the health care needs of a broad range of communities while blazing new paths through groundbreaking research and providing the most innovative education available to train outstanding optometrists and vision scientists.

Students relaxing in the new Center for Student Life and Learning.

MID-HUDSON

Dutchess Community College

State University College at New Paltz

Orange County Community College

State University College at Purchase

Rockland Community College

Sullivan County Community College

Ulster County Community College

Westchester Community College

If Rip Van Winkle were to awaken from his slumbers in the region surrounding his beloved Catskill Mountains today, he would be struck by the variety of landscapes it offers. This region, especially the river, serves as a link between rural upstate New York and downstate New York City and its suburbs. But more than a bridge between two cultures, the Mid-Hudson prides itself on its history and its distinctive range of settlement patterns. Many of the businesses and much of the population works and lives in the southern areas immediately north of New York City, while vast stretches to the north maintain a rural, even wild character. The Mid-Hudson is home to one of the most scenic areas in the state, long a summertime playground, which has added popular winter sports to its long list of attractions.

The Mid-Hudson region is a place of extraordinary natural beauty. Washington Irving gave an evocative description of the Catskill Mountains in his story "Rip Van Winkle": "Every change of season, every change of weather, indeed, every hour of the day, produces some change in the magical hues and shapes of these mountains . . ." In addition to the Catskills there are important waterways such as the upper branches of the Delaware River and the expansive Hudson River. Preservation of this ecosystem, which was threatened by industrial waste several decades ago, is vital to tourism and economic growth throughout the region. At Poughkeepsie, pedestrians use the Walkway over the Hudson, which, at 212 feet tall and 1.28 miles long, is the longest elevated pedestrian bridge in the world, to observe the beauty that prompted the Roosevelt family to build its home at Hyde Park.

The backbone of the region is the scenic Hudson River, named for the English explorer working for the Dutch East India Company, Henry Hudson. Hudson explored the river in 1609, claiming it for the government of Holland, and it soon formed the spine of the Dutch colony of New Netherland. The beauty of the river and its surrounding landscape has provided inspiration for American writers as well as the painters of the Hudson River School, those mid-nineteenth-century landscape artists whose romantic style fell out of favor by the end of the century.

After the turn of the century, the rural nature of the mountains to the west of the river, the Catskills, attracted wealthy Jewish city dwellers who fled the heat of New York City summers but were denied entry into many resorts. In response, Jewish entrepreneurs built a series of hotels, the most famous of which were Grossinger's and the Concord, centers of what came to be known as the "Borscht Belt," the venue that gave birth to many of the most prominent

Walkway Over the Hudson, between Poughkeepsie and Highland.

Opening ceremony at Woodstock, August 14, 1969.

Jewish comedians in the second quarter of the century. The hotels have now passed, victims of declining ethnic barriers after the barbarism of World War II and increased availability of air travel, which shrunk time and distance to other places, such as Las Vegas, dramatically. They survive only in fading memory or the gauzy nostalgia of films like *Dirty Dancing*.

The Mid-Hudson created memorable musical moments at midcentury. In the 1950s, it was home to the Weavers, the folk group, with lead singer Pete Seeger, that helped bring folk music to a much broader audience, preparing the way for Bob Dylan a decade later. And in the summer of 1969, Max Yasgur's farm hosted Woodstock, a three-day music festival of thirty-two of the most important musicians of that time, opening with Richie Havens and closing with an electric performance by the legendary Jimi Hendrix. The musicians played for peace—and varying amounts of cash—to a crowd that was esti-

mated at four hundred thousand. Despite inadequate food, water, and sanitation, the love-in was fueled by a genuine spirit of shared purpose, and more than a little weed, in time achieving a cultural currency unmatched by any other music festival.

Today, diversity is a primary characteristic of the Mid-Hudson region: tourism continues its appeal, with Woodbury Commons the second most frequented American destination by Japanese tourists; the region still offers a wide mix of rural, suburban, and urban areas within its seven counties; and today it houses the headquarters of a vast array of commercial enterprises, including the corporate headquarters of IBM in Armonk. "Big Blue" has been—and continues to be—one of the largest employers in the region.

As the region moves to encourage greater investments in high technology, which brings with it more high-paying jobs, the presence of a large num-

Mohonk Mountain House, New Paltz.

County Community College and Westchester Community College were housed in the former estates of rich industrialists. Ulster County Community College broke the pattern, however, offering its first classes in a modest renovated elementary school in Kingston, the county's most populous city.

While each of the colleges offers different opportunities to its county's residents, all are bound by a common purpose to offer that region what it needs, ranging from gateway programs for Westchester County's large immigrant population to New Paltz's extraordinary outreach to the community through the arts. Their understanding of common purpose led Orange, Rockland, Ulster, and Sullivan community colleges to create the Hudson Valley Educational Consortium, which provides broader access to academic programs and workforce training throughout the four-county region.

Both of the four-year SUNY colleges in the region, SUNY New Paltz and Purchase College, demonstrate the variety among SUNY schools and the different needs of the Mid-Hudson region. New Paltz, which began offering a normal school curriculum in the 1880s, has recently added a School of Science and Engineering, building on its emerging strengths in the sciences. Purchase College, one of SUNY's newest campuses, has focused its curriculum on the arts and has developed close relationships to the various arts communities in neighboring New York City.

The Mid-Hudson region, which stretches for a hundred miles north from New York City, carries a strong respect for its environment and history as it looks to innovate for the economy of the twenty-first century. SUNY's institutions have partnered with the region's residents for over a century and will be even more important to their future, providing residents with the educational opportunities they will need to meet the challenges of the decades ahead.

ber of private and public colleges and universities promises the region will continue to offer potential investors and companies a highly skilled workforce, one that is more highly educated than either the state or national average.

The eight Mid-Hudson SUNY campuses are important economic generators in their own right, enrolling more than fifty-five thousand students and employing more than seven thousand, with annual payrolls totaling $256 million. The SUNY colleges in the region are noted for combining their distinctive respect for the natural surroundings with innovation.

In the late 1950s and early 1960s, SUNY fostered the opening of six community colleges in the Mid-Hudson region. Some of these colleges, created to provide accessible and affordable education for the region's citizens, have emerged as leaders in ecologically sound technologies: Sullivan County Community College is particularly strong in this area, offering associate degrees in Green Building Maintenance and Management as well as Wind Turbine Technology. Like many such institutions, the earliest classes were offered in existing historic structures. Dutchess Community College (1957), for example, occupies the site of a former tuberculosis hospital; while Rockland Community College's first class was in the former Rockland County Almshouse. And, both Orange

DUTCHESS COMMUNITY COLLEGE

n the mid-1950s the community leaders of Dutchess County, in the heart of the Hudson Valley, decided to test support for a community college to provide affordable and accessible education for its residents. With only forty community colleges in the nation, they were on the cutting edge of higher education. In the fall of 1955, a committee formed to spearhead the project held a series of public meetings throughout the county and commissioned a feasibility study. Both indicated strong support across the county. Based on these positive reports, their proposal was accepted by SUNY and Dutchess Community College was born.

The search was on for a suitable home. Ultimately, they selected the former site of Bowne Hospital, an abandoned tuberculosis sanitarium built in the 1920s on a hill overlooking Poughkeepsie. Its

three buildings were renovated, a Board of Trustees named, and plans were finalized for admitting the first freshman class in September 1958. That the college

The Class of 1960 become the first of more than forty thousand Dutchess Community College alumni.

A majority of Dutchess County's nurses train at the college.

was meeting a need was immediately apparent. The initial projection of around two hundred students was quickly made obsolete by the 252 full-time and 412 part-time students who enrolled. When the Middle States Association of Colleges and Schools granted full accreditation in 1964, it noted that few community colleges—Dutchess was already serving over three thousand students—matured with such speed.

The enrollment at the college has grown steadily to nearly ten thousand. The college also reaches

Fire Science students regularly demonstrate firefighting techniques and technology during test burns.

beyond its 170-acre campus to offer courses in communities around the county. And a satellite campus in Wappingers Falls serves students living in the southern part of the county. To accommodate the expanding student body, the physical plant of the college has steadily expanded from the original three to thirteen buildings.

As the student body grew, so too did the academic offerings. By 1982 there were thirty-two registered academic programs, fifteen years later there were forty-two, and today nearly sixty programs lead to AA, AS, and AAS degrees and certificates. Liberal arts and science and fine arts programs prepare students for transfer to baccalaureate colleges. Applied programs prepare students to serve Dutchess County's immediate needs. For instance, more than seventy percent of the area's nurses graduated from the college. Other programs prepare students in a variety of applied fields, including architecture and construction, business, criminal justices, fire science, health care, and human services.

Curricular growth was accompanied by a corresponding emphasis on student satisfaction and academic excellence. That commitment is symbolized by the presence of a strong academic library. A program of endowed faculty chairs encourages and rewards academic excellence among the faculty, and annual Honors Convocations recognize the academic achievements of outstanding students. The Conk-

The Francis U. and Mary F. Ritz Library offers comfortable study spaces and extensive resources.

lin Scholarship for Academic Excellence offers two years' free tuition to Dutchess County high school students graduating in the top ten percent of their class. The Dutchess Community College Foundation, incorporated in 1975, underwrites many other scholarships, supports faculty research, and helps keep the college abreast of technological developments.

Public art has featured prominently on the Dutchess campus since the early 1970s when the Armenian sculptor Ludvik Durchanek donated two pieces, *The Family* and *Prometheus*. The collection has grown steadily and today over thirty-five sculptural works grace the campus. Among the most notable is *Administration, Faculty, and Students*, by Carrie Jo Hatchel, the country's first female ironworking

sculptor. The college has been committed to exposing students to art and sculpture as well as encouraging the public to visit and enjoy the art. This commitment to public art enables Dutchess Community College to enhance the cultural life of Dutchess County. In 2001 the college was awarded the Dutchess County Executive's Award for Art in Public Places.

Building a sense of community continually challenges community colleges, in which most or all students are commuters. From its very beginnings, Dutchess Community College has offered students the opportunity to take part in activities and organizations in order to build that sense of belonging and pride in their school. A student-run newspaper, *The Spectator*, and a yearbook, *Chronos*, chronicle life at DCC. A wide variety of clubs reflect not only academic interests but also extracurricular activities as well. One of the earliest, and one that continues to loom large on campus today, is participation in the Model United Nations. Dutchess began sending representatives in 1959 and, in collaboration with Vassar College, continues to do so more than fifty years later.

The Cardinal brightens winter campus walks.

In 2012 Dutchess opened its first dormitory, Conklin Hall, giving over 450 students an on-campus experience. The Falcons athletic teams compete in seven sports. The Falcons baseball team is the first community college team ever to go to the Division III championships three years in a row.

Music, theater, and other cultural events are important parts of the Dutchess experience. The current Masquers Guild traces its roots back to the drama club that was formed in the college's first year. The Dutchess Community College Jazz Ensemble, also created in the early years of the campus, is a regular fixture at college functions. Through the Lyceum Series, inaugurated in 1972, speakers of national importance are brought to campus to deliver speeches to both students and the community.

Dutchess Community College continues to fulfill the mission set out over fifty years ago, to offer high-quality, affordable education. One-third of Dutchess County's high school graduates attend the college. DCC takes pride in giving students an education that fits them for success at four-year schools or for the twenty-first century workforce. The farsighted pioneers of the 1950s would be gratified to see how their vision led to an institution that has served Dutchess County so well.

A Falcon slides home.

STATE UNIVERSITY COLLEGE
AT NEW PALTZ

I n 1828, the New Paltz Classical School opened its doors to what would in time become the State University College at New Paltz. The Classical School added Greek and Latin to the usual offerings of reading, writing, and arithmetic. In 1833, it was reorganized into an academy on Huguenot Street in New Paltz. For more than fifty years the academy educated the children of the city until a serious fire in 1884 compelled it to rebuild.

Once rebuilt, the academy shifted its mission and became a state Normal School, training teachers for the growing public schools. But even then, New Paltz innovated by also offering an academic course of study to students who were not interested in becoming teachers. Yet another fire destroyed the school in April 1906, and it was rebuilt on a new location, a ten-acre hillside plot about a mile from the Wallkill River. The new building, dedicated in January 1909, still stands, refurbished and known affectionately as "Old Main."

In 1938, the New York State Education Department authorized a four-year curriculum, which gave

Old Main, built in 1909, now the School of Education.

the school collegiate status and a new name: the State Teachers College at New Paltz. Within a decade, the college began to offer graduate studies in education. With SUNY's formation in 1948, New Paltz was among the founding schools. Within SUNY, it continued to thrive and innovate.

In the 1960s, the college entered a period of great change, with new bachelor degrees in the liberal arts and sciences available to students. No longer a state teachers college, it officially became State University of New York College of Liberal Arts and Science at New Paltz.

The curriculum in that decade reflected important social currents, as the faculty created survey courses in African and Asian cultures, presaging the development of a Black Studies program. The Experimental Studies program (later renamed the Innovative Studies program) offered innovative courses, both credit and noncredit, in a variety of topics, such as video art, camping, dance therapy, clowning, and eco-design. Even more innovative was its structure: instructors were hired by the students and

Van den Berg Hall, built in 1930, today houses the School of Business.

paid through student activity fees.

During the turbulent 1960s and early 1970s, the campus at New Paltz, like many others across the country, was the site of student unrest and protests, most notably against the Vietnam War. As the period progressed, attention shifted to civil rights. In time, New Paltz students, like so many others, soon returned to the academic work at hand, whether in classrooms, laboratories, studios, or gyms, leaving behind a rich heritage for the future.

The 1960s and 1970s were also marked by significant building on the campus, including two residence hall complexes; a lecture hall; classroom, laboratory, and faculty office buildings along the new Excelsior Concourse; a gymnasium; an administration building; and a new student union. In 1982, the van den Berg School of Practice closed, one of many SUNY "campus schools" to suffer similar fates, later to become home to the School of Business.

By the 1980s, New Paltz settled into a period of relative quiet, with the college developing professional degree programs in Journalism, Accounting, and Nursing. Despite

Construction of the Concourse, 1967.

Student Union Atrium, 2010.

Graduation, 2014.

the growth of programs in the liberal arts and sciences and pre-professional areas, teacher education has remained an important part of the college's mission, the centrality of which is demonstrated by the recent renovation of "Old Main" to house the School of Education.

The campus has acquired a well-deserved reputation for service to the arts. The Samuel Dorsky Museum of Art, which opened in 2001, is one of the largest in SUNY, with a permanent collection that comprises more than five thousand works of American art (with emphasis on the Hudson Valley and Catskill regions); nineteenth-, twentieth-, and twenty-first-century photography; metals; and an international collection of art and artifacts. Through its exhibitions and public programs the Dorsky serves as a center for Hudson Valley arts and culture.

Fifty years after the introduction of art education, the college's Master of Fine Arts program would be ranked in the top 100 Best Graduate Schools by U.S. News & World Report, which also ranked the Metal/Jewelry program first in the nation. There are other distinctions that the college earned in the past decade. Adding to its long history of international education—the college had welcomed fifty female students from Cuba in 1901—New Paltz received the Heiskell Award from the Institute of International Education in 2015 in recognition of its successful programming to create study-abroad opportunities for economically disadvantaged and historically underrepresented students.

Since launching the Hudson Valley Advanced Manufacturing Center in spring 2013, the college's groundbreaking 3D printing initiative has integrated its strengths in engineering, computer science, technology, and the arts. New Paltz has added state-of-the-art 3D printing equipment, created a certificate program in Digital Design and Fabrication, forged public-private partnerships with industry leaders, garnered over $12 million in state and private funding, and promoted collaboration among students, faculty, and regional businesses on 3D design projects.

Cuban student, following the Spanish-American War, 1901.

Today's campus, set on 216 beautiful acres, has improved dramatically, with both new and renovated residence halls and an Athletic and Wellness Center. Other renovations include the Student Union Building, with the addition of a now-iconic pyramidal glass Atrium, Old Main (2012), the Sojourner Truth Library (2016), and Wooster Hall (2016). A new science building will open in 2017, and planning proceeds for a new engineering innovation hub, scheduled for completion in 2018.

While the campus, with 143 programs organized into six schools, would be unrecognizable to the founders of the Classical School almost two centuries ago, SUNY New Paltz maintains its traditional commitment to serving the educational needs of the Hudson Valley and other regions of New York State with excellence and creativity. That the founders would readily recognize.

ORANGE COUNTY COMMUNITY COLLEGE

After World War II Orange County, a predominantly rural farming region about fifty miles northwest of New York City, urgently needed a college. Its veterans, who upon returning from World War II qualified for a free college education under the GI Bill, found there were few institutions of higher education in the region. In addition, a recent report revealed that of all the counties in New York State, Orange County had the fewest high school graduates pursuing a college education. In response to this crisis, local education and business leaders established the Middletown Collegiate Center, a temporary solution offering evening classes in Middletown High School.

When the center closed in 1949, Orange County's recently formed Committee on Higher Education began waging a public relations campaign to convince local government officials and citizens of the need for a permanent college. A college education should be available to all, they argued, not just the privileged few. *Look* magazine reported that when the committee members "discovered that the youth of (their) community couldn't afford to go away to college, (they) brought the college to the community.... 'What we need here, ... is a college for the kids who have to stay home. One within reach of the bus or family jalopy.'" In the end, the committee's efforts paid off. New York State agreed to supply half of the funding if Orange County would provide the remainder. All that was needed was a campus.

Although other sites were considered, the Morrison estate in Middletown won out. The existing facilities would serve immediately as classrooms and offices, and the extensive property would allow for

Morrison Hall, the oldest building on the campus, was built by the Hortons and later was the home of John H. and Christine Morrison.

Days before the first day of classes in September 1950, horses were still in the barn during last-minute conversions.

future expansion. Webb Horton, a retired tanner and industrialist, had built the mansion on the estate, later named Morrison Hall, in 1910. He bequeathed the estate to his cousin, John H. Morrison, whose wife Christine donated the mansion and the property to Orange County to house the proposed community college after his death in 1950. In September the first entering class began its studies in a building that had once been the Morrison estate barn and carriage house.

The student population grew exponentially; the college quickly outgrew its facilities, and funding was provided to accommodate the growth. Four new buildings were constructed in the first decade: Hudson Hall, Harriman Hall, Sarah Wells Library, and the Orange Hall Student Center. Popular programs were added, notably the first two-year nursing program in the nation, which was approved by New York State in 1952. This program attracted nationwide attention and served as a model for similar programs in other community colleges.

The college also began to offer courses off campus. Through the Extension and Community Services Department, English, psychology, mathematics, and music courses, among others, were taught throughout

Orange County. Evening and weekend classes began in 1951 and were an immediate success. By 1955 the college was offering forty-six evening courses enrolling 1,390 students. Enrollment on the main campus also grew dramatically; by 1965 it neared one thousand, and by 1991 more than five thousand full- or part-time students were studying at the campus.

Throughout the decades, the college not only expanded, but it transformed itself to reflect changes in the surrounding community and the nation. In 1960 the student body responded to the burgeoning national civil rights movement by students refusing to hold the college's spring dance at the racially segregated Elks club; they insisted the dance be open to all students. College president Robert Novak declared that the college favored a "strong policy of total integration." In October of 1966, students reactivated a chapter of the NAACP to "attack local barriers to integration." And the college responded to the increasing demand for greater accessibility to higher education throughout Orange County by offering evening courses in Newburgh and at Mount Saint Mary College.

Kaplan Hall, an eighty-five-thousand-square-foot classroom and laboratory building, opened on the new SUNY Orange Newburgh campus in January 2011.

The 1970s was a time of change for women and minorities in the nation and on campus. In 1972, SUNY Orange hosted a conference on women's roles in education, careers, and politics. That same year, the College's Black Student Union drove a van from Middletown to Newburgh to encourage young children and teens to consider a college education.

Eventually, SUNY Orange established a permanent presence in Newburgh. In 1990, the college leased the former Broadway Elementary School on the corner of Broadway and Robinson avenues in Newburgh, and more than three hundred students registered for courses at the site. In 1998, the Newburgh satellite campus relocated to a larger facility overlooking the Hudson River. Enrollment continued to grow, necessitating another move. After years of deliberation, a permanent site was agreed upon. Construction began in 2009, and Kaplan Hall opened on the Newburgh campus in January of 2011. The campus buildings, in the center of Newburgh's downtown,

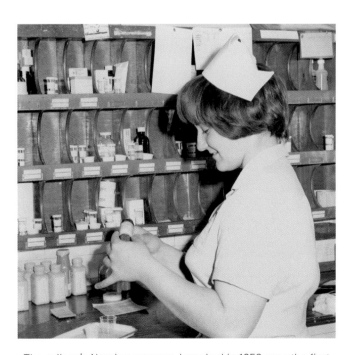

The college's Nursing program, launched in 1952, was the first associate degree nursing program in the country.

The Rowley Center for Science and Engineering facility on the Middletown campus dramatically expanded technology offerings.

offer breathtaking views of the Hudson River and the surrounding area.

SUNY Orange's Middletown campus also continues to grow. The Rowley Center for Science and Engineering, completed in the summer of 2014, is a new 107,000-square-foot science center developed to expand the science, engineering, and architecture programs. The SUNY Orange Foundation raised the funds for this project as well as for remodeling the Devitt Center for Botany and Horticulture and construction of the Morrison Lab School.

SUNY Orange continues to be closely involved with its surrounding area and community, with the Office of Educational Partnerships (OEP) extending the educational mission of the college beyond its Middletown and Newburgh campuses by offering classes at satellite centers in local high schools. The Community College in the High School Program (CCHSP) enables qualified high school students to take college courses at their high schools during the regular school day. The

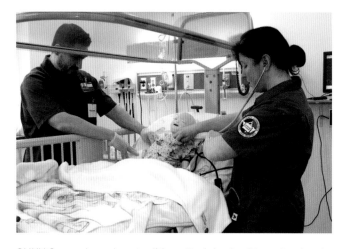

SUNY Orange has a long tradition of training health professionals.

Cultural Affairs department's programming enriches the lives of students and the community through art exhibits, lectures, concerts, master classes and films, and the college's Continuing and Professional Education (CAPE) program offers classes to community members desiring to improve skills or acquire new ones.

SUNY Orange reaches out to students of various ages, with the Morrison Lab School in Middletown and the Lab School in Newburgh offering convenient, affordable early childhood day care. Meanwhile older learners are served by SUNY Orange's Encore program, which offers noncredit courses and travel experiences for lifelong learners age fifty-five and older. In the years since the first students began their college careers in a converted carriage house shared with a horse on the Morrison estate, Orange County Community College has grown into a leading educational and cultural resource for Orange County residents of all ages.

STATE UNIVERSITY COLLEGE AT PURCHASE

Long a patron of the arts, Governor Nelson A. Rockefeller was the driving force behind creating SUNY's newest university college, one with a unique mission. His vision was to create a publicly funded college that combined liberal arts and sciences programs with professional conservatory training in the performing and visual arts. Chartered in 1967, this pioneering college, created with the idea that scholars and artists are vital to one another as well as to a culturally enlightened society, was built on a five-hundred-acre estate in Westchester County twenty miles north of Manhattan. The mission and the location combined to inspire the college motto, "Think Wide Open."

A college founded according to this unique vision had to be architecturally noteworthy as well. Edward Larrabee Barnes was commissioned as master architect, and he set out to create "a city within the country," a campus in which nearly all the buildings clustered around a large open space preserving the fields and meadows of the original farm and estate. The plan called for preserving many of the existing buildings, including the current administration complex that had been built in the 1920s. With Barnes providing the overarching vision, nine architectural firms were commissioned to design individual structures, including the first college campus building in America devoted solely to dance.

The Neuberger Museum of Art was the first building completed. It opened in 1974 with the core comprised of Roy R. Neuberger's collection of American masters, featuring works by Georgia O'Keeffe, Jackson Pollock, Mark Rothko, and Willem de Kooning, among others. The Neuberger now houses more than six thousand objects and enjoys an international reputation for its dedication to excellence in its pro-

Fulfilling Rockefeller's vision, the Neuberger Museum of Art educates students while serving as a cultural center for the wider community.

A tense moment on stage.

gramming and exhibitions focusing on modern, contemporary, and African art.

The initial campus design reached completion with the opening of the Performing Arts Center in 1978. Its four theaters anchor the campus and community cultural life, bringing audiences of more than 166,000 a year to over three hundred public events. The facility is used by many of the college departments as well as by arts organizations in the greater community.

Reflecting its mission, great care has been taken to integrate art throughout the campus. One of the most striking of the outdoor sculptures is Henry Moore's *Large Two Forms*. The Neuberger Museum of Art, the primary exhibition space, is augmented by two smaller galleries on campus. The exhibitions in the Richard and Dolly Maass Gallery, located in the School of Art+Design, provides a professional context for students, giving them the opportunity to work with an exhibiting artist who is not a member of the college's faculty. A team from the Neuberger Museum,

Purchase also prepares those who work behind the scenes.

the Performing Arts Center, and Campus Technology Services developed the Passage Gallery, which exhibits student work in a prominent location just across from the Performing Arts Center box office.

Purchase enrolls approximately 4,200 students in the School of the Arts and the School of Liberal Arts and Sciences. Though known for its world-class arts programs, it also ranks nationally in the top tier of public baccalaureate institutions for the number of its biology and psychology graduates who receive their doctorates. Purchase College students choose from forty-seven undergraduate majors with thirty-two concentrations and four graduate majors with eleven concentrations.

Since the college aims to provide students with an education that will enable them to secure professional employment following graduation, there is an emphasis on cross-disciplinary studies. This is clearly illustrated by the newest unit, the School of Film and Media Studies, whose students take courses in a variety of disciplines integrating production experience with critiques of modern media and its place in the culture.

This focus on interdisciplinarity can be found outside of the arts as well. Casa Purchase: An Out-

A metal sculpture student refining his welding skills.

reach Center for Latin American Studies was begun by a member of the history faculty. Casa Purchase represents a "coordinated effort to weave together the educational, artistic, and research opportunities of Purchase College with the needs of local residents and officials, their schools, and their organizations."

While Purchase College's mission is unique, it also provides a traditional campus life for students.

A Panther prepares to pounce.

inclusion in *The Princeton Review's Guide to 332 Green Colleges*.

Purchase has a long tradition of fulfilling Rockefeller's vision of the college becoming a distinguished cultural center for the region. In 1968, Purchase admitted its first students into the Continuing Education program, four years before the first full freshman class came to campus. That commitment to cultural expansiveness continues. Today, its Neighborhood Bridges and Performing Arts Workshops bring the arts to local schools. And pre-show introductions and post-performance workshops with artists amplify Purchase's cultural impact.

Over two-thirds of students reside on campus in three apartment complexes and more traditional dormitories. Two dormitories are devoted to the First Year Experience to ease the transition to collegiate life. Seventeen Panther teams compete in the Skyline Conference with other SUNY and private colleges.

In 2014 Purchase College received a $5 million gift from Emily and Eugene Grant that established three new funds to support the Provost's Office for Faculty and the Conservatory of Music. This generous gift covers the Opera program's production expenses, offers faculty incentive rewards, and creates a pool of unrestricted funds to be used by the Conservatory of Music.

Despite Purchase's focus on the arts, the campus continues its efforts to create a greener community. In 2014 the EPA awarded the college a substantial grant through the New York State Clean Water Revolving Fund's Green Innovation grant program to facilitate the installation of green infrastructure. The commitment to sustainability is ongoing. Purchase employs a full-time senior energy manager to increase the emphasis on creating a green campus. In 2014, these efforts were rewarded by the college's

The quiet before unleashing the tympani.

ROCKLAND COMMUNITY COLLEGE

In the spring of 1959, community leaders convinced the County Board of Supervisors that the county needed and could support a community college. It was close, a slim 3–2 vote in favor of commitment, but ever since, Rockland County has embraced the college and the college has played a vital role in the life of the community. This reciprocity is clear in the college's mission as "an open admissions institution," characterized by an "accessible, responsive, student-centered learning environment."

The Barn, home for RCC theater productions until it was destroyed by fire in 1979.

RCC's first 139 students began classes in what had been the Rockland County Welfare Home. The sturdy brick edifice, renamed Brucker Hall, became the administration building and remains so today. The 26.5-acre farm surrounding the campus also included a dairy barn renovated into a multi-purpose space housing the College Barn Theater.

In the years following its founding, the college experienced two decades of tremendous growth, with the physical plant expanding to meet student need.

During this period, the college added two academic buildings, a student union, a library, and a fieldhouse, which housed the athletic and physical education programs and hosted numerous trade shows and community events. In 1983, the new Cultural Arts Center, with a 504-seat theater, replaced the College Barn Theater.

Recognizing the need to create access to a college education for those with limited access to transportation to its main campus in Suffern, the college in 1969 received federal funding to launch off-campus extension centers in Haverstraw and Spring Valley and added a satellite center in Nyack a year later. The Haverstraw Center continues to thrive today, having undergone a $1.5-million expansion featuring a 3D printing "smart lab" and other services to promote advanced manufacturing, business, and employment throughout the county.

Rockland Community College prides itself on being a vital resource for the community, offering both cultural and business enrichment to the region. More than two hundred thousand visitors come to events on the campus each year. One of the most important institutions on the RCC campus is the Holocaust Museum and Center for Tolerance and Education. The museum was founded in 1984 and moved to the campus in 2012, and sponsors a variety of events each year designed to educate the populace about that dark event in human history.

International education provides a distinct opportunity for Rockland students. In the 1970s the college launched its Study Abroad program, the first of its kind at a community college. Fifteen students traveled with an instructor to Alvescot College in Oxfordshire, England, for a semester of overseas study, living in small individual "flats" with their English peers. Since that modest start, *The Chronicle of Higher Education* has recognized RCC's international study program as the nation's finest among community colleges no fewer than ten times. In 2014, RCC

Cupola, Brucker Hall.

Autumn on campus.

Send-off tea for students embarking on a Cambridge study trip.

was one of only three American community colleges to send students to study at the prestigious University of Cambridge in England.

Like the Study Abroad program, RCC's Mentor/Talented Students honors program has achieved distinction. Founded in 1977 the Draper M/TS program (later renamed for one of its founding professors) was awarded a coveted FIPSE grant in 1997 from the US Department of Education to serve as a model for community college honors programs throughout the country. Ivy League schools and Tier One colleges recruit RCC honors students for transfer because of the rigorous program's reputation for excellence.

Rockland Community College responds to the changing needs of its increasingly diverse student population with a similarly diverse curriculum. From only six associate degrees in 1959, RCC's academic menu has grown and offers its seven thousand students choices from among forty associate degrees and eleven one-year certificate programs. Students

can find a program to fit their particular needs, whether it is preparation for transfer to a baccalaureate program, preparation for employment in a specific field, or simply a desire to learn something new. The college meets the needs of all students, at all ages.

RCC students have many opportunities to participate in activities beyond the classrooms, including, but not limited to, intercollegiate sports; a literary magazine; the student newspaper, *Outlook Student Press*; or productions in the Multimedia Production Center, the home of RCC-TV. Together with outstanding faculty, they have created a lively, engaging, and committed learning community.

In 2006, RCC opened a one-hundred-thousand-square-foot, state-of-the-art Technology Center, the first new permanent construction on campus in more than twenty years and the first "green" building constructed by Rockland County. On Earth Day 2008, the college formally signed the American College

The Technology Center, which opened in 2006, is RCC's first certified "green" building.

and University Presidents Climate Commitment, which pledged RCC to sharply reduce and eventually eliminate all of its global warming emissions.

As is evident in the new campus master plan, the college is committed to serving a wide variety of students by innovative programs. With its proposal for residence halls to attract more international students, the campus will enhance its traditional support for international education and demonstrate the growing need to better understand the global community of which all students are a part. RCC is also expanding its high school program by providing capable high school students the opportunity to complete college-level courses in the high school, better preparing them for the transition to demanding postsecondary academic work. And the national push to improve STEM (Science, Technology, Engineering, and Math) education is evident in SUNY Rockland's innovative curriculum enhancements in its STEM and Health Professions Division.

Finally, the college values cultural pluralism, as is underscored in the current effort to develop a formal diversity plan. Situated in one of New York's most ethnically and religiously diverse counties, Rockland Community College honors many cultures by sponsoring a wide range of heritage celebrations throughout the year. These provide part of the many supports necessary for each student to succeed. That commitment to all who want to learn has been an essential part of the college's mission and history and will continue to guide its future.

Commencement—a testament to success for Rockland Community College students.

SULLIVAN COUNTY COMMUNITY COLLEGE

Located on 405 acres of former farmland in the lovely Catskill Mountains, Sullivan County Community College prides itself on providing personalized education in its bucolic setting.

In September 1962, SUNY's Trustees acknowledged the need for a two-year community college in rural Sullivan County. A year later the first freshmen arrived at a modest campus in the former South Fallsburg High School. Additional temporary buildings were erected on the football field, a former bank served as office space, an unused steel-framed loft found new life as an art studio, and revamped private homes became administrative and faculty offices.

The college soon outgrew those limited quarters and plans were drawn up for a new campus in Loch Sheldrake, set against the backdrop of the Catskill Mountains. Though located in the countryside, the modern and sophisticated architecture, the work of famed architectural firm Edward Durrell Stone and Associates, reflects the college's determination to embrace its rural location while enhancing it. The design took into account the sometimes-harsh Catskill weather with nine interconnected buildings. Only trips to the Paul Gerry Fieldhouse required braving the elements.

The first freshmen—all seventy-two of them—who walked through the doors on September 23, 1963, could choose among two business programs and a liberal arts and sciences program. These limited offerings were taught by a faculty of nine. Today, the student body of about 1,750, sixty percent of whom are Sullivan County residents, choose from

A student pondering our genetic makeup.

Arts and Design, Simulation and Game Development, and other computer-based programs prepare graduates for the modern cybernetic world. Programs in business and healthcare prepare students to fill important needs in Sullivan County and New York State. Students aspiring to a baccalaureate degree can choose from a variety of liberal arts and science AA and AS programs that prepare them to transfer.

Sullivan's small size encourages a close-knit student life. Approximately four hundred students call either the Lazarus I. Levine Residence Hall or the EcoGreen Townhouses home during the academic year. Kaplan Student Union offers a base for a variety of student clubs and organizations as well as a place to relax.

Intramural and intercollegiate athletics are housed in the thirty-five-thousand-square-foot Paul Gerry Fieldhouse, which provides facilities for basketball, net sports, racquetball, and a fitness center. The Sullivan Generals compete in twelve intercollegiate sports. The men's basketball team is four-time National Junior College Athletic Associa-

among more than thirty-five programs and majors that either prepare graduates for immediate entry into the workforce or for transfer to a four-year college or university.

As one of the major purposes of a community college is training the regional workforce, many of Sullivan County Community College's offerings reflect its rural location and its commitment to align the curriculum with the regional economy. As befits a college in an agricultural area, SCCC is particularly known for its programs in food management and the culinary arts. Fire Protection Technology, Recreation Leadership, and Emergency Management degree programs, along with a Tourism certificate program, also address the special needs of the Catskills.

Other degree programs turn toward the wider world. Graphic

On-campus living facilities have strengthened the sense of community.

tion (NJCAA) Division III national champion. Connecting the Gerry Fieldhouse to the college's geothermal heating and cooling system made it the largest air-conditioned facility in the area. In addition to college sporting events, the fieldhouse is a popular venue for community events and gatherings.

Sullivan County Community College takes its role in the community seriously and works to maintain strong links beyond the campus. The school provides a varied Community Learning program in which students can take courses ranging from belly dancing, to craft beer brewing, to an introduction to plant-based eating. Several of the courses are designed specifically for children, thus offering a truly lifelong learning experience for Sullivan County residents.

The Division of Workforce Development, Continuing Education, and Lifelong Learning provides another link to the wider community by offering

A student relaxes in Kaplan Student Union.

learning opportunities to businesses and individuals that contribute to the success of companies and Sullivan County residents. The division prides itself on its flexibility, continually retooling its offerings to provide those that are applicable in today's rapidly changing business environment.

Future chefs learn the culinary arts.

Like many SUNY campuses, Sullivan County Community College places a strong emphasis on sustainability. A geothermal heating and cooling system, a photovoltaic array, and a wind turbine have been installed to feed the power grid as well as train students in renewable energy techniques. The campus is home to an organic community garden providing healthy, fresh produce to the campus dining services. In turn, students collect and compost over three thousand pounds of food leftovers and scraps each year. In an agreement with Sullivan Solar Garden, a nine-acre solar farm has been installed on the campus.

Recognizing that sustainability is not only good practice but also a source of employment opportunities, sustainability education is strongly repre-sented in Sullivan's curriculum. Students can earn associate degrees in Green Building Maintenance and Management. Those wishing to take a more sci-entific approach to the ecological issues that face the world can enroll in the Environmental Studies program. Indeed, the emphasis on sustainability is carried throughout Sullivan's curriculum, with more than sixty courses focusing on the issue.

Although only a two-hour drive from New York City, Sullivan County Community College reflects a very distinct part of our varied state. The college has offered students valuable liberal arts and professional training in a close academic community for over a half century. And its alumni, in turn, have contributed greatly to the economy, vitality, and quality of life in Sullivan County and beyond.

Hands-on renewable energy training is delivered at Sullivan's 3 kW photovoltaic array.

ULSTER COUNTY COMMUNITY COLLEGE

Ulster County Community College is a small, rural community college in the hamlet of Stone Ridge, New York. The county of Ulster borders the east side of the scenic Hudson River valley, ninety miles north of New York City and fifty miles south of Albany. With an area of 1,130 square miles, much of which is forested and lies within the Catskill Forest Preserve, Ulster County is almost the size of Rhode Island with a population of only just over 180,000. Ulster serves as a pastoral retreat for many New York City residents as well as home to small municipalities, retail strip malls, small and midsized businesses, an emerging tourism and agricultural industry, and Woodstock, a vibrant arts community.

Despite Ulster's sparse population, the desire to provide educational opportunity within its borders was strong. Thus a referendum to establish a community college was passed overwhelmingly by the voters in November 1961. Dale Lake, the college's first president, set Ulster on the course of establishing a strong transfer program by recruiting the founding faculty from four-year colleges when many community colleges were recruiting from high schools. In September 1963, Ulster opened the doors of its temporary campus in the historic old Ulster Academy in Kingston. Two years later Ulster graduated its first class of forty-eight students, the first of over fourteen thousand alumni.

Meanwhile, ground was broken for Ulster's permanent campus, located on ninety acres of meadowland and apple orchards in the hamlet of Stone Ridge, between the Shawangunk and Catskill mountains, ten miles south of Kingston, the county's largest city.

Some of the first students relax in front of the temporary campus.

By moving to Stone Ridge, the campus was situated in the geographic center of Ulster County. Classes began on the new campus in the fall of 1967.

The Ulster voters' optimism was justified and the campus grew quickly. By the early 1970s eight buildings graced a campus that had expanded to 165 acres. The library's maturation reflects the dramatic changes. The original one-room library held five thousand volumes. By 1985 over seventy thousand volumes were housed in a purpose-built twenty-one-thousand-square-foot facility. Today, with the wonders of the Internet, students can sit in the rural splendor of the Stone Ridge campus and access over eighteen million volumes.

But the early 1990s brought great challenges to Ulster County and the Mid-Hudson region. The county was devastated by the closure of IBM's Kingston plant, which had over eight thousand employees at its height. The departure of IBM had a domino effect of business downsizings, closures, and failures. Real estate markets plummeted; new construction all but halted. The economic depression seriously undermined the local tax base, the county's finances, and

the psychological well-being of a community that had been secure in the faith that IBM would always be the backbone of its economy. Outmigration followed, as many residents sought employment elsewhere.

Ulster County Community College became actively involved in the economic revitalization of the county, working with federal, state, and local officials to establish a Business Resource Center in Kingston. Opened in 1995, it housed a small business incubator and a regional New York State Small Business Development Center with a staff of business counselors to work with potential entrepreneurs as well as dislocated businesses. It also became the home of the college's extension site with state-of-the-art classrooms and computer labs and Continuing Education offices. Relocating the Continuing Education unit to Kingston increased its accessibility for retraining the workforce and for the community.

Ulster's leadership role in economic development has been recognized in the region and beyond. The "one-stop shop" for business was of immediate interest to public officials. Peer SUNY institutions sent delegations to observe the Business Resource

Ulster graduate celebrating with a future graduate?

Center, and CNN did a feature story on it that spurred the interest of colleges nationwide.

As the county economy recovered, Ulster embarked on ambitious changes in programs, recruitment, technology, administrative, and academic systems. Further initiatives included the addition of eighteen new academic programs, including an online degree, and a renewed focus on increasing student retention. Facilities were renovated, relations with the county's arts community strengthened, and the campus technology infrastructure upgraded. By joining with SUNY's community colleges in Orange, Rockland, and Sullivan counties in the Mid-Hudson Educational Consortium, the campus has enabled students to obtain degrees in important programs that it otherwise could not afford.

The college promotes cultural awareness among its students and the community. The Muroff-Kotler Visual Arts Gallery holds a permanent collection that enriches the campus. The five-hundred-seat John Quimby Theater provides a venue for student and professional theatrical productions, concerts, dance presentations, poetry readings, guest lectures, and other featured events.

The fine arts play a prominent role in Ulster's campus life.

Veterans prepare for civilian life.

1777, Ulster's athletes compete as the Senators in the Mid-Hudson Conference and the National Junior College Athletic Association.

While Ulster offers transfer, career, vocational, and continuing education programs, it concentrates on a range of associate degrees, in both the liberal arts and sciences, as well as the more technical fields (such as engineering, fashion design, and nursing) necessary to maintain its tradition of successful academic transfer to four-year institutions. Typically about seventy percent of Ulster's graduates pursue a baccalaureate degree after their associate degree. Among programs leading directly to employment after graduation are Accounting, Criminal Justice, and Veterinary Technology.

Outside the classroom, students participate in clubs focusing on interests as wide as chess, veterinary technology, fashion, gaming, or the Veterans' Club. Befitting Kingston's historic role as the site of the first meeting of the New York State Senate in

Ulster County Community College has been shaped by its environment. It remains a small and close-knit campus of two thousand students where faculty and students have a strong sense of community. In a county that has faced economic adversity, the college has played an important role in overcoming it and in maintaining a high quality of life.

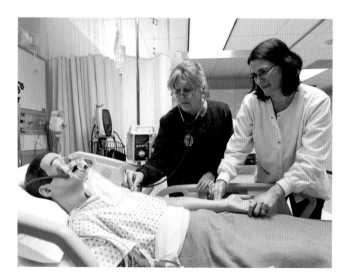
Learning the applications of modern medicine.

Ulster prepares students to tend to animals as well as humans.

WESTCHESTER COMMUNITY COLLEGE

Westchester Community College was a postwar baby. As World War II came to a close, the Dewey administration saw an urgent need to train technicians and appointed committees to recommend a policy for training youth based on predicted occupational trends. Following the recommendation of these committees, the New York State Legislature created five community-centered institutes of applied arts and sciences that would provide tuition-free education to prepare youths and adults to enter semi-professional employment. One of these institutes was at White Plains.

The institute opened its doors in September 1947 with a mission to address both the needs of returning servicemen and the economic needs of the region. As a postwar housing boom was anticipated,

one of the first programs offered at the institute was building construction technology. Thus, the school immediately began to fulfill the emerging community college mandate to provide accessible, affordable, vocationally centered education tailored to the specific needs of a region.

To this end, the institute also offered academic programs in Electrical Technology, Mechanical Technology, and Food Service Administration Technology. These curricula attracted a largely young, male student body. The gender and age makeup of the student body began to expand in the second year when the school initiated a Medical and Dental Office Assistant Technology program that attracted women and older students. The first graduation in 1949 awarded degrees to 183 men and twenty-three women in seven programs.

Compassionate care is part of the curriculum at Westchester.

The five institutes that opened in 1947 were given five years to prove their efficacy, which they did. In 1952 the Institute of Applied Arts and Sciences at White Plains was welcomed into the SUNY system as Westchester Community College. Secure in its future, the college started searching for a permanent campus. Initially, classes were held in a wing of a White Plains junior high school. But by 1953, as the college was being incorporated into SUNY, a move became inevitable. The City of White Plains needed to reclaim the space for its own needs, and SUNY Westchester had simply become too large to remain there.

The search led to Valhalla, the picturesque Hartford estate. The Hartfords, heirs to the A&P grocery store fortune, had willed the estate to Yale University, which used it as an environmental research facility. When Yale decided not to continue using the Hartford estate, Westchester County purchased it for the col-lege with support from SUNY. In 1958 classes began on the new campus in the English Tudor Hartford mansion and its greenhouses and farm buildings. The first library was in a converted garage. But soon an expansive building program transformed the campus. Thus today's lovely campus mixes modern and tra-ditional architecture in a rolling terrain with mature trees and plantings.

The curriculum also expanded. As early as 1947 the chair of the institute's Board of Trustees pre-dicted that the school of technology would eventu-ally teach a wide range of general college subjects. That came to pass. The college offers a wide range of AA degrees leading toward liberal arts and sciences baccalaureate degrees, while fourteen AS degrees lead toward applied majors in four-year colleges. The Environmental Science programs echo Yale's original use of Valhalla. Numerous AAS degree and certifi-cate programs train students for immediate employ-ment and help the workforce raise its standards.

In keeping with its initial creation to serve the educational needs of returning World War II veterans, in the 1970s the college turned its attention to address-ing the needs of veterans returning from Vietnam. In 1972, it established the Growing Options for Adults through Learning program in order to meet the needs of those returning from war. In addition, the grow-ing number of women returning to college convinced

Can any other campus claim to have held its first classes in Valhalla?

SUNY Westchester's students learn to observe nature more closely.

counselors that "mature" female students needed an expanded support system to help them negotiate the demands of college. This led, in 1975, to the creation of the women's forum to help working-class women succeed in a collegiate environment.

In the decades that followed, Westchester's outreach mission has shifted to meeting the needs of special populations, including the educationally disadvantaged, mature students, and students for whom English is a second language. The recently opened seventy-thousand-square-foot Gateway Center provides programs targeting the needs of recently arrived Westchester residents. It also houses the Gateway for Entrepreneurship and the Center for Financial and Economic Education, the products of public-private partnerships. In addition, the Welcome

Center serves as a port of entry for those exploring the college's offerings.

The college also reached out geographically, creating extension campuses around Westchester Country where it offers day, evening, and weekend courses. In the mid-1990s, Peekskill sought Westchester's help in turning its dilapidated downtown into a haven for artists. The college responded by establishing an extension campus offering fine arts, computer graphics, multimedia, and general education courses, which has contributed mightily to the city's recovery. The Westchester Community College Center for the Arts in White Plains enriches that city's cultural life while offering students courses in digital photography, ceramics, sculpture, and other art mediums.

Today's students learn skills that were not even imagined when the college was founded.

Extension locations in Mount Vernon, Yonkers, Ossining, Mahopac, New Rochelle, Port Chester, and Shrub Oak as well as online courses make the college accessible to residents in every part of Westchester County.

Today, nearing its seventh decade of serving Westchester, the county's college enrolls fourteen thousand students in credit-bearing courses. The region has much greater economic needs than the name "Westchester" normally conjures up. So, too, does the county's extraordinary ethnic, racial, and linguistic diversity defy its image. The college has consistently worked to meet the needs of its diverse student body and to address the county's challenges. Toward that end, it has the largest continuing education unit in New York State, offering noncredit courses that are fully integrated into the offerings of the academic departments and geared to changing regional needs. In its nearly seven decades, Westchester Community College has grown dramatically in enrollments, facilities, and faculty, while remaining true to its roots by adapting to meet twenty-first-century social and economic needs.

Students of many origins are introduced to higher education at the Gateway.

Tomorrow's healthcare workers learning the trade.

CAPITAL REGION

Adirondack Community College

University at Albany

Columbia-Greene Community College

Empire State College

Hudson Valley Community College

SUNY Polytechnic Institute

Schenectady County Community College

I n many ways the eight counties that make up the Capital Region can be thought of as the heart of New York State. In its early history, this area played a significant role in both the initial European settlements and the American Revolution. As the new nation embraced the possibilities brought on by the industrial revolution, this region was quick to seize the opportunities. This enthusiastic approach to economic growth has continued into the twenty-first century with the region's SUNY colleges and universities serving as major drivers of that success.

The European presence in the Capital Region dates back to 1540 when French fur traders built a fort on Castle Island in what is now Albany. The first permanent European settlers in the area were the Dutch, who based their occupancy on the 1609 claim registered on their government's behalf by Henry Hudson. Kiliaen van Rensselaer founded the Manor of Rensselaerswyck in 1630; this Dutch patroonship encompassed much of what is now the Capital Region. However, the Dutch did not hold on to the area for long.

By 1664 the British were in control, although they faced competing claims from the French over

"The Pavilion," Fort Ticonderoga, pathway in a walled garden started in 1757. Fort Ticonderoga was restored by Stephen Hyatt Pelham Pell.

the fur trade and strained relations with the Native American tribes. The centrality of the region and its rich resources made it a point of contention between competing powers, culminating in the French and Indian War in the mid-eighteenth century. The French defeat freed land north and west of Albany for further settlement by British colonists. During the American Revolution, Fort Ticonderoga changed hands several times, and the Battle of Saratoga was a vital turning point, convincing the French to forge an alliance with the new nation.

As the non-Native population grew following the establishment of the United States, conflict with the Iroquois tribes of the region ensued. The Cherry Valley Massacre of November 11, 1778, in which Iroquois and British attacked the nearby fort and village of Cherry Valley, resulted in the retaliatory Sullivan Expedition the next year. The carnage of the expedition eliminated the threat to European expansion by the Iroquois tribes in the region. As international politics had shaped the region in the eighteenth century, Albany's designation as New York State's capital in 1797 brought another form of political activity to the area, one that would become a growth industry a century and a half later.

The region was an early center of industrialization; its river-laden geography made the use of the waterwheel particularly efficient. The same rivers and creeks that facilitated waterpower also facilitated easy water transportation. The flat terrain allowed for efficient overland transport as well. The Great Western Turnpike was opened in 1799, and a decade later, Robert Fulton chose Albany as the site to demonstrate the economic viability of steamboats. During the War of 1812, the Watervliet Arsenal, one of the first large-scale industrial complexes in the area, was built to provide supplies for the army.

In October 1825 the 363-mile Erie Canal opened to its full length, connecting Albany to Buffalo and the Great Lakes region beyond. The canal, built by thousands of imported laborers at a cost of $7 million, was a technological marvel that encouraged both industrial growth and immigration by lowering transportation costs dramatically.

In the second quarter of the nineteenth century, Albany emerged as a rail center, and manufacturing in the region continued to grow. Eponymous Gloversville emerged as a center of the glove-making industry while Cohoes, known as the Spindle City, developed as a leader in textile manufacturing. Ironworks anchored the economy of Troy, which also eventually housed Cluett, Peabody & Company, the makers of Arrow brand shirts. Thomas Edison located his Edison Machine Works in Schenectady in 1887, and, on the shirttails of that industry, in 1892 that city also became the headquarters of the General Electric Company. In 1901, the American Locomotive Company, the result of the merger of eight locomotive manufacturers, was headquartered in the city. Eventually, Schenectady became known as "The City That Lights and Hauls the World" as well as the "Electric City."

The industrial base built in the nineteenth century began to erode in the twentieth, with industries either moving out or closing down altogether, especially in the decades after World War II. The Capital Region, with a little more than a million residents, came to rely more and more on government as its primary employer. Today, more than twenty-five percent

Watervliet Arsenal under construction, 1865.

of the workforce works in one government office or another—state, national, or local—with health care and education as the next largest employment sectors. Most recently, however, the alliance between high-tech industries and the College of Nanoscale Science and Engineering at SUNY Polytechnic Institute and Rensselaer Polytechnic Institute has led to a surge in high-tech employment, creating what many now call "Tech Valley."

Higher education has played a central role in economic development, producing the region's highly educated workforce, the basic research, and the inno-

vations needed to propel that growth forward. The Capital Region is home to four community colleges, SUNY's most innovative comprehensive college, and the oldest campus in the SUNY system. Hudson Valley (1953), Adirondack (1961), Columbia-Greene (1966), and Schenectady County (1967) Community Colleges, like so many others across the state, are rooted in their localities' educational needs, providing pathways for regional students to attain skills as well as college degrees. Empire State College (1971), the brainchild of SUNY's distinguished chancellor Ernest L. Boyer, was designed to accommodate the

General Electric Company, Schenectady Works, 1907.

Federal Lock and Dam on the Hudson River, north of Troy.

most prestigious awards the literary world has to offer. Reflecting that reputation, the renowned Pulitzer Prize–winning author, William Kennedy, is one of the distinguished faculty members at the university.

The University at Albany was also the seedbed for one of the most distinctive colleges in the country. The College of Nanoscale Science and Engineering began as a unit within the university, but its distinct vision of adapting the latest scientific research to technological companies led to a separation of the two. Its singular emphasis on technological innovation made it an ideal partner for the SUNY Institute of Technology in Utica, and the two merged in 2014, forming SUNY Polytechnic Institute.

The important role that the schools of the SUNY system have played, and will continue to play in the future of the region, can be seen in the vision of the Capital Region Economic Development Council's language: to "foster and strengthen the region's Economic Ecosystem in which the private sector, academia, and government work in partnership to stimulate the economic growth." This partnership has characterized SUNY's institutions in the region for more than a half century, and it promises to contribute to the region's bright future.

needs of working adults; ESC's flexibility in delivering courses has long been a point of pride for its faculty and alumni.

The University at Albany, the oldest state-supported campus in the SUNY system, was founded in 1844 as the state's first teachers' college. Today it spans the gamut of modern academics, from its high-tech research laboratories in the East Campus to the New York State Writers Institute that has hosted more than 1,200 writers, many of whom have won the

Postcard of the American Locomotive Works factory, Schenectady, 1920.

Troy Gas Light Company, Gasholder House, Troy.

ADIRONDACK COMMUNITY COLLEGE

SUNY Adirondack is nestled amid the natural beauty of Lake George, Saratoga Springs, and the Southern Adirondacks that lend the college its name. It is a community college that offers innovative instructional and student support programs designed to fulfill the college's primary mission of responding to the educational needs of its community and stimulating economic development, regional partnership, cultural enrichment, and intellectual leadership.

Today's SUNY Adirondack represents the collective support of Warren and Washington counties to provide open-access educational opportunities to this region and beyond. The initial vision for the founding of a community college in the region came largely from Merritt E. Scoville, an electrical engineer working at General Electric's Fort Edward plant. Soon,

others in the region joined his efforts to found a community college for Warren County.

Since Warren County could not support such a venture on its own, neighboring Washington County was invited to join as co-sponsor in funding and governance. A joint action committee drummed up popular support for the venture, surveyed parents and potential students, printed pamphlets, and held meetings. In April 1960, both the Warren County and Washington County supervisors approved the plan and presented it to New York State. On June 10, 1960, Adirondack Community College was officially established as a part of the State University of New York.

Adirondack Community College opened its doors to 315 students on September 12, 1961, in a temporary campus on the south edge of Hudson Falls. Two years later, the college graduated its first class of fifty-six

Adirondack Community College found a temporary home in the Griffin Lumber Company building in Hudson Falls.

Adirondack Community College has also reached out to residents of northeastern Saratoga County. Located near Saratoga Springs, the recently modernized Wilton Center offers students credit-bearing General Education and vocational courses, including a pre-nursing track, as well as noncredit courses.

As with the physical campus, SUNY Adirondack's curriculum has evolved over the years to fit the needs of the region and fulfill its vision to be the educational provider of choice and a pathway to success. Currently more than four thousand students are enrolled and are taught by nearly three hundred faculty. Small classes allow for a focus on each student's needs and learning style. Students can select from nearly thirty degree programs. Adirondack's academic offerings are tailored to prepare students either for immediate employment or to transfer to a four-year institution to pursue a baccalaureate degree.

students. Meanwhile work had begun constructing a permanent campus on 141 acres donated by the Glens Falls Insurance Company in Queensbury, a few miles south of Lake George. Since completion in 1967, the Bay Road campus has been the heart of the college. Seven buildings were erected for $4.5 million, and Adirondack Community College welcomed 1,334 students to the new permanent campus for the fall 1967 semester.

Recognizing the importance of tourism and recreation to the regional economy, the college offers many programs designed to enable students to work in those fields. The college has vibrant Commercial Cooking and Culinary Arts programs in which student chefs serve lunch to the public twice a week. Each week a different student serves as chef of the week and creates the menu as part of a portfolio project.

In keeping with the importance of the natural surroundings, SUNY Adirondack offers an AAS degree in Adventure Sports: Leadership and Management in which students participate in outdoor education and expeditions designed to develop management and leadership skills within the context of outdoor adventure sports. The AAS degree in Hospitality and Tourism provides students with the knowledge and hands-on skills they need in order to take their place in a rapidly growing field that is critical to the Adirondack region's economy.

SUNY Adirondack's Extension Center brings the college's offerings to Saratoga County residents.

While many students are commuters with complicated schedules, others are able to take part in a

Future chefs learning how to continue the long tradition of Adirondack hospitality.

Learning the ropes of rock climbing in the High Peaks' trails.

wide range of cultural and athletic activities. In 2013, SUNY Adirondack proudly opened its first on-campus housing facility, allowing its students to gain the full college experience of a residential campus. The new four-hundred-bed residence hall offers students a full range of amenities and extracurricular activities.

The arts remain an integral part of SUNY Adirondack's contribution to the cultural life of the region. The Writers Project, sponsored by the English Division, the Student Association, and the Foundation, with support from the National Endowment for the Arts, brings nationally known writers to campus throughout the academic year. It exposes the community to the work of established writers and provides writers at the beginning of their careers with a venue for readings, workshops, and retreats. Adirondack's Visual Arts Gallery, which opened in 1984, hosts shows by regional, national, and international artists, with an emphasis on the work of artists from the Southern Adirondack and Capital regions. Each spring semester concludes with a student art exhibition.

In order to fit the needs and schedules of its surrounding community, SUNY Adirondack offers a variety of certificate programs, continuing education, and online courses. In 2014, the college began

SUNY Adirondack students enjoy a variety of forms of recreation.

offering a one-year Entrepreneurship and Business Management certificate program designed to prepare students for employment in a wide range of business-related fields. Adirondack's Continuing Education programs offer a variety of career-readiness and workforce courses in such areas as Emergency Medical Technician, Notary Public Exam Preparation, and Bartending, as well as recreational courses such as calligraphy, building greenhouses, and beer brewing. Online courses, taught in six-week blocks, are offered on a schedule designed to meet the needs of those who cannot attend regular college courses. The courses are led by instructors who strive to provide a lively, interactive learning environment.

For more than fifty years, SUNY Adirondack has provided the students of Warren and Washington counties and the Capital Region of New York State with educational opportunities designed for their needs. In that more than half century it has become an integral pathway to success for students and for enriching the larger community.

Now SUNY Adirondack students can experience collegiate residential life.

UNIVERSITY AT ALBANY

The State Normal School at Albany opened its doors on December 18, 1844, to twenty-nine students and two instructors with a mission to educate common school teachers "in the science of education and in the art of teaching." The first teacher training school in the state to receive public support, the third in the nation, it sent graduates to teach throughout the state and assume leadership of state normal schools in states as far away as California. Students were drawn from every county

The Lodge and Howard Building, 1849.

in the state to train to be teachers for the "common schools" (i.e., grades 1–8). In 1890 the mission expanded to include high school teachers and administrators, and the name changed to the New York State Normal College.

In December 1905 the New York State Board of Regents dramatically revised Albany's two-year curriculum and admission standards to mirror those typical of New York's private liberal arts colleges. But the repurposed State Normal College was still committed solely to

97

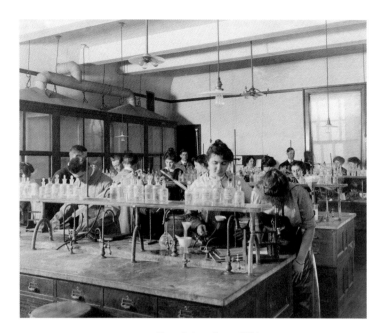

Chemistry class, 1916.

Dormitory Authority, which added three new buildings on the quadrangle in the 1950s.

While the college had been granted the right to confer master's degrees in 1890, it took another quarter century before the graduate degrees were strengthened to include both extensive coursework and a thesis. During the 1920s and 1930s the undergraduate and graduate curricula were tightened, admission requirements raised, and faculty encouraged to earn doctorates through sabbatical leaves.

The more rigorous curricula and more highly educated faculty led to plans to offer a doctoral degree in education as early as 1946. These early plans to expand the graduate student population provided the basis for the campus's successful transition to a university center in the 1960s. When newly elected governor Nelson A. Rockefeller fostered SUNY's dramatic expansion in the early 1960s, the State University of New York College of Education, its official title at the time, was prepared for the change, which was realized in 1962 when the college became the State University of New York at Albany, one of four new university centers proposed for SUNY.

training teachers and school administrators, and students in turn had to commit to remain in the state and teach in New York's high schools. The change to a four-year college was officially recognized in 1914 when the Regents renamed the school the New York State College for Teachers.

By 1909 the college had moved to a new campus between Western and Washington avenues several blocks west of the Capitol Building. During the next two decades, the school doubled in enrollment, leading the college's Alumni Association to undertake a special project: dormitories, first for women in 1935, and shortly thereafter for men. These buildings formed the Alumni Quadrangle, two blocks west of the campus. The Alumni Association's successful plan to build and operate the new residence halls provided a model for the later creation of the State

Mayor Erastus Corning of Albany and Governor Rockefeller view a model of the new campus.

The Downtown Campus could not accommodate the anticipated thousands of additional students, and a new site was chosen five miles to the west. The internationally acclaimed architect Edward Durell Stone offered a unique design for the new campus, with four residential hall towers anchoring a multi-building quad that contained classrooms, offices, and libraries surrounding a central bell tower. It was distinctive and particularly appreciated by Governor Rockefeller, who was a devotee of modern architecture.

The shift to a University Center drove an explosion of undergraduate majors and graduate degrees, as well as a dramatic expansion of the faculty. In 1962 the university offered one doctoral degree, nineteen master's degree programs, and one certificate; eight years later the *Graduate Bulletin* listed twenty-six doctoral programs, fifty-two master's programs, and seven certificate programs. The faculty grew from 115 in the early 1950s to 244 in 1962 and then tripled to 740 by 1970. As the campus grew, it added new research centers, such as the Atmospheric Sciences Research Center (1961) that studies atmospherics across the globe. The Center for Women in Government (1978) led the way in exposing pay disparities and the glass ceiling for women in the 1980s and 1990s.

The student body grew as well, and many of the new students came from downstate, especially Long Island, which changed the campus climate. Soon almost one-third of the students were Jewish, which created new demands for kosher meals and observances of the Jewish High Holy Days. More adjustments followed the 1968 creation of the Educational Opportunities program, which recruited sizable numbers of African American and Latino (initially, mainly Puerto Rican) students, as well as promising students from impoverished educational backgrounds. Early expectations that these students would blend into the existing student body were quickly dashed, and the university initiated a series of support systems designed to enable first generation college students to succeed in the Albany environment. These groups, and others, whose political consciousness was raised during the 1960s, pushed successfully for the creation of academic programs that reflected their interests: Africana studies (1969), Judaic studies (1970), Puerto Rican studies (1972), and Women's studies (1972) were all developed during this period.

By the mid-1970s, the University at Albany, like all SUNY campuses, suffered dramatic budget shocks, a fallout from the threatened default of New York City, and the need for a state rescue. But, the campus quickly recovered and began to develop new

Students protest, 1969.

areas of inquiry, despite the failure of state support to keep pace with enrollment. The School of Public Health (1985) brought together the resources of the university with the scientific expertise of the New York State Department of Health. A decade later, in 1996, the university acquired ninety-six acres in Rensselaer, which provided a site for the School of Public Health and laboratory space for collaboration with private industry in building biotech companies. The newest research center on the East Campus opened

Student intern with Cancer Research Center mentor.

Albany's successful lacrosse teams, men's and women's, reflect the Native American heritage of the region.

Albany students teaching in the Albany Promise program.

in 2007, commonly known as the Cancer Research Center, is committed to discovering the genetic origins of cancer.

The Center for Thin Film Technology became the most successful of the new programs that integrated disciplines. Founded in the early 1990s and featuring collaboration between physicists and chemists, the center developed into Albany Nanotech Institute, a successful international collaboration of academics, government, and businesses. In 2014, the College of Nanoscale Sciences and Engineering merged with SUNYIT in Utica to form a new school, SUNY Polytechnic Institute. Since its inception in 2009, the Uptown Campus's RNA Institute has researched RNA tools and technologies to address critical human health problems. In 2015, the university unveiled the College of Emergency Preparedness, Homeland Security and Cybersecurity, a first-of-its-kind academic center devoted to the nation's security, and the College of Engineering and Applied Sciences, the region's first public engineering option.

Obviously, the past forty years have witnessed dramatic changes at the university, with a new emphasis on collaboration with business and industry; greater awareness of the broader world, as illustrated by the school's theme, "The World Within Reach"; a more diverse, international, and larger (seventeen thousand) student body, and eighteen NCAA Division I intercollegiate athletic teams that compete in the America East Conference for postseason play.

Despite these changes, today's State University at Albany continues "to diffuse throughout the state a . . . fund of moral and intellectual wealth," as it had been urged by the superintendent of common schools in 1844. Admittedly, today's stage is larger, encompassing the nation and the world, and the engagement with the community is much more complex, with threads to businesses, social agencies, political bodies, scientific and technological laboratories, as well as the arts. But the mission has remained constant, to discover knowledge, teach students, and work with communities to address the most pressing social problems of the day.

COLUMBIA-GREENE COMMUNITY COLLEGE

Columbia-Greene Community College enjoys a spectacular setting, one made famous by the works of Frederic Edwin Church, the famed Hudson River School painter. Thirty miles south of Albany, the campus vistas are dominated by the Catskill Mountains to the west and the Taconic and Berkshire hills to the east.

The idea of establishing a community college reaching across the Hudson River to serve Columbia and Greene counties was first promoted by a Citizen's Survey Committee in 1966. The Columbia County Board of Supervisors and the Greene County Legislature quickly supported the idea and, later that year, the SUNY Board of Trustees chartered and authorized funding for Columbia-Greene Community College. The college logo illustrates the cooperation of the two counties connected across the Hudson River by the Rip Van Winkle Bridge.

A temporary campus was prepared in Athens, on the west side of the Hudson Valley, in a former elementary school. Faculty were hired, a curriculum was developed, and a former Pick Quick Market was purchased to house the library. The fifteen faculty worked through the summer of 1969 without pay to prepare the facility. In September the doors opened to 175 students. The first graduation, held at Catskill High School in June 1971, awarded associate degrees to thirty-five students in a dozen areas of study.

Meanwhile, plans were afoot for an exciting permanent campus across the river near Hudson. The New York State Historic Trust deeded over nearly

Facilities were limited in the early years as in this chemistry class on the Athens campus in the early 1970s.

rounded out its basic curricula in science and liberal arts with new vocational programs, noncredit classes, training for business and industry, and training for disadvantaged students through the Federal CETA program. Enrollment swelled to over 1,400 credit students and more than six thousand noncredit students by the mid-1980s.

Physical expansion followed. The campus saw sweeping expansion in the arts and technology with the construction of a day care center, an arts center, and a technology building. With the inclusion of new programs in Fine Arts, Automotive Technology, and Nursing, and the creation of a traditional college quadrangle, Columbia-Greene was on its way to becoming a mature and comprehensive community college.

Despite a downturn in enrollments in the 1990s, the college embarked on a major renovation

150 acres adjacent to the Olana Historic Site, Frederic Church's dramatically sited Moorish mansion, which was about to reopen as a museum.

Architect Edgar Tafel designed an innovative megastructure that housed all facilities under one roof and fit harmoniously into the landscape. The design won an award at an architecture conference in Paris. Ground was broken in the autumn of 1972 for the 131,355 square-foot building. Classes began on the new campus September 16, 1974, even though much of the college's equipment was still in crates.

As enrollments and faculty grew, the campus

Classrooms, such as this "smart" biology laboratory, have been revolutionized since the 1970s.

of the original main campus building. With support from Columbia and Greene counties, ground was broken to implement a $13,000,000 reconstruction plan in spring 1996.

The result was a totally rewired and revitalized facility that included: a skylighted Student Services Court with centralized student services, including registration, bursar, and financial aid; an Academic Support Center with 140 Internet-connected computers installed adjacent to the library to create a university-style research center; four new science laboratories and a nursing center, including state-of-the-art fixtures, ventilation, and "smart" teaching stations ready for connection to computers, multimedia equipment, and the Internet; renovated classrooms, lecture halls, and administrative offices; spacious and skylighted student lounges and study rooms; and an environmentally friendly geothermal heating, ventilation, and air-conditioning system.

Vocational programs prepare students for immediate employment.

And with renewed bricks and mortar and electronics came new academic programs. The Ford ASSET program was added as an option for automotive technology students, which complemented the Automotive Technologies Department's core program and Toyota option. An Automotive Technology certificate program for service and parts professionals began in the fall of 1997.

A certificate program in Computer Graphics and Design was launched in the fall 1998, followed by an associate degree program in Massage Therapy the following year. The college also established a Hudson River field station in Athens, the college's original home on the west side of the Hudson. It provides a laboratory and living environmental studies classroom for the college's students as well local public school students.

Students relaxing and studying.

Art thrives in the shadow of Frederick Church's Olana and nearby Hudson.

In addition, a twenty-year commitment to business and industry training was reaching a new threshold, highlighted by the Saland Employee Educational Development program, implemented with the assistance of New York State senator Stephen Saland, who secured $540,000 in state funding for the plastics industry program. The college also continued to administer federally funded job training programs under the Job Training Partnership Act and, later, the Workforce Investment Act. Noncredit programs also grew throughout the 1990s, reaching annual enrollments of over eight thousand by the decade's end.

The new century saw a dual enrollment baccalaureate degree program in teacher education launched in cooperation with SUNY New Paltz. And completion of the Professional Academic Center rounded out the campus's quadrangle.

While many students can only come to campus for classes, other students enjoy a traditional campus life with a variety of organizations. The Twins compete in eight intercollegiate sports in the Mountain Valley Conference. Opportunities for informal exercise abound with lakes, campgrounds, and three ski resorts nearby.

Columbia-Greene Community College has contributed to the city of Hudson's revival as an arts center. The campus is home to five galleries. The largest is in the Arts Center, which provides exhibition space as well as studios for students in the popular fine arts program. Frederic Church would approve.

C-GCC has come a long way since the early days in a converted elementary school. Today over two thousand students from the two counties and surrounding area benefit from a modern campus in a spectacular location, while many more take advantage of noncredit offerings.

EMPIRE STATE COLLEGE

By the late 1960s, the SUNY system had established a widely distributed network of college and university campuses across New York that offered a broad range of readily available educational opportunities that kept the SUNY promise to have a campus within thirty miles of every state resident. Then, in the early 1970s, newly appointed chancellor Ernest L. Boyer encouraged a number of experiments, one of which was a new college that focused on meeting the needs of nontraditional college students across the state. From its beginnings in 1971, SUNY Empire State College was designed to remove the barriers of time, place, and curriculum by introducing much greater flexibility in the ways that degree programs were delivered, especially to working adults.

Chancellor Boyer intended Empire State College to serve nontraditional students by nontraditional means, focusing on the educational needs of

Former SUNY chancellor Ernest L. Boyer, one of the most influential educational leaders of the late twentieth century.

Whether learning takes place online, onsite, or through a combination of both, Empire State College pairs each student with a faculty mentor.

and, in early 2014, the college was among a select group of schools from across the nation to propose that students be allowed to access federal financial aid for direct assessment. In 2016, ESC was selected by the US Department of Education for an experimental program, making federal financial aid available to students who were previously denied. These experiments support the ability of low-income students to complete their degrees more quickly while gaining employable skills.

Since the 1970s, the setting and modes of Empire State College's instruction have evolved with

An Empire State College student explains her research project to a professor.

individual students, as opposed to offering a conventional academic structure at a residential campus. To accomplish this goal, resources were assembled in centers across the state to bring them closer to prospective students, who worked with faculty mentors individually or in small groups to create their own degree programs in one of twelve broad areas.

"Prospectus for a New University College," Chancellor Boyer's blueprint for Empire State College, introduced greater flexibility in class schedules, encouraged part-time studies, and reduced institutional requirements. SUNY championed this visionary reconfiguration of higher education long before modern educational planners began discussing prior learning assessment or distance education, both of which were available at Empire State College by the late 1970s.

Empire State College's tradition of innovation continues today. The college has a long history of being a national and international leader in prior learning assessment. Recently, the college has emerged as one of the leaders in competency-based learning

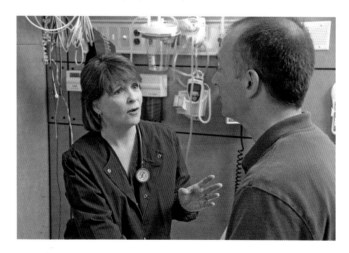

Students in the nursing programs take courses online and learn with professional clinicians at healthcare facilities in their communities.

changing technologies and changing educational needs. In the 1990s, for example, the growth of the Internet enabled SUNY to create the SUNY Learning Network, a delivery system that linked courses from different campuses. With its long-standing mission to work with nontraditional student populations in individualized ways and its experience in distance education, Empire State College has led SUNY's innovative pedagogical initiatives through its Center for Learning and Technology.

Another unique characteristic of Empire State College was the choice to offer entire programs of study in distance formats that led to completed degrees. Undergraduate students, in both the associate and bachelor's degree programs, choose to concentrate in one of a dozen designated broad areas, while graduate students select from among eleven graduate programs. The graduate programs are almost all fully online, including the programs offered to nursing students.

In order to better serve the needs of students, Empire State College developed robust partnerships with the military, organized labor, and other organizations in both the private and nonprofit sectors.

The Center for Labor Studies educates union members through partnership programs.

From its inception, the college has worked to serve the needs of active service military, a mission now undertaken by the Office of Veteran and Military Education. Through Empire State College military personnel can gain college credit for their military experience. The importance of this relationship to both the state and the college has led to the permanent assignment of a representative of the New York State Division of Veterans' Affairs at the Saratoga Springs campus.

To further its partnership with labor, Empire State College created the Harry Van Arsdale Jr. Center for Labor Studies. The center, in keeping with its role as part of ESC, offers instruction through a combination of online, in-person, and group study. Students working with the center's faculty and staff pursue studies that explore the cultural, social, and institutional ramifications of work and its impact on workers' lives in both the contemporary world and within a historical context. The center also offers specialized programs for union apprentices that lead to college degrees. Two union locals require their apprentices to earn an Empire State College associate degree as part of their overall education and training.

Empire State College's reach extends well beyond New York's boundaries. As part of the college's mission to make education accessible beyond national borders, the Center for International Programs (CIP) offers programs to students who live in Albania, the Czech Republic, the Dominican Republic, Greece, Lebanon, and Turkey, again providing rich educational opportunities where students live and work. The center's baccalaureate degrees are identical to those awarded in the United States.

Today, SUNY Empire State College seeks to maintain its well-deserved reputation as a national and international leader in educational innovation by serving nontraditional learners more efficiently and effectively. The college community is working together to build on its tradition of faculty closely mentoring students, individualized learning, credit for college-level learning—regardless of how it was acquired—and flexibility in terms of when, where, and how students learn.

Triumphant SUNY Empire State College graduate.

108

HUDSON VALLEY COMMUNITY COLLEGE

Strategically located in New York's Capital Region just minutes from the state capital, Hudson Valley Community College serves more than eleven thousand students each semester, employs more than 650 full- and part-time faculty members, and offers eighty-five degree and certificate programs. Its excellent support services for students has earned Hudson Valley a ranking in the top ten percent of community colleges nationwide.

The college's 120-acre campus is situated on the southeastern edge of Troy, New York, overlooking the Hudson River and offering many amenities beyond the extensive facilities that support its academic programs, including the 4,500-seat Joseph L. Bruno Stadium. When not in use by the college's Vikings and other community teams, the stadium is home to the New York-Penn League's Tri-City Valley-Cats Class A baseball team.

Troy, known as the "birthplace of America's Industrial Revolution," was a fitting location for the Troy Technical Institute, which trained World War II and Korean War veterans to reenter the regional industrial workforce. Hudson Valley Community College's history formally begins in 1953 when Rensselaer County assumed control of the Veterans' Vocational School. It later was renamed Hudson Valley Technical Institute and finally, in 1959, Hudson Valley Community College. The following year classes moved to a permanent campus on a spacious plot purchased by Rensselaer County.

The first degrees were awarded in 1955 in Air Conditioning, Heating, and Refrigeration Technology, Automotive Technology, Construction Technology,

Troy Technical Institute's home in downtown Troy
from 1953 to 1959.

ences—and currently ranks fifty-eighth of 1,123 community colleges nationally in the number of associate degrees awarded annually. Eight out of ten Hudson Valley students come from the Capital Region, with the remainder coming from different areas of New York State, as well as other states and countries.

The college's Associate in Applied Science (e.g., Civil Engineering Technology, Computer Information Systems, and Dental Hygiene) and Associate in Occupational Studies (e.g., Advanced Manufacturing Technology and Electrical Construction and Maintenance) programs lead to immediate employment in industry, business, government, and health agencies. The college's Associate in Arts (Liberal Arts and Sciences—Humanities and Social Sciences) and Associate in Science (e.g., Criminal Justice, Engineering Science, Fine Arts) programs prepare students for transfer to four-year colleges and universities. Hudson Valley has articulation and transfer agreements with nearly 250 colleges and universities. The college also offers certificate programs for selected

Electrical Technology, and Mechanical Technology. These programs are still offered along with many new programs, such as Photovoltaic Installation and Semiconductor Technology, which were beyond the imagination sixty years ago. Today's college has four schools—Business, Engineering and Industrial Technologies, Health Sciences, and Liberal Arts and Sci-

President Barack Obama visits HVCC to emphasize the role of community colleges in training the twenty-first-century workforce.

The home of science at HVCC since 2013.

occupational specialties that can be completed in one year. In addition, its Workforce Development Institute provides training in building trades, health careers, transportation, and more. More than twenty of the college's degree and certificate programs can be completed entirely online.

The college's newest building is the one-hundred-thousand-square-foot Science Center opened in August 2013 with twenty-five state-of-the-art laboratories for the study of biology, chemistry, physics, biotechnology, earth science, and forensics; eleven classrooms; faculty and staff offices; conference spaces; a science study center, greenhouse, and café. Approximately seven thousand students utilize the facility each semester. An administration building, opened in 2007, houses classrooms and the Teaching Gallery in addition to financial and business offices.

As a result of its most recent Facilities Master Plan, Hudson Valley Community College now is a pedestrian-friendly campus with several open green spaces and quads, including one with a monument honoring those who have served in the five branches of the United States military. Vehicle traffic and park-

ing are restricted to the campus perimeter lots and to an 800-space parking garage.

Major renovations of the college's library were completed in fall 2012 when the new Marvin Library Learning Commons was unveiled. The new, student-centered spaces include dedicated silent areas for study and research, collaborative areas where students work together, and an atrium café where students may relax and talk with friends.

The college also offers courses at nearly ten satellite locations, including an extension center at 175 Central Avenue in Albany. Its Training and Education Center for Semiconductor Manufacturing and Alternative and Renewable Technologies in Saratoga County, TEC-SMART, offers more than a dozen state-of-the-art classrooms and laboratories to train the workforce in semiconductor manufacturing and clean energy technologies as well as offering business and liberal arts courses.

The highly successful Early College High School programs offered at TEC-SMART through a local school/college/business and industry partnership continue to grow; twenty school districts currently

Students studying and relaxing in the Marvin Learning Commons.

Students at work in the clean room at TEC-SMART.

participate. In addition, nearly two thousand students in thirty different school districts take college-level courses—either online or in their own classroom—as part of the College in the High School program. The college also operates the Capital District Educational Opportunity Center in downtown Troy that has offered free academic programs and occupational training to eligible adult learners since 1966.

Since its beginning, Hudson Valley Community College has been an excellent resource not only for enrolled students but the entire community. Today thousands of people visit campus each semester to participate in an ever-growing variety of noncredit courses and enjoy lectures by visiting authors, film series, theater performances, and more in the 350-seat Maureen Stapleton Theatre. Each year, the McDonough Sports Complex houses public events such as craft and garden shows, high school basketball, and track and field competitions. Hudson Valley Vikings compete in seventeen intercollegiate athletic sports. Fifty-eight scholar-athletes have been inducted into its Hall of Fame since it was established in 1979.

The number and scope of the college's degree and certificate programs have grown immensely

since its beginning, as have the alumni, who now number more than seventy-five thousand. Growing from a small technical institute, Hudson Valley has served Rensselaer County and the Capital Region in ways its founders could not have imagined, but they would recognize the commitment of the college to providing the community with the best postsecondary educational opportunities possible.

Vikings on the field.

SUNY POLYTECHNIC INSTITUTE

SUNY Polytechnic Institute (SUNY Poly) was officially formed on March 19, 2014, when the State University of New York Board of Trustees unanimously approved SUNY chancellor Nancy L. Zimpher's recommendation to merge the SUNY College of Nanoscale Science and Engineering (CNSE) in Albany and the SUNY Institute of Technology (SUNYIT) in Utica. The transformative merger was the product of a pioneering vision and leadership to create an entity rooted in academia and capable of driving significant and sustained industrial and economic growth across the state of New York. As a result, SUNY Poly has emerged as a unique institution in the SUNY system with more than seven thousand scientists, researchers, engineers, students, faculty, and staff working at a number of sites across New York State, anchored by two coequal academic locations.

The history of SUNY Poly's Utica site dates back to 1966, when the Upper Division College at Herkimer/Rome/Utica was founded and began offering graduate programs to students using classrooms at a local elementary school. In 1971, the college began operating in a former mill in West Utica, which was gradually remodeled into classrooms, offices, and a library. With growing enrollment, the institution leased three additional buildings in West Utica and one in Rome and adopted a new name in 1977: State University of New York College of Technology at Utica-Rome.

In 1981, construction began on a new campus in Marcy. The first building, Kunsela Hall, was completed in 1984, and the college operated two campuses during a transitional period until the new campus was completed for the 1987 fall semester. In 1989, the college name was changed again to the State University

Donovan Hall houses computer labs, classrooms, and faculty offices on the Utica site.

of New York Institute of Technology at Utica-Rome, but the curriculum was still limited to upper-division courses in a number of disciplines clustered around technology.

In early 2002, the campus mission was expanded when the SUNY Board of Trustees authorized lower-division programs in professional, technological, and applied studies. SUNYIT admitted its first class of freshmen the following fall, creating a full, four-year institution. SUNYIT also continued to offer graduate degree programs, including a unique MBA in Technology Management. Steady growth and construction on the campus has continued over the years, including

Adirondack Hall is a townhouse-style residence hall on the Utica site.

a $13 million student center, a $20 million fieldhouse and athletic fields, and a $23.5 million residence hall, all completed in 2011.

SUNY Poly's College of Nanoscale Science and Engineering, located in Albany, began as a distinct part of the University at Albany with a vision that combined the strengths of government, academia, and industry. The goal was to propel New York State to technological leadership that would spark economic development. The institution has become the academic cornerstone in the push to develop New York's high-tech industries. Four key drivers comprise the strategy: select an overarching discipline (nanotechnology); invest in state-of-the-art infrastructure; focus on world-class, hands-on education and training incorporating the entire supply chain; and leverage public-private partnerships. And, the strategic vision has yielded remarkable results within a very short period.

SUNY Poly CNSE's first building was NanoFab 200 (also known as the Center for Environmental Sciences and Technology Management, or CESTM), completed in June 1997. This seventy-thousand-square-foot, $16.5 million facility set the stage for the creation of today's NanoTech Complex, including the $50 million NanoFab South (2004), the $175 million NanoFab North (2005), the $150 million NanoFab East and NanoFab Central (2009), and the $365 million NanoFab Xtension (2013).

Today, SUNY Poly CNSE is a fully integrated research, development, prototyping, and educational facility spanning 1.65 million square feet and boasting more than $24 billion in high-tech investments with over three hundred corporate partners on site, including IBM, Intel, GlobalFoundries, SEMATECH, Samsung, TSMC, Applied Materials, Tokyo Electron, ASML, and Lam Research.

The current education-driven economic development strategy has enabled construction projects that continue to add to the landscape at both of SUNY Poly's academic locations. The Computer Chip Commercialization Center (Quad-C) in Utica represents the first phase of Governor Andrew

President Barack Obama and Governor Andrew Cuomo tour SUNY Poly CNSE's clean rooms in May 2012.

Cuomo's $1.5 billion Nano Utica initiative, a public-private partnership spearheaded by SUNY Poly that will support thousands of new high-tech jobs. Meanwhile, the $191 million Zero Energy Nanotechnology (ZEN) Building in Albany serves as a living laboratory for clean and renewable energy technologies. Both buildings opened in 2015 and will result in the creation of thousands of jobs, groundbreaking academic programs, and cutting-edge workforce training opportunities.

In the midst of cutting-edge technology, traditional collegiate life continues. SUNY Poly is a member of the National Collegiate Athletic Association (NCAA) Division III, the Eastern Collegiate Athletic Conference (ECAC), and the North Eastern Athletic Conference (NEAC). The SUNY Poly Wildcats compete in baseball, softball, men's and women's basketball, cross-country, lacrosse, soccer, and volleyball.

SUNY Poly also operates the Smart Cities Technology Innovation (SCiTI) Center at Kiernan Plaza in Albany, the Solar Energy Development Center in Halfmoon, CNSE's Central New York Hub for Emerging Nano Industries in Syracuse, the Smart System Technology and Commercialization Center (STC) in Canandaigua, and the Photovoltaic Manufacturing and Technology Development Facility in Rochester. The last was an essential element in the recent decision of the Department of Defense to locate a $600 million public-private-funded photonics center in Rochester, expanding the region's high-tech industries.

Quad-C anchors the Nano Utica initiative, the state's second major hub of nanotechnology research and development.

The Zero Energy Nanotechnology Building brings cutting-edge technology to Albany.

In addition, SUNY Poly manages the $500 million New York Power Electronics Manufacturing Consortium, with nodes in Albany and Rochester, as well as the Buffalo High-Tech Manufacturing Innovation Hub at RiverBend, Buffalo Information Technologies Innovation and Commercialization Hub, and Buffalo Medical Innovation and Commercialization Hub.

SUNY Poly represents a new paradigm for public and affordable higher education in science, engineering, and technology, one that is respectfully cognizant of the customary academic enterprise while fostering and enabling the fast-evolving culture of discovery and innovation in today's knowledge-driven global economy.

In addition to developing a revolutionary academic model, SUNY Poly

Graduation at the SUNY Poly Utica site.

has been a critical cornerstone in the state government's high-tech strategy to establish New York State as a global leader in the nanotechnology-driven economy of the twenty-first century and serves as a worldwide resource for pioneering research and development, technology deployment, education, and commercialization for the international nanoelectronics industry.

With access to world-class facilities and innovative career preparation, SUNY Poly offers unmatched opportunities for students, at both the Utica and Albany locations. The same commitment to cutting-edge academic and research programs that distinguished both institutions in the past makes SUNY Poly a unique, high-tech global leader in public higher education.

SCHENECTADY COUNTY COMMUNITY COLLEGE

Schenectady County Community College's rich history is evident whenever prospective students and their families first enter Elston Hall, descend two grand staircases, and emerge into the Student Commons. In this one snapshot, the college's history seamlessly fuses with the modern architecture of the main area where students now socialize, grab a bite to eat, and study. Inevitably, their eyes gaze up to the brick façade framed by the President's Office and the elegant Lally Mohawk Room, further sharing the college's history with today's students.

The brick façade was once the outside of the grand Hotel Van Curler, built in 1925 in the heart of the city of Schenectady. The stairs led to the terrace where guests of the well-known hotel had tea and dined. The Lally Mohawk Room, now the location for open houses, guest lectures, and student events, was the hotel lounge.

After decades of serving as a landmark in Schenectady, the hotel closed its doors in February 1968. While the hotel was entering its final phase, the Board of Supervisors of Schenectady County appointed a group of forty-nine citizens to a special Community College Study Committee to assess the feasibility of a community college in Schenectady. The Board of Supervisors accepted the committee's positive report in December 1966, later designating the Hotel Van Curler as the college's location.

In September 1969, amid much community excitement, Schenectady County Community College opened its doors to the first entering class. The former hotel was renamed Elston Hall, in honor of a member of the original Board of Trustees. One by one, hotel

Students relax in the reflected splendor of the old Hotel Van Curler.

rooms became elegant faculty offices, still the envy of colleagues at many other colleges. Today, Elston Hall houses a Student Center with a cafeteria, a lounge, the College Bookstore, a café, and the School of Hotel, Culinary Arts, and Tourism's Casola Dining Room.

Through the decades, the fifty-acre campus on the edge of the city of Schenectady has expanded. In 1978, a multipurpose building was constructed to house the Begley Library, which is open to the public, and the Carl B. Taylor Community Auditorium, home to musical and theatrical performances and special events.

In fall 2012, the college opened a new $3.9 million School of Music building, which was designed to meet the needs of students in the nationally accredited music programs. The School of Music includes teaching studios, an industry-standard live recording studio, two specialized music classrooms, practice rooms, recital space, teaching studios, faculty offices, and a student lounge.

On any given day or evening, the sounds of the college's student ensembles, professional ensembles in residence—the Empire Jazz Orchestra, Capital Region Wind Ensemble, and Musicians of Ma'alwyck—as well as guest artists fill the Taylor Auditorium. Members of the community ranging from high school students, music teachers, and families to senior citizens and students from other colleges enjoy performances.

The Center for Science and Technology, at the other end of the campus, opened in 1987. This unique facility contains the college's nanoscale materials technology classrooms and labs, physics and chemistry laboratories, as well as specialized laboratory facilities for circuits, electronics, vacuum science, and computer networking. The Nanoscale program is tied closely with local companies to ensure that SCCC's courses are offering the skills needed in the industry. Students intern at the College of Nanoscale Science and Engineering as well as in regional firms, such as GlobalFoundries, leading to employment in this booming field after graduation.

Campus architecture echoes the old hotel to create a harmonious quadrangle.

As the successful Early Childhood program gained momentum, Schenectady's Gateway Building opened in 2000. The colorful one-story building houses general classrooms, a childcare center, the Gateway Montessori Preschool, and offices. Students work directly with children in the preschool, and the childcare center fulfills an important need in the community.

The Culinary Arts program has long been a signature program at the college. To accommodate students choosing to enter the burgeoning field of hospitality, an impressive Culinary Arts Expansion in Elston Hall was completed in August 2007. It houses the Casola Dining Room and its dedicated kitchen, two culinary arts laboratories, a bak-

ery outlet, and a seminar room. Members of the public enjoy gourmet cuisine in the Casola Dining Room, where students gain training in dining room management, baking, *garde manger*, and culinary a la carte service. Guests can then enjoy mouthwatering confections available in Pane e Dolci, a full-scale bakery outlet. Finally, the Boucherie offers handcrafted fresh sausages, smoked meats, charcuteries, and appetizers produced in-house by students.

In addition to the physical campus, SCCC's virtual student community is able to take online courses and programs, some of which, such as Criminal Justice, are available entirely online. And, through an innovative partnership with SUNY Delhi, after receiving their associate degree, graduates can take all of their classes on the Schenectady campus as they pursue bachelor's degrees.

SCCC has a deep connection to its city and county. In fall 2011, the college began offering classes at Center City in downtown Schenectady, integrating the college even more into its urban location. The men's and women's basketball teams practice and play all home games at the YMCA while college faculty

Music enhances the cultural life of the college and community.

Nanoscale students on the cutting edge of science.

teach drama classes in the historic Proctor's Theatre across the street. In 2014, the college opened a center at the Albany County Building at 112 State Street in downtown Albany.

The college's more than 6,200 students and faculty are vital members of the Schenectady community, raising families, working, and contributing to the local economy. With the addition of student housing, those living at College Suites frequent downtown restaurants and shops. Students also volunteer their time to local nonprofit organizations conducting afterschool activities for local youth, helping to stock food pantries, collecting toys for needy children, and writing to governmental leaders to advocate for funding children's programs.

Schenectady County Community College has a history that is evident in the elegant former Hotel Van Curler. The college continues to build on this important history and carve out a significant place as a successful urban community college that has changed the lives of thousands of graduates and their families and helped Schenectady navigate its economic and social challenges.

Culinary Arts students bring pleasure to their colleagues and the community while learning their trade.

The SCCC City Center brings the college more intimately into the city's life.

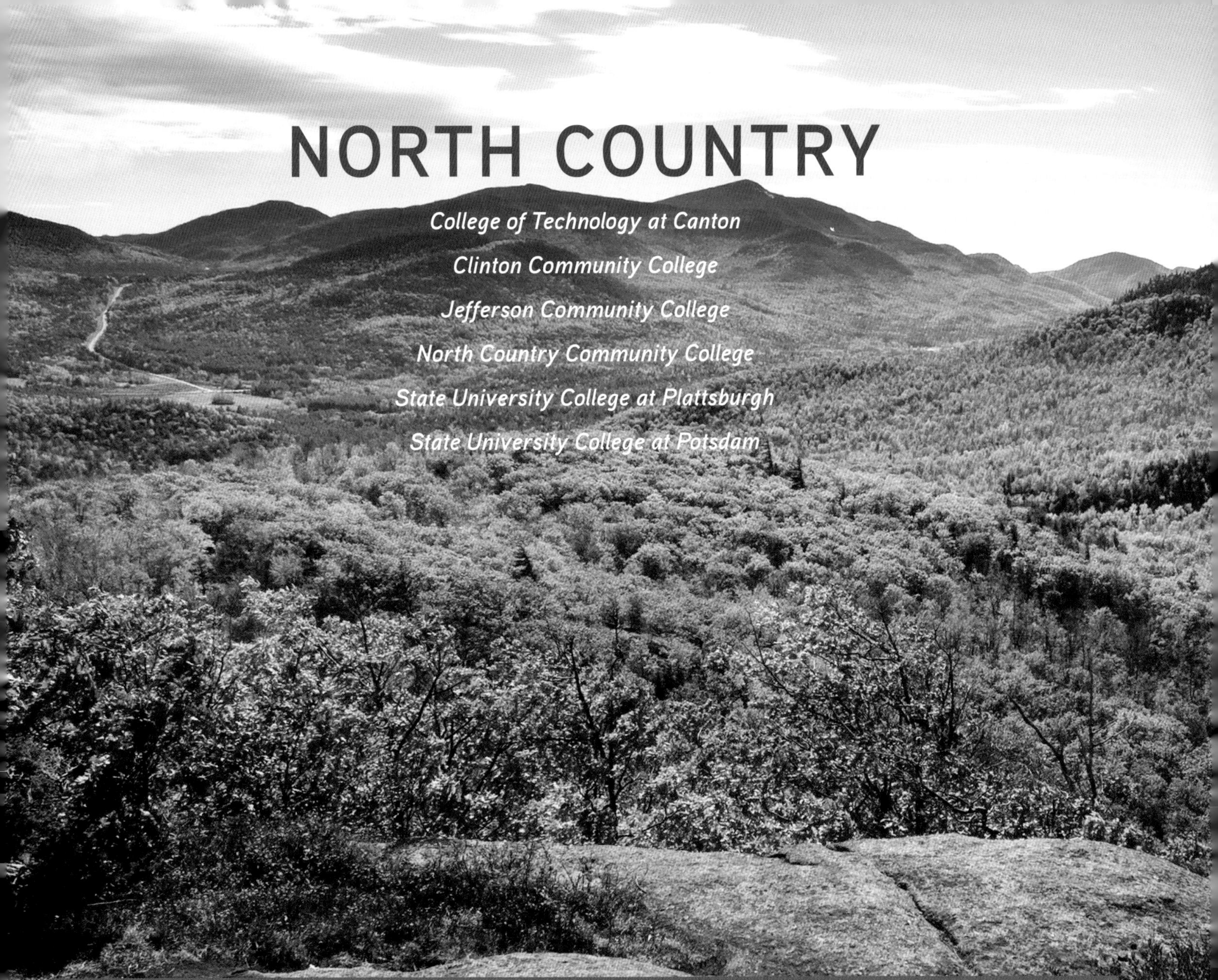

NORTH COUNTRY

College of Technology at Canton

Clinton Community College

Jefferson Community College

North Country Community College

State University College at Plattsburgh

State University College at Potsdam

Home to the Adirondack Park and the High Peaks, the North Country is the largest and most sparsely populated of New York State's economic development regions. Stretching from the eastern shore of Lake Ontario to the western edge of Lake Champlain, this vast area gives both residents and visitors plenty of elbow room to enjoy its natural beauty and tranquility. Home to the Thousand Islands, the St. Lawrence River, Lake Champlain, and the two thousand square miles of the Tug Hill Plateau, which averages the highest snowfall east of the Rocky Mountains, the North Country is an ideal venue for winter sports and summer recreation.

The North Country is anchored by the cities of Plattsburgh in the east and Watertown in the west. Plattsburgh, situated near the Canadian border in the area explored by Samuel de Champlain, has long had a French influence, the vestiges of which remain; for example, the town was designed without the traditional English "Main Street." While Plattsburgh's status as a city is relatively new (dating from 1902), settlement in the region dates back to the fur traders of the seventeenth century. When the

Crown Point, French Fort St. Frédéric in foreground.

French lost the region in the aftermath of the French and Indian War, the area that became Plattsburgh was transferred into British hands. Plattsburgh then played a critical military role as the site of important battles in the American Revolution and the War of 1812 and, later, as the home of Plattsburgh Air Force Base, the Strategic Air Command's primary East Coast wing during the cold war.

Watertown, the largest community in the North Country with a population of just over twenty-seven thousand, was settled in 1800 as part of a large wave of migration leaving New England after the American Revolution. Settlers saw the industrial potential in the Black River as well as the agricultural promise of the St. Lawrence River valley. The classic American "five-and-dime" was conceived in Watertown by Frank Winfield Woolworth while working at a local

store in 1878. Today Watertown is closely tied to nearby Fort Drum.

There are two Native American settlements in the North Country. The St. Regis Mohawk Reservation (better known as Akwesasne to residents) has a population of approximately eight thousand and straddles the New York–Canada border. The controversial Akwesasne Mohawk Casino was built on tribal lands in 1999. The 2008 movie Frozen River, made in Plattsburgh, is set on the reservation. The second, Ganienkeh, is a Mohawk community located at Miner Lake outside of Altona. Ganienkeh is a rare case of Native Americans reclaiming land from the United States; in the 1970s members of the Mohawk nation successfully gained control of the land based on eighteenth-century treaties. A small number of families established a nonreservation settlement and

The 1838 Old Stone Barracks at Plattsburgh.

claimed sovereignty over the land. Its residents claim the unique status of being the only nation governed under the Constitution of the Iroquois Confederacy, without interference by either the American or Canadian governments.

Nestled in the Adirondack Mountains, Lake Placid hosted the Winter Olympics in 1932 and in 1980, the latter games being famous for the USA hockey team's unlikely triumph. The North Country is no stranger to continued displays of excellence on the six SUNY campuses in the region: two state university colleges, three community colleges, and a college of technology.

The North Country's SUNY campuses reflect both the rich history of the SUNY system and their rapid growth in the last third of the twentieth century. While the history of two of the six SUNY schools stretches well back into the nineteenth century, the three community colleges came into existence in the expansive 1960s. All of the schools take their roles

St. Regis Falls, Franklin County.

as economic drivers in the region very seriously by offering programs designed to prepare graduates to take a role in the changing world of the twenty-first century with particular focus on the unique opportunities provided by the area.

SUNY Potsdam and SUNY Plattsburgh, both founded in the nineteenth century, were among the original members of SUNY. Founded as academies, both evolved into normal schools featuring teacher training and then into state teachers' colleges before joining SUNY. As the North Country shares a two hundred-mile border with Canada, it is fitting that Plattsburgh is home to the most comprehensive undergraduate program in Canadian studies in the United States. Potsdam was the site of the "Potsdam Miracle" of the 1980s, when a nearly moribund math department was transformed into an international leader in the field.

The College of Technology at Canton, founded in 1906, was the first postsecondary, two-year college in the state of New York. Despite its long history, Canton looks to the future, as exemplified by its 2007 selection of the kangaroo as its mascot, because that animal—like the college—can only move forward.

True to its mission, Canton has embraced new energy technologies; its Wind Energy and Turbine Technology program is a national leader.

Between 1963 and 1969, the state of New York responded to the pressing educational needs of the dispersed population of the North Country by transforming and expanding the state teachers colleges into colleges of the liberal arts and sciences as well as opening three community colleges: Jefferson (1963), North Country (1967), and Clinton (1969). The community colleges are tied very closely to the region and their communities, as they prepare students for a variety of possibilities, from completing their undergraduate studies at a four-year college to moving immediately into the workforce. Exemplifying the six SUNY colleges' close relationship with this unique region, North Country Community College was the official college of the 1980 Winter Olympic Games held at Lake Placid, New York.

Lake Placid Olympic Jumping Complex.

COLLEGE OF TECHNOLOGY AT CANTON

ew SUNY institutions have been more closely tied to their environment than Canton. The college originated in 1906 as the School of Agriculture of St. Lawrence University. The college owes its origins to the efforts of St. Lawrence University's president, who successfully petitioned state legislators to pass the requisite legislation. But supporters feared that Governor Charles Evans Hughes might not sign the bill. In order to convince him to wield his pen, concerned residents undertook a letter-writing campaign prompting Governor Hughes to joke that he "did not know there were so many inhabitants in all the North Country." As early twentieth-century St. Lawrence County was experiencing an agricultural boom, spurred particularly by the dairy industry, the new college filled a void and provided a valuable service to the citizens of the region.

In its first decades the college focused on agriculture and home economics. The latter drove the school's growth as annual enrollment in the agriculture program remained under one hundred into the

A food preparation class in the Domestic Science program whose enrollments helped keep the School of Agriculture open.

Peter Nevaldine, founder of the Engineering Technology program, speaking in front of Canton's exhibition at the 1938 New York State Fair.

Students relaxing in the early days of SUNY.

mid-1930s. Then, in 1937, engineering and technical courses were added to the curriculum, creating a new orientation that would shape Canton's future. The new offerings were foreshadowed in a 1935 report, "A New York State Technical Institute," in which New York State's Department for Vocational and Extension Education argued for the creation of institutions to train students for industrial jobs. Canton's curriculum added industrial chemistry and technical electricity. Reflecting the expanded mission, the school was renamed New York State Agricultural and Technical Institute in 1941. The college made important contributions to the war effort training technicians in the following years.

Over the years, there were periodic fears that SUNY Canton was slated to be closed, due to anemic funding and the decline of St. Lawrence County agriculture. In 1934, the damage wrought by the Great Depression prompted talk that the School of Agriculture was on the chopping block, but an enthusiastic lobbying campaign by the director and local supporters convinced Albany to keep the doors open.

In 1948, New York State Agricultural and Technical Institute joined SUNY as a charter member.

Advanced technology programs were added to the curriculum in the 1950s and 1960s, leading to a name change to the State University of New York Agricultural and Technical College at Canton.

Then, another threat appeared in 1961 when St. Lawrence University announced that the school would have to move off its land. Canton's unusual history of having been founded by, and then separated from, St. Lawrence University created the anomalous situation of a SUNY institution surrounded by the property of a private university. Some saw an opportunity simply to close the school. Others believed that the college would be better off moving away from the small town of Canton. But once again determined efforts by local supporters ensured that the institution survived and remained in Canton. The result was a spacious new 555-acre SUNY Canton campus overlooking the Grasse River, encircled by miles of beautiful trails offering scenic landscapes. Fittingly, two footbridges connect the college to the Village of Canton. And the college continues to offer cutting-edge technology education on its "new" campus.

During the last two decades of the twentieth century, Canton shifted its emphasis decisively away from agricultural education toward technical offerings. In 1987, the present name, State University of New York College of Technology at Canton (conventionally called "SUNY Canton") was adopted in order to reflect that changing emphasis. However, the agricultural heritage continues through the veterinary sciences management and veterinary technology degrees as well as joint programs with SUNY's College of Environmental Science and Forestry.

For much of its history, SUNY Canton offered one-year certificates and two-year associate degrees. Currently, the offerings include over ten certificate programs and twenty associate degree programs. And since 1997 the college has been adding four-year baccalaureate programs. With these additions, students in many fields may follow a "ladder curriculum" that allows them to earn a one-year certificate in seven fields, then one of twenty-two associate degrees, and finally a bachelor's degree in one of twenty-three majors. The college organizes its degree programs into three academic schools: the School of Science, Health, and Criminal Justice; the Canino School of Engineering Technology; and the School of Business and Liberal Arts.

SUNY Canton has fully embraced the emerging technologies and needs of the twenty-first century; all of its bachelor's degrees are offered online as well as on campus. This gives the college a global presence, with students as far away as Japan, Russia, and Ukraine completing degrees through this campus in a small village in northwestern New York.

One of two covered bridges that connect the modern campus to the Village of Canton, whose citizens' support was crucial to the school's founding and survival.

Students in the Engineering Technology program build a bridge to scale.

Canton, named a Top Ten Pet-Friendly College by Petside.com, has offered a Pet Wing housing option since 1997.

The Department of Criminal Justice recently began offering students a major in homeland security as well as a minor that quickly became the most popular minor in Canton's history.

The college also continues to find new ways to serve local needs. Recent years have seen the campus become the home of the Small Business Development Center and the David Sullivan/St. Lawrence Country Law Enforcement Academy. The university's offerings are enhanced by membership in the Associated Colleges of the St. Lawrence Valley with St. Lawrence University, Clarkson University, and SUNY Potsdam.

SUNY Canton has innovated in other ways as well. In 1997 it opened its Pet Wing housing option. This permits students to bring their pets with them to live at the school, thus easing their transition into higher education. In recognition of the support given by the college to pet-loving students, NBC Universal's Petside.com twice named the school as a Top Ten Pet-Friendly College in 2012 and 2015. With the inauguration of bachelor's degrees came varsity athletic competition. Canton's football team had the unusual distinction of being coached by a renowned former NFL coach, Lou Saban, in its early years.

So the State University of New York College of Technology at Canton entered the twenty-first century with a sense of purpose and a clear trajectory of growth—today serving over 3,500 students. In 2007, the growing Canton athletic programs inspired the adoption of a new mascot, Roody Roo. As kangaroos are remarkable in the animal kingdom for only being able to move forward, the marsupial reflects the college's mission. And its foreign pedigree underscores the college's global focus.

CLINTON COMMUNITY COLLEGE

Situated at Bluff Point on a forested height overlooking Lake Champlain, Clinton Community College's spectacular setting and rich history provide a distinctive environment in which today's students live and learn. But, they are far from the first to use the site. For over a millennium, Native peoples used the abundant resources of the Champlain valley and Adirondack Mountains, with Bluff Point's "recent" history dating from French explorer Samuel de Champlain's 1609 arrival on the lake that bears his name.

During the French and Indian War (1754–1763), England and France fought over Lake Champlain to control shipping between the Hudson River and the lower St. Lawrence. As the highest promontory on the lake's western shore, Bluff Point provided the best vantage point from which to watch ships pass-ing between Canada and the French outposts at Crown Point and Ticonderoga. On October 11, 1776, the first battle between the newly formed American naval force under the command of Benedict Arnold and a British fleet took place below Bluff Point. Just twenty-eight years later, during the War of 1812, American naval commander Thomas Macdonough Jr. defeated a superior British force at Plattsburgh Bay, just north of Bluff Point.

Beyond its strategic importance, Bluff Point has also long been valued for its panoramic view and heal-ing environment. In 1888, the Delaware and Hudson Company purchased the site and built the luxurious Hotel Champlain. The original Victorian wood-framed building featured five hundred rooms and seven cot-tages on the grounds. Three massive towers atop the building provided literally a "bird's-eye view" of

The Victorian hotel as President and Mrs. McKinley would have seen it.

the lake, nearby islands, and the surrounding mountains of New York and Vermont, while bridle paths, a steamer dock, a yacht club, hiking trails, a private beach and bath house, and children's playrooms provided guests of all ages with an almost limitless variety of daily activities.

On May 25, 1910, the wood-framed hotel burned completely to the ground. Construction began almost immediately on a replacement, and the next summer a modern concrete and steel hotel welcomed eager guests back to their Adirondack retreat. Throughout Hotel Champlain's sixty-year history, its register read like a *Who's Who* in international business, politics, and sports. Among the notables who signed in were US presidents William McKinley, Theodore Roosevelt, William Howard Taft, Franklin D. Roosevelt, and Warren G. Harding; New York governors Charles Evans Hughes and Al Smith; Britain's Lord Beaverbrook; and New York Yankees' "Babe" Ruth.

By 1951 the hotel was operating at such a loss that it was sold to the Society of Jesus to house Bellarmine College, which prepared Jesuit priests. Twenty-one years later, it was sold to Clinton County

Early-automotive-age guests arrive at the Hotel Champlain, the center of today's campus.

for a million dollars and was reborn as the main campus for the new community college. In 1956, the County Board of Supervisors began to explore the feasibility of a community college for the region, appointing an exploratory committee chaired by the president of SUNY Plattsburgh. A decade later, when Governor Nelson A. Rockefeller authorized the establishment of Clinton County Community College as a two-year college within SUNY, events proceeded quickly. During the next year, Clinton County officials (by a 9–6 vote) agreed to establish and support the college. The breathtaking view from Bluff Point, once reserved for the few, now belonged to the citizens of Clinton County.

Clinton Community College first opened its doors to 189 full-time students in the fall of 1969, truly fortunate to make the splendid former Hotel Champlain its home. Today Clinton enrolls over 2,300 full- and part-time students. Over the years Clinton's campus added the William H. Forrence Health,

Physical Education and Recreation Center and the Ronald B. Stafford Center for the Arts, Sciences and Technology, with the Institute for Advanced Manufacturing scheduled to open in 2017. While these new buildings provide the modern equipment and facilities necessary for today's educational needs, each has been designed to be consistent with the campus's distinctive architecture and spectacular natural setting. Refurbished cottages from the Victorian hotel era continue to serve the college and the community. Alumni Cottage is home to the Office of Institutional Advancement.

Clinton Community College is an integral part of the community, offering students access to a variety of educational programs taught by a highly dedicated faculty, illustrated by the courses and programs that had been designed for the men and women at Plattsburgh Air Force Base. The base closed in 1995, and five years later, in 2000, the college opened its first of two residence halls in a refurbished building on

Biology students are instructed in laboratory techniques and exploration.

New and old buildings combine to create a spectacular campus overlooking Lake Champlain.

One of the first graduates of the Wind Energy and Turbine Technology program enjoys his achievement and the view.

what had been base property, arranged in suites with easy bus transportation to the main campus.

Cutting-edge technology degree programs including Wind Energy and Turbine Technology, Environmental Technology, and Renewable Energy Technologies have provided new opportunities for Clinton graduates and made the college a first stop for local industries to train and expand their workforce. Many students earn a two-year degree or certificate and then transfer to a four-year university. Others attend more briefly to meet a specific educational need or enter directly into the workforce after graduating with an associate degree.

The college's notable accomplishments in recent years include designation as a Military Friendly School and winning the 2010 National Championship Women's Soccer tournament. Clinton Community College is proud to be part of the rich history of Bluff Point, striving to help students create a brighter future for themselves and Clinton County.

JEFFERSON COMMUNITY COLLEGE

Located in Watertown, Jefferson Community College is nestled in northwestern New York State, near the junction of Lake Ontario and the St. Lawrence River. The proximity of the Thousand Islands and the Seaway Trail, the abundance of recreational lakes and rivers, and the area's rich history and natural resources make travel and tourism important regional economic drivers.

A community college for Jefferson County was first proposed in the late 1950s when, at the urging of a handful of advocates, the matter was put to a vote of the people. In November 1959, the referendum was voted down by a mere eight votes. In response, a dedicated band of citizens crusaded in earnest for the establishment of this community's college. Through a door-to-door and mail campaign, meetings with organized labor and civic groups, and televised pro-

grams with high school students, the Citizens Committee won a second referendum in November 1961 by a landslide of nearly three thousand votes.

Jefferson opened its doors in September 1963 to 114 full-time and 200 part-time students and offered academic programs in business, engineering science, accounting, liberal arts, and secretarial science. As the college leadership sought a site for a permanent campus, the fledgling college held its first classes in a converted elementary school in downtown Watertown and its sporting contests at the local YMCA and at nearby Fort Drum.

In June 1964, groundbreaking ceremonies were held for construction of a permanent campus on Coffeen Street. Jefferson students selected school colors of cranberry and white and an athletic mascot, the Cannoneer, a reference to the region's history and

A reminder of the area's early conflicts and inspiration for the "Cannoneer" nickname.

nearby Sackets Harbor, the US Navy's Lake Ontario headquarters in the War of 1812. In 1966, Congressman Robert C. McEwen presented the college with a Civil War–era, three hundred–pound cast iron cannonball that now rests in the foyer of the college gymnasium. The next year the college received a War of 1812 cannon that is now a focal piece of its quad, and each year on the eve of commencement, members of the graduating class covertly decorate the cannon as a testament to throwing off classroom decorum.

Through the remainder of the 1960s and the following decade, the college added new academic offerings including nursing, data processing, retail merchandising, criminal justice, and hospitality and tourism. In tandem, student activities and athletic programming were enriched. New transfer pathways and one-plus-one programs with other colleges and universities provided students with new opportunities.

By the time Jefferson celebrated its twenty-fifth anniversary in 1986, enrollment had grown to 1,870 full- and part-time commuter students. The academic curricula had expanded to twenty associate degree programs and six certificate programs, and the campus was bustling with student activities and special events. During this time, notables Charles Kuralt and Ralph Nader made appearances on campus and the college hosted performances by nationally known musicians Harry Chapin, John Denver, Arthur Fiedler and the Boston Pops, and Blood Sweat & Tears. Student government wrestled with campus life issues of the day, and student activism and a student newspaper, *The Word*, thrived.

The student union's image of our third president, whose name graces the county and its community college.

As the world of online learning opened up in the 1990s, Jefferson joined the SUNY Learning Network to make individual courses and then entire programs available to students in an online format. Today, more than five thousand credit hours of the college's programming are taken online and six academic programs are offered fully online.

Increasing access to higher education for area residents has always been a focal point of the college's mission. Jefferson has a robust concurrent enrollment program and offers college coursework to area high schools via interactive video (ITV) classes. The only college campus within fifty miles of Watertown, Jefferson partners with both SUNY and private colleges to bring bachelor's- and master's-level programs to the community at the Jefferson Higher Education Center. These upper-division programs provide flexible scheduling to fit working adults' lives.

Jefferson also enjoys a very close relationship with the US Army 10th Mountain Division stationed at Fort Drum located just ten miles from the campus. More than one-third of Jefferson's four thousand students are either active-duty military, family members, or veterans of military service. The college participates in C-TAMS, GoArmyEd, and SOCAD programs for members of the military and also offers contract coursework for military units at Fort Drum.

Jefferson continually assesses community and workforce requirements to ensure that its programs are meeting the needs of the region. The college has recently added curricula in winery management and marketing, renewable energy, sports management, and agri-business. The college has also expanded its Nursing and Allied Health programs and offers tuition assistance for nurses who want to pursue bachelor's- and master's-level nursing credentials.

Alongside its credit-bearing programs, the college offers a variety of workshops, seminars, and workforce training opportunities. Cultural events, open to the public, routinely include film and theatrical events, lectures, seminars, and art exhibitions. Library resources are open to the public and community members are encouraged to use them. Personal,

Jefferson Community College values its especially close relationship with Fort Drum.

The Culinary Arts program prepares Jefferson's students to serve the local economy and encourages them to remain in the region.

academic, and vocational counseling are provided to both students and the community. The Center for Community Studies at Jefferson conducts community-based research and provides a forum for discussing issues of community significance.

The first-ever residence hall opened at Jefferson in the fall of 2014, enabling 294 Jefferson students to live on the campus and give student life new dimensions. In addition, the newly constructed Deans Collaborative Learning Center opened its doors in March 2016, providing students with direct access to essential academic support services, library resources, breakout rooms for team projects or group study, and technology-rich classrooms all in a collaborative learning environment.

Jefferson Community College marked its fiftieth anniversary in 2011, celebrating its rich history and recognizing the efforts of those who worked so hard to found Jefferson Community College and in the five decades since to bring higher education to the region. At commencement 2013, Jefferson Community College celebrated the awarding of its twenty thousandth degree, a testament to the value that the college brings to Jefferson County and this region of New York State.

Proud graduates joining more than twenty thousand alumni.

Cherry blossoms on the Jefferson campus.

NORTH COUNTRY COMMUNITY COLLEGE

N orth Country Community College is the only public college in the Adirondack Park, the location of which resulted in its being named the Official College of the Winter Olympics in 1980. This designation in turn generated a relationship with the US Olympic Training Center that continues to the present day. Several Winter Olympians, such as Jimmy Shea, a gold medalist in 2002, have attended the college. Students, staff, and faculty also remain actively involved in Saranac Lake's Winter Carnival, a regional favorite since 1897. From its home in the beautiful but thinly populated North Country, the college has had a profound impact on the region's development.

In the 1950s a group of concerned citizens in the Saranac Lake region decided that the region needed a college; the area's low population and lack of capi-

tal proved to be obstacles. During that decade they came close to achieving their goal several times, once by nearly creating a new technical college, once in nearly relocating a state college, and yet another time by almost funding a private four-year college. However, it was not until 1964 that their plans began to come to fruition when the SUNY Trustees issued a Master Plan that recognized the need for a community college or technical school in the region. The Regents State-Wide Plan (1965) mandated further research.

The resulting study, commissioned by the Board of Regents, acknowledged the challenges facing an institution of higher education in the region. Despite widespread support for the establishment of such a school, the low population density meant that the region did not meet the state-mandated financial requirements. The decision to build the college in a

The annual Saranac Lake Winter Carnival.

central location, Saranac Lake, in order to serve two counties, Essex and Franklin, resolved the problem.

From the time of its initial planning beginning in February 1967, a conscious effort was made to link the curriculum of the new community college to both the educational and economic needs of potential students in the area. The result was curricula that offered both vocational education for immediate employment and transfer programs in preprofessional fields and the liberal arts. Fitting with the economics of the region

The Malone (above) and Ticonderoga campuses help North Country serve its vast region.

at the time, the early curricula emphasized business and paramedical fields.

As the Board of Trustees began planning prior to the initial opening of the college in September 1968, the community rallied behind the new school. Three local organizations provided temporary facilities for the school, underscoring the widespread community support. In the 1970s state construction funds underwrote classroom, laboratory, and library buildings, creating a permanent central campus. Expanding beyond Saranac Lake, in 1969 and 1970 branch campuses opened in Malone and Ticonderoga. These enabled North Country Community College to reach across the largest community college district in New York, stretching over 3,500 square miles from the Canadian border to Lake George.

Today, North Country continues its tradition of actively seeking public and private partners for a variety of projects that enhance its role in the region. For example, the proximity of the Saranac Lake campus to Lake Placid and the Olympic venues enables the Department of Health, Recreation, Sports, and Wellness to offer an associate degree in Wilderness Recreation Leadership. This program, created in 1979, trains outdoor educators, professionals, and guides for entry-level employment in various aspects of the outdoor industry or to transfer to a four-year program. The program provides a balance of hands-on practical instruction with theoretical training.

Students at North Country Community College are able to earn their Wilderness First Responder certification through a seventy-hour summer course provided by Wilderness Medical Associates.

Currently, North Country offers two Associate of Arts degrees, eight Associate of Science degrees, and eleven Associate of Applied Science degrees, as well as six certificate programs. Its eleven academic departments continue its historical role by preparing students for either entry into the workforce or transfer to a four-year college. The curricula at North Country continues to emphasize the business and medical fields that formed the core of the initial curriculum. In order to better meet the needs of its students, many of whom are not traditional college-age students, North Country offers a wide variety of online courses, making it possible for students to complete up to half of their program online as well as one fully online program in the liberal arts and sciences. Looking to the future, the NCCC faculty are exploring adding other associate degrees in a fully online format, giving the college even greater opportunities to overcome distance across the vast North Country.

North Country Community College serves the larger community through a number of programs that benefit citizens who are not currently enrolled. For

Students in the Wilderness Leadership program learn to endure the challenges of an Adirondack winter.

Paddling on an Adirondack lake.

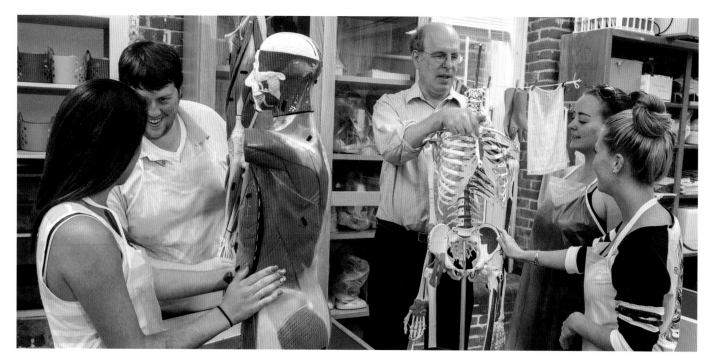

North Country continues its long-standing commitment to training nurses.

Students take comfort from the warmth and friendship of dining together.

example, NCCC offers a College Bridge program enabling Essex and Franklin county high school students to earn college credits while fulfilling high school graduation requirements. North Country's Center for Lifelong Learning offers noncredit programs for children as well as adults.

For nearly a half century, North Country Community College has set out to meet the North Country's educational needs. The region's unique character has presented both challenges and opportunities for the college as it has matured. North Country has accepted these challenges and made the most of the opportunities to provide an educational experience specifically tailored to the region's needs. As it proudly proclaims, North Country offers "a rich Olympic heritage, vibrant arts community, recreation and nature, the power of SUNY, and quality hands-on education at a price you can afford."

STATE UNIVERSITY COLLEGE AT PLATTSBURGH

Located on the western shore of Lake Champlain, just north of the Adirondack Park and south of the Canadian border, SUNY Plattsburgh has been an integral part of the regional community for over 125 years, offering liberal arts–based education to prepare students for career opportunities at local, regional, state, national, and global levels. The natural beauty of the surroundings enriches the quality of life of both students and faculty; the college reciprocates with a strong commitment to community service.

Chartered in 1889, the Normal and Training School

The Class of 1904 poses in front of Old Normal, Plattsburgh Normal School's first building, which served all campus needs until the 1929 fire.

at Plattsburgh was the last "normal school" built in New York State. In the 1880s, Plattsburgh boomed, boasting the luxurious Hotel Champlain, a new county courthouse, railroad depot, bridges, streets, and new housing. Prominent Plattsburgh citizens of this growing but rough-and-tumble mining, logging, and shipping community wanted to bring higher standards to the region and believed establishing a normal school would raise moral values and cultural standards to match the area's material progress.

Normal Hall opened in 1890—an imposing three-story,

red brick and buff sandstone building, built in the Richardson Romanesque architectural style. The building housed classrooms, the library, two auditoria, science laboratories, woodworking and print shops, a gymnasium, administrative offices, and a dining facility. Fourteen faculty were hired to teach fewer than one hundred students, including only two men.

As a normal school, Plattsburgh focused on teacher training. On the ground floor, an elementary school of 150 children enabled future teachers to do their "practice teaching" under the supervision of "master teachers." Upstairs, the normal school's curriculum included courses in English, Latin, and Greek; American and European history; the natural and physical sciences; art and music; personal health and hygiene; and even beekeeping. Most graduates then taught in the region's one-or-two-room schoolhouses. Courses in business skills (accounting, typewriting, taxation, and financial planning) were soon added to the summer courses, drawing students from across New York State to Plattsburgh's "Summer Institutes."

On a cold Saturday, January 26, 1929, disaster struck when a fire began and quickly spread to the

Hawkins Hall—the administrative center of campus since the 1930s.

highly varnished floors, woodwork, and stairways, causing the windows to implode and accelerating the blaze. The roof and towers collapsed in less than a half hour. In fact, everything not in the school's safe was destroyed. Fortunately, a professor giving a music lesson to community children managed to drop them from a first-floor window before escaping himself.

Many feared that Plattsburgh's institution would move south to Glens Falls, which wanted a normal school. The city elders, however, moved quickly to rebuild. Classes for the normal school students resumed in Plattsburgh's City Hall the following Wednesday, while the school-aged children were temporarily absorbed into the city's school system. A new Normal Hall (later Hawkins Hall) hosted classes for the first time in September 1932. Coming on the eve of the Great Depression, the construction project gave a welcome boost to the local economy.

A new principal, Charles C. Ward, responded to the challenges of the Depression-era's tightened budgets by instituting the Cadet Teacher program, forging connections between local schools and the normal school, instituting a pioneering four-year

Residential campus life began with the postwar construction of McDonough Hall.

Au Sable Hall, new home to the Business and Economics and the Computer Sciences departments.

Home Economics Teacher program, and, shortly after World War II began, creating the Cadet Nurse Corps, which became the School Nurse–Teacher program. Under Ward's leadership, the normal school became Plattsburgh State Teachers' College, making its graduates more competitive with private college graduates for teaching posts. During World War II, students picked apples from the area's orchards, learned how to pilot aircraft, operated shortwave radios, and became weather forecasters, among other wartime tasks. After the war, returning veterans utilizing the GI Bill swelled enrollment, necessitating the construction of Macdonough Hall, the first of several dormitories.

In 1948, the college, along with New York's other state teachers' colleges, joined the new SUNY system. In time, that relationship spurred a revised mission into a comprehensive, selective, four-year liberal arts college that also offered master's degrees in education and other academic disciplines.

Spurred by Governor Nelson A. Rockefeller's vision of a network of state-funded two- and four-year colleges within an hour's driving distance of every citizen of the state, Plattsburgh grew rapidly in the 1960s and early 1970s. Increasing enrollment necessitated new construction, including the award-winning Feinberg Library, a college center, a field house and playing fields for athletic events, and several multilevel dormitories along the northern bank of the Saranac River. The Plattsburgh campus, still dominated by Hawkins Hall, has grown to thirty-six buildings. The newest, Au Sable Hall, dedicated in 2014, houses the Business and Economics and the Computer Sciences departments.

Across the campus, opportunities abound to take learning beyond the classroom walls. Much of this "experiential" learning takes advantage of the region's natural resources. Expeditionary studies majors go climbing, skiing, and kayaking in the Adirondacks, while environmental science majors gain experience at an 8,600-acre center for teaching about the region and undertaking research on behalf of groups such as the Adirondack Park Agency.

Art suffuses the campus. The Plattsburgh State Art Museum houses more than 4,600 historical and contemporary objects. The museum adopted Andre Malraux's idea of a "museum without walls" to become an open visual art resource for the college and the Northern Adirondack/Champlain valley region, by integrating the arts across the campus and into the community. Epitomizing that connection, Brower Hatcher's twenty-foot-high *Adirondack Guide*

Art meets international relations with the Amitié Plaza sculpture reflecting Plattsburgh's longstanding ties to our northern neighbor.

A light moment in an intense history seminar.

Monument commemorates the college's connection to the nearby mountains.

The close tie between the school and the Canadian nation is underscored by William King's sculpture of two figures shaking hands in Amitié Plaza, the center of the campus, representing the friendship between the United States and Canada. In fact, Plattsburgh offers the most comprehensive undergraduate Canadian Studies program in the United States. For decades its students have studied at Canadian universities and undertaken internships in Canada.

SUNY Plattsburgh is committed to community service. For example, students in the Art Department participate in the annual Empty Bowls dinner to benefit the local food pantry, pairing with local fifth graders and other community members to craft the bowls used at the fundraiser. In 2013–2014, 3,873 students gave more than 382,000 hours in community service to the greater Plattsburgh area, including that of seventy students who spend spring vacation working in Habitat for Humanity's Alternative Break program.

College students communicate through *Cardinal Points*, the weekly award-winning student newspaper, and the student-operated PSTV broadcasts to approximately six thousand students and eighteen thousand off-campus households. The Plattsburgh Cardinals—especially the ice hockey, basketball, soccer, track, and cross-country teams—offer exciting contests for students and the community.

Currently, SUNY Plattsburgh enrolls over six thousand students in more than sixty majors, organized into three academic divisions: Arts and Sciences, the School of Business and Economics, and Education, Health, and Human Services. But, true to SUNY Plattsburgh's normal school origins, education remains the largest major on campus.

The college emphasizes academic excellence and takes its motto, "A Proud Past, a Strong Future," to heart. In 1890, an unknown writer described the first Normal Hall: "everything about the premises is in excellent order, and the future of the school is bright with promise." It is even brighter now, over 125 years later.

STATE UNIVERSITY COLLEGE AT POTSDAM

Potsdam proudly stakes its claim as the oldest unit in the SUNY system, tracing its roots to the founding of St. Lawrence Academy in 1816. The academy's first class of forty-two students was taught in a one-story, 24-by-36-foot wood-framed building. The student body grew rapidly; 114 students were enrolled by 1820. Despite the challenges of early 1800s travel, the reputation of the St. Lawrence Academy drew students not only from the region but also from as far away as Montreal and elsewhere in Canada. Rising enrollments soon required more space, and in 1825 the new North Academy building welcomed its first students.

Teacher education has a long history at SUNY Potsdam. When Reverend Asa Brainerd arrived in 1828, he brought a commitment to more professional training for teachers. Brainerd was the first school principal in

New York State to offer specialized teacher-training courses and this innovation reverberated throughout the state. In 1835, the New York State Legislature acted to strengthen programs for public school teacher preparation by designating one academy in each senatorial district to receive funding to create and sustain a teacher-training department. St. Lawrence Academy's selection for this distinction marked the official start of SUNY Potsdam's long tradition of teacher education. The first teachers' diplomas were awarded in 1836. Establishment of a teachers' department further increased demand for Potsdam's programs, resulting in the need for more space. The South Academy building opened in November 1837.

When the New York State Legislature committed to Horace Mann's "normal school" system for training teachers, it opened competition among New York's

SUNY's oldest college, Potsdam traces its roots to the St. Lawrence Academy, founded in 1816. It soon outgrew the original building.

academies to gain that designation and public funding. In 1867 the Village of Potsdam was chosen to be one of the first four, due in part to St. Lawrence Academy's reputation for teacher training but also to effective lobbying by the St. Lawrence Academy trustees and the surrounding communities' financial commitment. Thus, the St. Lawrence Academy became the Potsdam Normal School, which opened in a new building in April 1869 and graduated its first class in February 1871.

Music has been a Potsdam hallmark from the college's early years. Music first appeared in the St. Lawrence Academy's curriculum in 1831. The Crane Symphony Orchestra, formed in 1839, is the second earliest college orchestra in the country after Harvard's. In 1884, Julia Crane took charge of Potsdam's Music Department and founded the first normal school course to train public school music teachers in the United States. In 1886, she launched the Special Music Teachers Curriculum within the newly incorporated Crane Normal Institute of Music. Soon its graduates were teaching music throughout New York State and across the nation.

As the college moved into the twentieth century, physical and curricular changes followed. The original Normal School building was demolished and replaced by a new classroom administration building in 1919. The two-year teacher and music education curricula were initially lengthened into three-year and, by the late 1930s, four-year programs. Potsdam Normal School became the State Teachers College at Potsdam in 1942, the first year that bachelor's degrees were granted. Master's degrees were authorized in 1947. When SUNY was established the following year, the campus entered the system as the State University of New York Teachers College at Potsdam.

At midcentury the college relocated from downtown Potsdam to the present Pierrepont Avenue campus; the first buildings in the new location opened in the early 1950s. Once the clock tower was constructed on the main building for the new campus, it quickly became the enduring symbol of the

The Spring Festival of the Arts, begun in 1932, has brought numerous artists and speakers such as Eleanor Roosevelt.

Satterlee Hall, opened in 1954, initially contained all of the classrooms on the new Pierrepont Avenue campus as well as the administration. Its clock tower is the college's symbol.

college. Additional buildings were constructed from the mid-1950s to 1973, creating the campus as we know it today.

Further name changes occurred in 1959, when the college became the State University College of Education at Potsdam, and in 1961, when the name changed to the State University of New York College at Potsdam. This latter name change reflected the expansion into more liberal arts programs. The strength of the college's programs in the arts and sciences continue to attract students, and the importance of the college's strong liberal arts tradition is evident in a variety of fields within the arts, sciences, social sciences, and humanities.

Potsdam's long tradition and its high reputation for preparing music teachers continues today. Over half of New York State's music teachers graduated from the appropriately named Crane School of Music. Other graduates, including Renée Fleming, have gone on to successful performing careers. Crane's performing groups have appeared under famous guest conductors, including Nadia Boulanger, Leopold Sto-

kowski, and Robert Shaw. Crane's graduates also teach in every state in the country. The 1980 Winter Olympics in Lake Placid provided an international showcase for Crane's students, who performed compositions by the faculty.

The entire community benefits from the extensive cultural enrichment afforded them by SUNY Potsdam's presence. The many lectures, programs, events, athletic games, as well as a wealth of musical, dramatic, and dance performances truly enhance life in New York's North Country. A special feature has been the Community Performance Series that has, since 1989, brought leading artists to perform at Crane. They also conduct master classes during their time at the school. A preconcert lecture is also given by a member of the faculty on the evening of the concert.

Throughout the long history of the campus, the college has been a strong presence in the community. The new Performing Arts Center, opened in 2014, provides Potsdam with the latest facilities for performing arts instruction and performances.

The campus Alma Mater, reflecting the campus's location, begins,
"On the banks of Raquette River,
With its hills of blue,
Stands our honored Potsdam College,
Stirring sight to view!"

Gunther Schuller, renowned American composer, conductor, and jazz musician, works with Crane students as guest artist-in-residence.

Student practicums and internships in the local community assist regional institutions. SUNY Potsdam's participation in the Associated Colleges, along with Clarkson University, St. Lawrence University, and SUNY Canton, provides its students with broad opportunities. The North Country benefits from the synergy created by their close proximity.

Over four thousand Potsdam students choose from over forty majors, fifty minors, and eighteen graduate degree programs. The academic departments are organized into three schools: the Crane School of Music, the School of Liberal Arts, and the School of Education and Professional Studies. Outside the classroom, Division III athletic teams offer students formal recreational opportunities. For those who want to explore the great outdoors, New York's extraordinary Adirondack Park beckons only fifteen minutes away.

For nearly two centuries, SUNY's oldest institution has benefited from and contributed to the North Country. And its influence, especially in music, extends across New York State and the rest of North America.

MOHAWK VALLEY

College of Agriculture and Technology at Cobleskill

Fulton-Montgomery Community College

Herkimer County Community College

Mohawk Valley Community College

Morrisville State College

State University College at Oneonta

Often known as "America's First Frontier," the six counties of the Mohawk Valley region have been particularly successful in reinventing themselves to meet the changing demands of the larger society. As the economic needs of the nation shifted, the industries in the region also shifted. In order to preserve this flexibility, the colleges and universities of the valley combine an awareness of the region's history with a dynamic vision for its future.

The Mohawk Valley was at the center of great events in the nation's history even before there was a nation. The area is the traditional homeland of the Iroquois Confederacy and the region where the British and French colonial ambitions for North America clashed in the eighteenth century, often allying with one of the several Native American tribes that lived in the valley. As chronicled by James Fenimore Cooper, these battles entailed shifting alliances among competing cultures. The five novels comprising Cooper's "Leatherstocking Tales" contributed to the widely held belief that the new American nation was indeed exceptional, a unique product of the confrontation of modern society with nature.

Caughnawaga Indian Village site, Fonda.

Market Street, Amsterdam, 1909.

The Mohawk River runs from the mountains east of Lake Ontario 150 miles to join the Hudson just above Albany. It provided a passage through the Appalachian Mountains to the west, serving as the main transportation route for Native Americans, Europeans colonials, and Americans in turn. Throughout its history the region has functioned as an important transportation corridor linking the eastern seaboard with the interior to the west. The Erie Canal runs through the region, paralleling the river in places and using it in others. Cheap transportation played a vital role in the area's industrialization. This transportation corridor was further enhanced with the 1853 merger of a number of railroads that ran from Albany to Buffalo into the New York Central Railroad, providing a complex of cheap transportation to the Midwest. In the twentieth century, the New York State Thruway followed the same general route, running along the river in several stretches as far west as Utica.

This effective transportation system facilitated the growth of the textile and metal industries in the cities throughout the valley, from Schenectady in the east to Utica in the west. Schenectady's economy boomed in the late nineteenth and early twentieth centuries due to Thomas Edison's decision to locate one of his major companies there, the forerunner to General Electric's massive plants. Amsterdam became a center for textiles, particularly the carpet mills that thrived until the postwar period, when more and more production moved to the southern states. And Utica in the early twentieth century was one of the wealthiest cities in the country, with an arms industry that developed in World War I and continued to prosper through the Second World War. But, all these cities experienced increasing economic difficulties in the last half century, as the industrial base of each city eroded, creating a Rust Belt along the Mohawk. In addition, the siting of Griffiss Air Force Base at the Rome Air Depot in the 1940s had proven to be a major new employer in the area in the immediate postwar years that in the 1990s, with the post–Cold War reassignment, cost the area six thousand jobs.

Consequently, the Mohawk Valley region had to reinvent itself, turning in recent decades to its institutions of higher education. This emphasis on education aims at producing a more highly educated regional workforce, which will enhance the region's twenty-first-century emphasis on technology, telecommunications, banking, insurance, tourism, and finance.

The Mohawk River, Erie Canal, and Erie Canalway Trail.

The Mohawk Valley region is among the most beautiful in the state, a distinct asset to regional tourism. The New York State Canal system meanders through the gently rolling countryside, and the Oneida Indian Nation has emerged as one of the region's largest employers, providing nearly five thousand jobs at the Turning Stone Casino and Resort. Beyond tourism, the former Griffiss Air Force Base has been redesignated as the Griffiss Business and Technology Park and is home to approximately six thousand employees. Continuing the region's long association with the US Air Force is the presence of the Air Force Research Laboratory, which has helped to attract other technology companies.

The schools of the SUNY system that call the Mohawk Valley home are taking a lead in the economic rejuvenation of the region, emphasizing the developing technologies that will make this region a strong economic force in the twenty-first century. This emphasis on technological growth is found on the campus of the former SUNY Institute of Technology in Utica, which has merged with the College of Nanoscale Science and Engineering in Albany to form SUNY Polytechnic Institute, a complex that has already attracted several high-tech firms to the region

with the Marcy Nanocenter. The new center is expected to bring more than fifteen hundred new, very well-paying jobs to the area.

The Mohawk Valley is home to two SUNY Colleges of Technology. SUNY Cobleskill emphasizes the development of "green" ecological initiatives that are such a central part of the region's vision for the future, while the other, Morrisville State College, boasts both its "green" initiatives and the development of Nelson Farms, which offers students the benefits of experiential learning. The State University College at Oneonta, which began as a teachers' college, has now developed a vibrant liberal arts program that fosters the strong critical thinking and communication skills needed by students in the global economy of the twenty-first century.

Herkimer County Community College pioneered international education opportunities and distance education technologies as ways of providing new educational pathways for students in the region. Fulton-Montgomery Community College offers a broad range of transfer and professional programs on its main campus in Johnstown, as well as at the branch campus in Amsterdam that serves students

Erie Canal, Schoharie Creek Aqueduct, Fort Hunter.

Otsego Lake, Cooperstown.

Rome Westernville Road Bridge spanning Mohawk River, Rome.

in the eastern region of the Mohawk Valley. Finally, to the west, Mohawk Valley Community College was the first such institution created in New York. Like the other community colleges of the SUNY system, the three that are located in the Mohawk Valley region are designed to equip students for either transfer to four-year schools or immediate entry into the regional workforce.

The Mohawk Valley, then, has been the site of a storied past, as a transportation gateway and string of industrial concerns that have had to painfully evolve through the past three decades into a new web of interconnected high-technology research and production sites. Essential to that future are the SUNY colleges that dot the landscape, providing thousands of residents each year with the intellectual capital needed to sustain a more variegated regional economy, enrich its social fabric, and enhance the cultural life of its communities.

COLLEGE OF AGRICULTURE
AND TECHNOLOGY AT COBLESKILL

Nestled in the rural Schoharie Valley of central New York, SUNY Cobleskill is one of the leading agricultural and technological colleges in the Northeast. Its academic and cocurricular programs are known for their emphasis on experiential learning, connections to industry and business, leadership opportunities, and community service. Students live and learn on a modern, 902-acre campus with outstanding educational facilities, accomplished faculty, and supportive staff.

Chartered in 1911 as the Schoharie School of Agricul-

Early Cobleskill students learned about real "horsepower."

ture, the New York Legislature mandated that the school teach "Agriculture, Mechanical Arts, and Home Making." Five years later, Cobleskill opened its doors to eight students with only one building and five faculty members on ninety acres. Soon a dairy barn was constructed, a herd purchased, and a poultry house completed. Originally devoted solely to the agricultural education of young men, the school college quickly expanded its offerings to include courses of study in home economics and nursery school teacher training for women. Enrollments grew

The agricultural college matures.

slowly, and the campus matured without significant additions between the wars.

A new era began in 1948 when the Institute of Agriculture and Home Economics joined the newly created State University of New York as a founding member. Three years later SUNY granted it the power to award the Associate in Applied Science degree as an accredited community college. Reflecting the growing role of technology programs in the curriculum, the name was again amended in 1957 to the SUNY Agricultural and Technical Institute. In 1964 the institute was renamed a college as enrollments began to soar.

A further step was taken in 1987 when the college awarded its first baccalaureate degree, a Bachelor of Technology in agriculture. The college now offers over fifty associate's and bachelor's programs, with enrollments divided between the School of Agriculture and Natural Resources programs and the School of Business and Liberal Arts and Sciences.

During the 1950s and 1960s, SUNY Cobleskill expanded its buildings and programs to meet the needs of a rapidly growing student body. The campus began to assume its modern look with the addition of academic buildings for Plant Science, Animal Science, and Agricultural Engineering, the library, a campus center, and administrative offices, as well as the first residence halls.

The early twenty-first century has seen another era of expansion. The college constructed the Cobleskill Campus Child Care Center, the Equine Center, a new two-hundred-head dairy barn, a new heifer barn, and the Center for Environmental Studies and Technology, supported by $8 million of federal grants for gasification projects. The new Center for Agriculture and Natural Resources provides state-of-the-art facilities for the plant and animal science pro-

The agricultural tradition lives on at modern Cobleskill.

Across its history, Cobleskill's equine program has included both heavy "workhorses" and sleek steeds.

grams, cold- and warm-water fish hatcheries, a meat processing lab, a conservatory, greenhouses, and green roofs. And Cobleskill has recently opened its first suite-and-townhouse-style residential housing.

Applied learning and field experiences are infused into academic programs. Culinary arts students apply their skills in kitchen laboratories and run a campus restaurant; histotechnology students complete a four-hundred-hour clinical rotation; aquaculture students raise fish at the campus fish hatcheries; and equine program students train horses in the campus's indoor and outdoor arenas. Students complete internships as the capstone for their Bachelor of Technology degrees, gaining experience at locations as diverse as Yosemite and Shenandoah National Parks, Bighorn National Forest, the National Wildlife Refuge, John Deere, Army Corps of Engineers, Smithsonian Gardens, MTV, Disney World, and the New York State Assembly.

Students also present research in international venues such as the World Aquaculture Conference and compete in national events such as the Philadelphia Flower Show.

In a wide variety of programs, including Fisheries and Wildlife, Equine Studies, Plant Science, Culinary Arts, Animal Science, and Early Childhood Education, students study abroad on faculty-led trips to various countries including Australia, New Zealand, China, the Netherlands, England, Ireland, Turkey, Peru, Anguilla, and India. Students also complete service trips abroad and participate in international programs offered through the SUNY system.

Although many Cobleskill students hail from Schoharie County and other rural regions of upstate New York, the college has a strong appeal for New England and Mid-Atlantic students, especially those interested in agriculture. Additionally, students from downstate New York, New York City, Long Island, and

Today's students learn how to harness a different form of horsepower.

Throughout its history, SUNY Cobleskill has never lost sight of its primary mission and has positioned itself as one of the leading agricultural and technological colleges in the Northeast. Faculty continue to distinguish themselves through innovative, applied approaches, and students continue to develop their skills for future careers and lifelong learning while the college continues to contribute to regional economic development. Modern SUNY Cobleskill, with more than forty buildings, one hundred faculty, and twenty-five hundred students on over nine hundred acres, is a far cry from its beginning with one building, five faculty, and twelve students a century ago.

overseas pursue a wide range of programs and add to the student body's cultural breadth.

Students enjoy a rich campus life. Ten residence halls enable students to profit from the total collegiate residential experience. Over fifty clubs and residential councils offer opportunities to participate in shaping the community. Fighting Tiger athletic teams compete in the North Eastern Athletic Conference, and the cross-country teams have been particularly successful.

The college has been frequently recognized for its dedication to service, listed for five consecutive years on President Obama's Higher Education Community Service Honor Roll. *Affordable Colleges Online* has listed SUNY Cobleskill as being among the "top schools in New York State for a lifetime return on investment." Victory Media counts SUNY Cobleskill as a "Military Friendly College" for ranking in the top twenty percent of colleges nationwide in serving the needs of veterans.

The arts are not forgotten.

FULTON-MONTGOMERY COMMUNITY COLLEGE

Situated in the southern foothills of the Adirondacks, the 195-acre Fulton-Montgomery Community College overlooks the Mohawk River Valley. In 1963 the Fulton and Montgomery County Boards of Supervisors proposed a joint community college. The State University of New York Board of Trustees quickly approved the proposal, creating SUNY's twenty-seventh two-year institution.

Temporary accommodations were soon leased in Johnstown High School and nearby buildings. In fall 1964 seventeen faculty began teaching 325 students in the liberal arts and sciences as well as applied programs such as accounting and secretarial science. The bookstore and the Humanities Division found a home in St. Mark's Lutheran Church. An English professor wound up teaching Flaubert's *Madame Bovary* in the church halls, while a social sciences professor drove fifty miles each Saturday to teach an extension class.

In 1965 the college acquired its current site and began building a campus around a traditional quadrangle. By the time it opened in 1969, more than one thousand students were enrolled. The permanent campus gave the college the resources to meet its vision of offering low-cost education while

Constructing the clock tower, the symbolic center of the campus's quadrangle.

This picture would have been science fiction to the college's founders.

tional students from more than fifteen different countries. As a comprehensive community college, Fulton-Montgomery offers a variety of academic programs ranging from Business to General Studies to Fine Arts to Health Professions to Engineering and Technology. The college's forty-four academic programs are designed to meet the needs of the region and its students by preparing them to transfer to a four-year college or to enter the workforce upon completion of a program. For those planning to transfer to a baccalaureate college, the college offers a wide range of courses in the liberal arts and sciences. The Honors program challenges highly motivated students to reach their full potential. The Cobleskill Partnership Bachelor of Business Administration provides seamless transfer to a sister SUNY institution.

providing services and facilities to residents of its two counties.

Over the following five decades, enrollments have risen dramatically, and today Fulton-Montgomery serves over 2,800 students including interna-

Other programs prepare graduates to enter the workforce. The flexibility of the college's Collaborative Career Learning program enables students to

A librarian's view of busy students.

All the world's a television stage for these students.

combine classroom education with internships, giving students hands-on experience. The Fulton-Montgomery Career and Technical Center, operated by the Board of Cooperative Educational Services located next door to the campus, provides laboratory work for courses in automotive technology and construction technology.

Programs from Fulton-Montgomery's early years in leather-making and secretarial science have yielded their place in the curriculum to more modern approaches. The Radiologic Technology Lab and the state-of-the-art, federally funded Demonstration Cleanroom serve the rapidly changing technological community and student needs. The latter, part of the college's Center for Engineering Technology, opened in 2010 as the only cleanroom at a community college in the Mohawk Valley region. The center represents a collaboration of academic science and technical programs ranging from automotive technology to engineering science. In the center professors and students learn in the Advanced Manufacturing Laboratory, in classrooms, with high-technology equipment, and of course, in the cleanroom. Previously,

Fulton-Montgomery's Electrical Technology students had to travel to Albany's Nanotech center to work in cleanrooms.

The Radiologic Technology Lab features a digital radiology machine with a picture archiving and communications system. The equipment includes an instructional mannequin that has an internal skeleton to teach students how to take images. With the assistance of the college's Foundation, the Radiologic Technology program has a phantom patient molded from a radiation-equivalent urethane formulation over an actual human skeleton. The phantom patient's moveable joints realistically simulate patient positioning, while radiographic images of the phantom patient also reveal replicated internal organs. These are created by hollow structures that allow each cavity to be injected with a contrast medium, just as would be the case with a patient in the hospital.

The Evans Library and Learning Commons anchors the students' intellectual experience. On a typical day, over 1,200 people come through the door. Once inside, they can access sixty-five thousand paper and e-book volumes, tap into databases

Following Voltaire's advice to tend their garden.

for over twenty-five thousand periodicals, or search among eighteen million items in SUNY's collaborative library system. Librarians offer research assistance that opens up new worlds to inquiring students. A variety of academic and student support services help each student succeed by providing advisement, counseling, academic intervention, and tutoring,

The main campus centers on a quadrangle anchored by its signature clock tower. In addition, the campus includes a childcare center, the Perrella Gallery for the fine arts, television studios, a theater, and study lounges. Recent additions include Raiders Cove, a social venue for students; Union Stations, a renovated cafeteria that now offers five serving stations; and the Books and Bytes Café.

Students have a vibrant campus life. Fulton, Montgomery, and Raider halls provide facilities for students wishing to call the campus home and partake in the complete collegiate experience. Freshmen from homes beyond commuting distance are required to live in campus housing. Students can participate in over thirty clubs, such as the Art Guild, Foggy Mountain Players, Outdoor Adventure Club, and the Students of the World Club. Seven Raiders athletic teams participate in intercollegiate sports, while other students participate in intramural sports.

Fulton-Montgomery also offers opportunities beyond the main campus, such as varied day and evening classes available at an extension site in Amsterdam's Riverfront Center. The college also offers a number of distance-learning opportunities through selected courses, both credit and noncredit, for delivery via the Internet and other electronic means. By taking advantage of these offerings, students can engage in higher education and lifelong learning from the comfort of their homes on a schedule that allows them to accommodate the competing demands of work, family, and other commitments.

In its first half-century Fulton-Montgomery has changed dramatically from a few hundred students in borrowed facilities into a mature comprehensive community college on an attractive campus. Repaying the investment by two counties and SUNY, Fulton-Montgomery Community College has brought quality education to thousands of students, thereby enriching the quality of life in the region.

Faculty trying on student work in the Perrella Gallery.

HERKIMER COUNTY COMMUNITY COLLEGE

Situated in the foothills of the Adirondack Mountains, Herkimer County Community College was first proposed by the Herkimer County Board of Supervisors in 1963, and the next year Herkimer County was included in SUNY's 1964 Master Plan as a potential site for a community college. After refinements to the proposal and a very close county-wide referendum, the SUNY Board of Trustees voted to establish its twenty-ninth community college in Herkimer.

Classes began in the fall 1967 semester with an enrollment of 221 full-time and 101 part-time students who were instructed by nine faculty. For the next four years classes were held in temporary quarters while a debate raged over the site for the permanent campus. Ilion, Mohawk, and Little Falls all showed interest, but Herkimer finally won, thanks to donations by several Herkimer residents that enabled the college to acquire a one-hundred-acre site on the edge of the village at no cost.

Fulfilling the mandate that community colleges should serve the practical educational needs of the community and make education affordable and accessible, Herkimer's early programs, such as Radio-TV Broadcasting, Travel and Tourism, and Automotive Mechanics, were essentially vocational. Since then, the college has built strong departments offering programs in the humanities, social sciences, sciences, and fine arts for students whose ambitions include pursuing a baccalaureate degree.

In 1971, the permanent campus was ready, and in September classes commenced there on a five-building, $7,700,000 complex designed to serve a potential enrollment of 1,100. But the college's enrollment

Students broadcast to campus and community on television and radio.

Assisted Design, Occupational Therapy, and Travel and Tourism. In 1999, expansion of both the McLaughlin College Center and the Physical Education Building were completed at a cost of $9,000,000. The campus has also expanded spatially, now covering nearly five hundred acres.

The arts play an important role in campus life. In 2000, HCCC's Cogar Gallery was underwritten by the George and Ann Cogar Foundation. The gallery hosts local, regional, and national art exhibitions throughout the year. The Robert H. Wood Great Artists Series, endowed by a longtime Ilion resident, presents classical music performances for the college and the local community.

By the end of the 1980s, demand for the college's services had grown to such an extent that the college began offering classes at Mt. Markham High School in mathematics and science. These were the first classes in the concurrent enrollment program currently called College Now. Nationally accredited, it offers an opportunity for local high school students to take college classes

had already grown to 884 full-time students, and with more than two hundred part-time students, further expansion was necessary.

As the school grew, so did its facilities, supporting new specialties. The campus's Nature Trail was dedicated in 1973 on fifty-five acres featuring an interpretative nature trail, a managed artificial pond, and a tree plantation. Soon after, the college added the Archeology Museum and the Natural History Museum, with exhibits of plant and animal life in the Mohawk Valley area. And a Child Care Center opened in 1981 to serve the needs of returning adult college students, college staff, and the community.

In 1991, a new thirty-three-thousand-square-foot Technology Center opened, providing classroom and laboratory space for study in Criminal Justice, Radio and Television, Computer Science, Computer

The child care center serves as a practicum site for Early Childhood majors.

Learning the art of modern physical therapy.

at a reduced rate in their high schools while earning both college and high school credit.

During the late 1980s and the 1990s, Herkimer County Community College began to be recognized for the high percentage of its students who graduate within two years, an achievement that continues. By 1997, enrollment had reached 2,467, a more than sevenfold increase in the college's first thirty years. The college made an early commitment to online learning, launching the Internet Academy in May 1999 with six complete degree programs. Since then it has grown to include twenty two-year degree—and three certificate—programs, as well as a variety of support services. Approximately twenty-five percent of the college's enrollment is now completely online.

Herkimer College is also engaged internationally. In July 1997, Herkimer signed an agreement allowing graduates of the Kamei School in Japan to complete an associate degree at HCCC in one year of study in a variety of programs. This marked the growth of an international program that began with twelve students in 1996 and now brings approximately ninety students per year from twenty different countries. In July 2010,

six faculty members traveled to China to teach high school students through the Bright Vision Education Group. In that same year, the new Center for Global Learning opened to provide educational programs designed to prepare students to become productively engaged citizens in a global society.

Herkimer has offered on-campus housing since 1991. Today, over six hundred students live in the apartment-style dormitories, enabling them to enjoy a full collegiate experience. Students participate in a wide range of clubs and organizations. The campus radio station, WVHC, broadcasts 24/7 all year round and is especially known for its jazz programming. Herkimer County Community College athletes compete in seventeen intercollegiate sports in the Mountain Valley Collegiate Conference. The Generals have won fifty-three national championships and have twice been ranked number one nationally among nonscholarship two-year colleges by the National Alliance of Two-Year College Athletic Administrators.

Established in 1967, the Herkimer County College Foundation supports over eighty scholarships,

Apartment-style dormitories enhance on-campus life.

Another victory for the Generals.

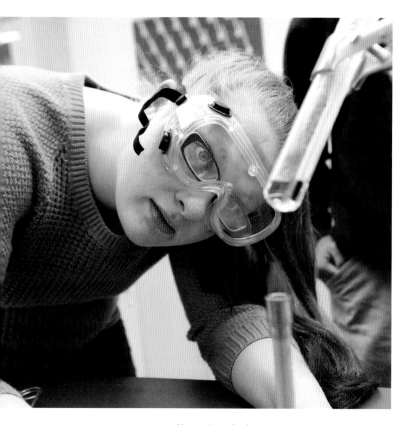

Natural curiosity.

awarding more than $120,000 annually to eligible students. By raising private funds, the foundation has been instrumental in acquiring additional land for the campus and developing student housing adjacent to the campus. The foundation's most notable fundraising event is the Herkimer County Arts and Crafts Fair, which has grown into a major annual regional event over the past four decades.

From its inception, Herkimer County Community College has supported the community in a variety of ways, providing lifelong learning opportunities, youth programming, health and wellness activities, personal interest courses, professional development and training, and cultural, athletic, and social events. The college emphasizes strong partnerships and alliances with business, educational, government, and nonprofit organizations that support regional workforces and economic development. And Herkimer County Community College has played an integral role in community revitalization through programs such as the Communities 2000 program, Keep America Beautiful, and Herkimer Now.

MOHAWK VALLEY COMMUNITY COLLEGE

The Mohawk River valley lies south of the foothills of the Adirondack Mountains. Opened to the world by the Erie Canal, then the New York Central Railroad, and the New York State Thruway, the valley was at the heart of the American industrial revolution, becoming an international textile center. That economic base, and its subsequent decline, has shaped Mohawk Valley Community College's history.

After World War II, New York State created five technical institutes to bolster the postwar economy by providing technical training, especially for returning GIs. One of those five was the New York State Institute

Early class technology reflected the valley's role in the industrial revolution.

of Applied Arts and Sciences in Utica. Its early curriculum was designed to serve the textile industry, which still employed over twenty-five thousand Uticans. The institute opened in the former Country Day School, in October 1946, with fifty-three students entering a business retail program designed to promote textile products. The sense of urgency in meeting postwar educational needs was such that faculty spent the previous weekend unpacking furniture and arranging classrooms. More than two-thirds of the first students were veterans, and tuition was free for New York residents.

Other programs designed to fit the needs of area industries soon followed. A second location opened the following year in the former Utica Steam Cotton Mill to house the Textile and Electrical Technology programs. These programs were created in the hope that their graduates would aid in solving the problems beginning to plague textile factories in the Northeast. As those companies shut down and were replaced by electrical and metalworking firms, the college adapted its curricula to train students to perform a variety of manufacturing activities—from drafting and design to quality control—as well as to develop the manual skills needed in such industries. Many students were former textile workers, retraining for the changing economy.

The institute joined SUNY in 1950 as the State University of Applied Arts and Sciences at Utica. But New York State's technical institutes were only a temporary postwar measure; in 1952, SUNY directed the institutes to find local sponsors that would take partial financial responsibility and convert them into community colleges. Under this plan, the state reduced its share of operational support from one hundred percent to one-third. And the state's capital support would be reduced to fifty percent.

Oneida County stepped forward as the local sponsor, creating one of New York's first community colleges under the name Mohawk Valley Technical Institute. Over the next decade, the number and variety of instructional programs continued to grow, and the curriculum expanded into the liberal arts and sciences and other nontechnical areas and began preparing graduates to transfer to baccalaureate colleges. In recognition of this broadening mission and changing emphasis, the institute was renamed Mohawk Valley Community College in 1963.

By then the main campus had moved to a permanent eighty-acre campus in southeast Utica. Opened in 1960, the new campus was designed by famed architect Edward Durell Stone, whose world-class projects included Radio City Music Hall and the Museum of Modern Art in New York City. Initial construction included the Academic Building, the Physical Education Building, and the College Center, all of which have been extensively renovated and expanded over the years. MVCC built its first four residence halls in 1966—making it the first New York community college to provide on-campus

The sciences and health sciences.

housing—and added a fifth in 2005. With these on-campus residence halls, Mohawk Valley's students have long been able to experience a complete collegiate experience. Later campus additions have included Payne Hall (1969), the Science and Technology Building (1989), and the Information Technology/Performing Arts/ Conference Center (2001).

Soon after receiving county sponsorship, the institute extended its services into western Oneida County. At the request of the US Air Force, the college began instruction at Griffiss Air Force Base in Rome in 1954. Some classes were held on base and others at Staley Junior High School. The present Rome branch campus opened in 1974 in the former Oneida County Hospital. The Plumley Complex was added to the Rome campus in 1991. In 2006 the Airframe and Power Plant Technology program began in Rome's Griffiss Business and Technology Park, giving students practical hands-on training with the most modern aircraft.

The more than ninety academic programs divide evenly between those leading to transfer to a four-year college and those leading directly to employment. Among the former are programs ranging across the fine arts and humanities, social sciences, and sciences and mathematics; among the latter are those leading directly to careers in health science, business, and information systems, as well as specialties such as fire protection, hotel technology, criminal justice, and cyber-security.

Students find an active life at MVCC. They may choose from among over fifty clubs, and the Mohawk Valley Hawks teams compete in twenty-two indoor and outdoor intercollegiate sports. The Robert R. Jorgensen Athletic/Events Center can host three thousand people for events such as the Boilermaker Road Race, which draws more than thirty-five thousand visitors to the city each July. Its other amenities include basketball, volleyball, and tennis courts; a fitness center; and an indoor track.

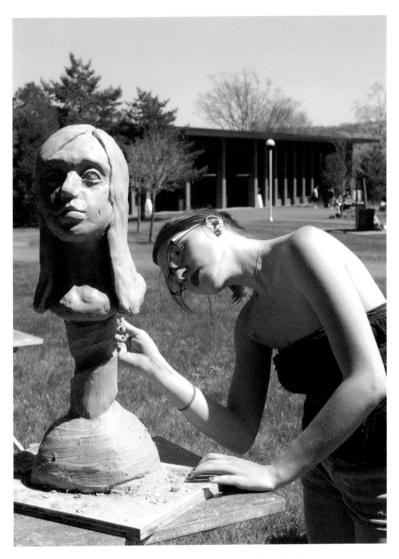

Student sculptors follow their passions in the Fine Arts and Crafts Club.

The Utica and Rome campuses host more than 150 community events annually. In addition, students, faculty and staff help raise funds for worthy causes through events such as the Alex Kogut Run/Walk, Making Strides Against Cancer Walk, American Heart Association Heart Run/Walk, and the Veteran's Center Food Drive.

MVCC's enrollment has risen steadily in recent years to over six thousand full-time equivalent students taking credit-bearing courses taught by over three hundred faculty. With an average age of over

The men's and women's lacrosse teams honor the area's Mohawk heritage.

technology boom centered on SUNY Polytechnic and Griffiss Air Force Base. The college's proud tradition of technical and trade education has positioned it to help meet the growing demand for students with degrees in science, technology, engineering, and mathematics, while its partnerships with other colleges in the state encourage students to easily transfer to four-year institutions. Mohawk Valley Community College will continue to contribute to the region's economic well-being and quality of life as it navigates the transition to a postindustrial society.

twenty-five, many are mature students, and over three-quarters live in Oneida County. The college also serves more than six thousand students in noncredit courses. In total, it is the largest college between Syracuse and Albany and the region's largest provider of college education and noncredit training.

Looking to the future, Mohawk Valley Community College will further align itself with the revival of the city of Utica and the surrounding area—including the arterial project—through the City of Utica Master Plan, the Utica Comets hockey team, and the nano-

The Hawk entertains a fan.

MORRISVILLE STATE COLLEGE

ocated in the center of New York State, thirty miles from both Syracuse and Utica, Morrisville enjoys a lovely rural setting in Madison County. Founded as an agricultural college, Morrisville now offers a wide range of academic programs as well as applied programs such as Automotive Technology, Equine Science, Dairy Management, Nursing, Renewable Resources, Resort and Recreation Management, and Information Technology. These programs, combined with state-of-the art facilities, present theoretical learning in real-world settings.

At the beginning of the twentieth century, New York State's farmlands and rural areas were

Early students studied and lived in the former Madison County Court House and jail.

being abandoned, while food prices were rising. Morrisville, for instance, had lost one-third of its population since 1890. Agricultural education was seen as one solution. On May 6, 1908, the New York State Legislature authorized the creation of the School of Agriculture at Morrisville in the hope that advanced education would both help farmers make a better living and aid the state's economy. Ideally, young men would learn new techniques and then return to their family farms where they would increase food production and lower food prices.

In 1910, the first students were accepted into six degree programs: Home Economics, Academics, Horticulture, Agronomy, Shop, and Animal Husbandry. They arrived at a campus created from buildings that had been abandoned when the Madison County seat moved from Morrisville to Wampsville. Two years later the Class of 1913, eleven men and two women, graduated.

Between the World Wars, the school grew, adding students and broadening its mission to include programs in Teacher Training, Automotive Technology, and Horology (watchmaking). In recognition of the growing role of technology courses, it was renamed the Agricultural and Technical Institute at Morrisville.

Governor Roosevelt, who was deeply committed to agricultural reform, visiting the campus.

In 1948, Morrisville became a founding member of the SUNY system and entered the new decade as an associate degree–granting institution, renamed the State University of New York Agricultural and Technical Institute at Morrisville. The 1960s were about growth and change as a new campus was constructed and more than a dozen new programs were established, pushing the student body population to over two thousand. The addition of academic programs prompted yet another name change in 1965, when the college took on its current title, SUNY College of Agriculture and Technology at Morrisville.

Today, although Morrisville offers much more than agriculture, it hasn't forgotten its roots. The college is a leader in technology as well as sustainability. The present state of agriculture is fused with science, reflected by the creation of degrees in renewable resources technology

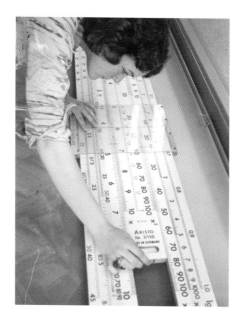
High tech in the 1960s.

and natural resources conservation. In addition to its two-year programs, Morrisville now awards four-year bachelor degrees in selected programs, such as Agriculture Business Development, Dairy Management, Equine Science, and Horticulture.

The college also plunged into the technological revolution and added degree programs in new fields such as Electronic Marketing and Publishing, Web Development, Journalism and Communication for Online Media, Renewable Resources Technology, Natural Resources Conservation, and Renewable Energy.

One of the most innovative elements in Morrisville's curriculum is Nelson Farms, a small-scale food incubator designed to provide business opportunities for entrepreneurial farmers and producers. Students use the facility as a hands-on laboratory in which they gain real-world experience in several areas of agriculture.

As students pursue these varied programs, they benefit from a modern campus that includes fifty buildings on more than one thousand acres of farm- and woodland. The college now boasts its own full-service, fine dining restaurant, the Copper Turret; equine and dairy complexes; and an award-winning automotive facility. The Equine Rehabilitation Center makes Morrisville the only college in the Northeast that offers students the opportunity to treat injured horses as part of their collegiate education. How appropriate, then, that among the Morrisville Mustangs seventeen intercollegiate sports are the Women's Hunt Seat Equestrian and Western Equestrian teams.

Morrisville State College features small classes that take a real-world, practical approach to education. Today's three thousand students are enrolled in more than seventy-five academic programs, including more than twenty that offer baccalaureate degrees. Nearly every bachelor's degree includes a full-semester internship as a capstone.

Technology continues to shape Morrisville State College's campus culture. In the late 1990s, Morrisville gained a national reputation as a leader in the implementation of technology on campus with innovative laptop, wireless, and cell phone initiatives. In the fall of 2008, the college established one of the first campus-wide wireless networks, providing students, faculty and staff with the fastest wireless network available at that time.

In addition to technology, Morrisville State College actively participates in the green revolution with a ten-kilowatt wind turbine, an anaerobic methane digester that has reduced the $4,000 monthly electric bill at the dairy complex to about $400, a biodiesel processor, and research on biodiesel feedstocks. These facilities provide renewable energy and, coupled with several projects currently in progress, allow students hands-on learning in a safe and technical atmosphere.

Equine studies remain a central feature of the Morrisville curriculum.

Harnessing solar power for the campus.

Morrisville's Controlled Environmental Agriculture (CEA) integrates fish farming and produce production with an innovative energy system that cuts costs by using waste from one process to fuel the next. Heat given off by an electric generator next to the greenhouse keeps the fish and lettuce warm during winter. The generator's carbon dioxide exhaust grows algae that feeds the fish. Fish waste is then used to fertilize the plants after being sterilized with ultraviolet rays.

Founded to solve an early twentieth-century agricultural crisis, today's Morrisville State College provides an education based on contemporary agricultural technologies that were unimaginable a century earlier. The Sheila Johnson Design Center encapsulates Morrisville's history, greeting visitors with a profile that echoes Morrisville's historic dairy barn while using the most modern sustainable technologies to house high-tech workshops.

The Sheila Johnson Design Center combines past and future.

STATE UNIVERSITY COLLEGE AT ONEONTA

In the northern foothills of the Catskill Mountains lies the city of Oneonta, a small settlement that numbered fewer than one thousand inhabitants well into the nineteenth century. But when the Delaware and Hudson Railway reached Oneonta and built the largest locomotive roundhouses in the world, new industries flocked to the Susquehanna River valley town. The population more than doubled in the 1880s, stimulating the ambitions of the boomtown's lead-

Old Main was the central building from 1889 until the 1970s.

ers, prompting them to make a successful application to New York State's Board of Regents to establish a Normal School.

By 1889 the Oneonta Normal School was ready to receive its first students in a stately building later dubbed "Old Main" sitting high above the Susquehanna Valley. It housed the entire campus until 1933 when the school expanded, opening the Bugbee School, named after the normal school's second principal, to provide on-campus training for student teachers. On the eve of World War II, like New York's other normal schools, Oneonta became a four-year, degree-granting institution.

Oneonta was a founding member of SUNY, entering as Oneonta Normal School. Three years later, in 1951, it adopted the name State University College of Education. In the early 1950s, the focus at Oneonta continued to be teacher education as it added home economics courses to the curriculum. In 1954 the Home Economics Building was constructed, and through the end of the decade several more buildings were added to the campus to accommodate expanding enrollment.

Growth sped up in the 1960s, forcing the college to resort to temporary solutions, including the use of mobile classrooms. Additional property was purchased as the campus grew. New buildings, including dormitories, classroom buildings, and the college's first separate library, appeared. The faculty's orientation also changed as the generation of faculty who had been hired to teach in a teachers' college retired and were replaced by those trained to teach more specialized courses in the liberal arts and sciences. During this decade the large broad-based departments, Science, Social Science, English, Speech, and Theater, divided into more focused units.

In 1963 Oneonta took another step in the transition toward becoming a multipurpose college when it accepted transfer students into thirteen liberal arts and sciences programs. Today, SUNY Oneonta offers seventy majors across the arts and sciences and another seven preprofessional programs.

Creating globally aware students has long been central to SUNY Oneonta's mission. As early as the 1930s an International Relations Club was popular with students. Faculty and students from the college presented papers on international education at conferences at St. Lawrence University and Syracuse University. In the mid-1930s German and Russian students enrolled, and after World War II there were student and faculty exchanges with colleges in China, England, India, and Syria. The college created an Office of International Education in 1967, which now promotes overseas studies through SUNY's numerous programs.

The Cooperstown Graduate Program, which awards the Master of Arts in History Museum Studies, is one of Oneonta's signature programs. Established in 1964, the program is a unique public/private partnership between SUNY Oneonta and the New York State Historical Association, the Farmers' Museum, and the Fenimore Art Museum in Cooperstown, twenty-five miles to the northeast. It is the one of the premier museum studies programs in the nation and is one of only two programs in the United States located in museums rather than on a university campus, thus giving students regular interaction with

The new sign over Old Main's entrance broadcast the 1962 name change.

Students take an in-depth look at the human body.

Contemplating the possibilities of studying abroad.

museum professionals. The program trains museum professionals who are expertly prepared to contribute to modernizing the nation's museums.

With a largely residential student body, Oneonta has a vibrant campus life. Students choose from nearly one hundred clubs and organizations and enjoy abundant social programming. The Red Dragons compete in nineteen intercollegiate sports in the SUNY Conference and have a particularly intense rivalry with SUNY Cortland. The Oneonta and Cortland basketball teams play a "Battle of the Red Dragons" each season.

From the beginning, Oneonta has worked to be a productive partner in the community. Since the 1990s the Center for Social Responsibility and Community has contributed to improved town-gown relations. In 2014 a thrift shop open to both the college and the community opened on campus, a result of a vigorous reuse and recycle movement on campus. SUNY Oneonta has earned a place on the President's Higher Education Community Service Honor Roll each year except one since the accolade was

Red Dragons with rhythm.

that provides educational, social, and recreational opportunities for students and faculty. The College Camp actively engages in forest stewardship and uses the facility to heighten students' understanding of the environment.

The campus's location also encourages an emphasis on environmental sustainability and green technology on the main campus. In December 2014 the school received $910,000 in funding as part of the New York State Green Innovation grant program for a project to reduce the impact of campus stormwater runoff. This grant is just one facet of a larger campus effort to integrate the issue of stormwater management into several academic disciplines.

For over a century and a quarter, from its early days as a Normal School, SUNY Oneonta has engaged closely with its community while educating students to look at a broader world. The college in the little town in the Catskills both embraces its specific geography and looks well beyond its borders. This duality of vision will continue to shape its mission in the years ahead.

established in 2006, for its programs designed to solve community problems and place more students on a lifelong path of civic engagement.

In September 2014 *Insight into Diversity* magazine named SUNY Oneonta one of the most ethnically diverse and inclusive colleges in the United States. This award is particularly telling of the advances that have been made on the campus since the infamous Black List of 1992, when the college administration had cooperated in identifying 125 African American male students who were then compelled to submit to a physical examination as the police attempted to track down a man who had attacked an elderly woman in town.

Oneonta's location in the Catskill Mountains has been a defining characteristic. In 1952 the Faculty-Student Association bought the sixty-three-acre Hoffman farm four miles north of the campus. This provided the nucleus for the current College Camp, a 276-acre tract of former farms and woodlands

The lodge draws students into the Catskill environment for education and leisure.

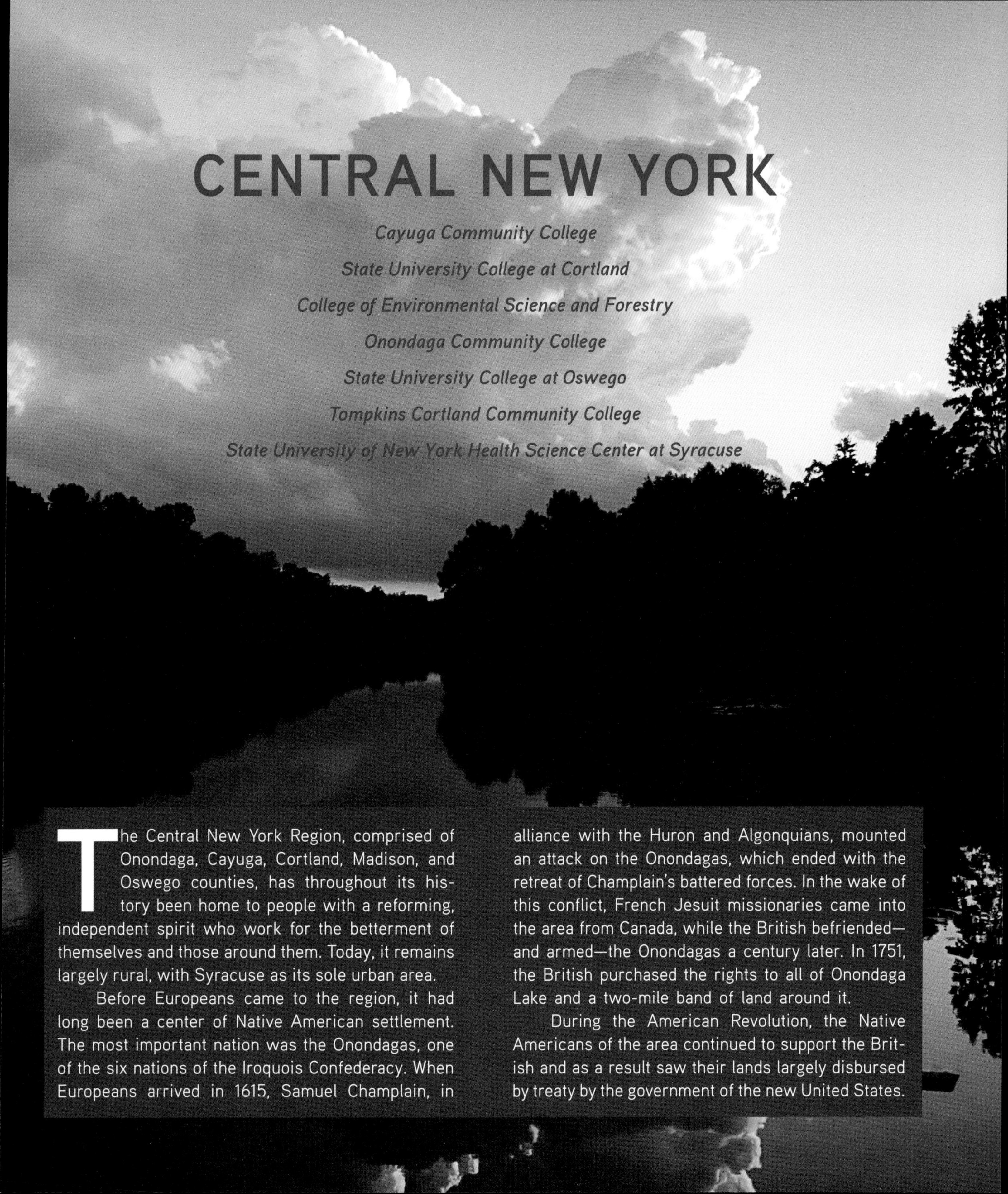

CENTRAL NEW YORK

Cayuga Community College

State University College at Cortland

College of Environmental Science and Forestry

Onondaga Community College

State University College at Oswego

Tompkins Cortland Community College

State University of New York Health Science Center at Syracuse

The Central New York Region, comprised of Onondaga, Cayuga, Cortland, Madison, and Oswego counties, has throughout its history been home to people with a reforming, independent spirit who work for the betterment of themselves and those around them. Today, it remains largely rural, with Syracuse as its sole urban area.

Before Europeans came to the region, it had long been a center of Native American settlement. The most important nation was the Onondagas, one of the six nations of the Iroquois Confederacy. When Europeans arrived in 1615, Samuel Champlain, in alliance with the Huron and Algonquians, mounted an attack on the Onondagas, which ended with the retreat of Champlain's battered forces. In the wake of this conflict, French Jesuit missionaries came into the area from Canada, while the British befriended—and armed—the Onondagas a century later. In 1751, the British purchased the rights to all of Onondaga Lake and a two-mile band of land around it.

During the American Revolution, the Native Americans of the area continued to support the British and as a result saw their lands largely disbursed by treaty by the government of the new United States.

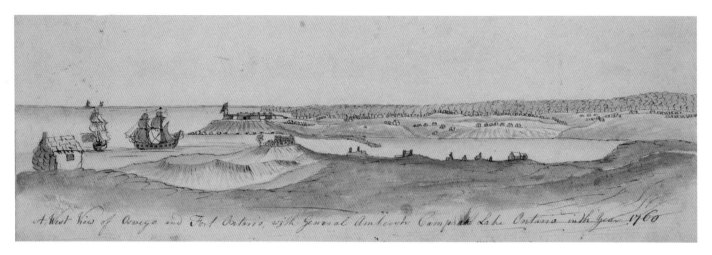

Drawing of Fort Ontario, 1760

The conclusion of the Revolutionary War brought more European settlers into the region, many drawn by the possibilities of trade with the Native Americans. In 1804, 250 acres of the Onondaga Salt Springs Reservation was laid out in a town that would become Syracuse. The opening of the Erie Canal in 1825 caused a spike in the sale of the region's salt production and improved the local economy. For much of the 1800s the majority of the salt used in the United States came from Syracuse. This industry anchored the Salt City's growth.

Central New York housed important stops on the Underground Railroad. Oswego's location on the shore of Lake Ontario made it a place of embarkation for fugitives heading for Canada. Syracuse became a center of the abolitionist movement largely due to the work of Gerrit Smith and those allied with him, largely drawn from the Unitarian and Quaker churches. In the years prior to the Civil War, Syracuse became known as the "great central depot on the Underground Railroad."

Among the most striking of the region's many natural attractions are the Thousand Islands. Straddling the United States–Canada border, the 1,800 islands in the Saint Lawrence River where it meets Lake Ontario are a haven for nature lovers. Yet, the area is probably best known as the birthplace of its namesake salad dressing, created by Sophia LaLonde to serve to her fishing guide husband's customers.

In the late nineteenth and early twentieth centuries, the Islands became a popular summer resort for the wealthy seeking to escape the heat of cities such as New York, Chicago, Cleveland, and Pittsburgh. Several grand hotels hosted visitors, and steamboats took them on tours of the islands. Today, the region continues to draw many vacationers and visitors, although not quite on such a grand scale as in the past.

While the Central New York region has always been decidedly rural, its major city, Syracuse, served as a major transportation hub in the nineteenth century. The Erie Canal intersected several of the other canals that were built in the early part of the century, and, shortly thereafter, rail connections were made to the west and south. In the 1950s, the New York

Iroquois Fort on Onondaga Lake, beseiged by Champlain in 1615.

Chittenango Falls.

State Thruway, a multilane, limited-access toll road stretching from New York City to the Pennsylvania border along the shore of Lake Erie, was completed, bringing another transportation link to and through Central New York.

In the late nineteenth century a number of industrial firms made their home in Syracuse, like Solvay Processing, a forerunner of a large chemical complex in the region, several automobile manufacturers, and furniture manufacturers. But, in the process, the industrial effluent dumped into Onondaga Lake made it one of the most polluted bodies of water on the North American continent.

By the mid-twentieth century, each of the Big Three American auto companies had major facilities in Syracuse, as did the Carrier Corporation and General Electric, which manufactured televisions at Electronics Parkway. Two decades later, each of these major industries had moved out, completely or in part, from the Syracuse area, leaving behind rising unemployment, a polluted lake, and a falling tax base. But, the area began to rebound with different industries, as illustrated by the fact that by the first decade of the twenty-first century, the area's largest employers were educational and medical institutions.

Looking to the future, the region has put six industries at the center of its strategic plan for economic development: financial services; tourism; clean energy; advanced manufacturing; health, biosciences, and biomedical services; and agribusiness. All of these will rely on the availability of highly skilled workers who will enable the region to expand its market share both at home and globally. And, many of these residents will be educated by the SUNY schools in the region.

Central New York's colleges and universities will play an important role in the rejuvenation of the region. They serve to attract young talent to the area as well as incubators of innovation. The State University College at Oswego long led the way in providing aspiring educators with instruction in revolutionary teaching techniques. Founded in 1861 as the Oswego Normal School, famed in the nineteenth century for the "Oswego Method," it became a degree-granting teachers' college in 1942 and a charter member of the SUNY system in 1948. The region's second state college, located in Cortland, halfway between Syracuse and Binghamton, also traces its roots to a normal school heritage. And, like Oswego, it has evolved over the years into today's

Wind turbine, Madison Wind Farm.

Pressure vessel, Nine Mile Point Nuclear Power Plant.

diverse comprehensive college, with twenty-eight academic departments, thirty-three graduate programs, and its distinctive "Main Street" initiative, which brings the campus and town communities closer together.

Central New York is also home to three SUNY community colleges that serve the region's demand for a skilled workforce. Cayuga Community College was the first community college developed wholly after the founding of the SUNY system, and today it hosts the Institute for the Application of Geospatial Technology. Both Onondaga and Tompkins Cortland community colleges offer specialized programs designed to serve the employment needs of major businesses in the region.

It is not at all surprising that the SUNY College of Environmental Science and Forestry (ESF) is located in the Central Region. This is a specialized doctoral-granting institution whose primary campus is in Syracuse, with branch campuses in several other locations, including Adirondack Park, the Thousand Islands, and Costa Rica. Fitting with the Cen-

tral Region's commitment to focus on "clean" energy, this institution offers nationally recognized programs in the management, sustainability, and understanding of the environment. Founded in 1911 as the New York State College of Forestry at Syracuse University, in 1913 ESF became a separate entity and in 1948 entered SUNY as a specialized college within the state system.

The area's largest employer, Upstate Medical University, proudly supports cutting-edge medical and biomedical research, runs the area's largest hospital, and offers education in almost every area of medicine and health care through its four colleges. In the past decade, enrollment at SUNY Upstate has increased thirty percent.

Central New York, known for its natural beauty and home to an independent population with a strong reforming spirit, uses its past as a foundation upon which it is committed to building a vibrant future. The schools of the SUNY system, long among the region's most important assets, are poised to contribute to and share in the growth.

CAYUGA COMMUNITY COLLEGE

The first community college developed in its entirety after SUNY was established, Cayuga Community College brought new hope to Auburn in the early 1950s. International Harvester had just closed its plant and the future looked bleak when the Auburn School District proposed creating a community college.

SUNY approved, and Auburn Community College opened its doors in a former elementary school on September 8, 1953, to sixty-nine students. The second year, the enrollment trebled to 210 full-time students, reaching the building's capacity. The notable successes of

Modest beginnings in a converted elementary school.

its students, many of them Korean War veterans, and continuously rising enrollments convinced the Auburn City School District's electorate to support a bond issue funding a new forty-acre campus on Auburn's east side. In August of 1959, the college moved from its overcrowded location to a modern campus it continues to call home.

The 1960s and 1970s were decades of growth for the college with both the enrollment and campus size increasing rapidly. In addition, a change of sponsorship opened new opportunities. In 1975 Cayuga County took over responsibility for financing the college from the Auburn Board of Education. In

The entrance to the new Fulton River Glen Campus Building.

The Regional Economic Center houses services for the college and community.

recognition of the enlarged mission, the name was changed to Cayuga Community College.

The county's backing enabled the college to play a larger role in the greater community. New degree programs were established, noncredit courses were offered to members of the community, off-campus classes were offered in neighboring communities, and training for local business and industry began. Among the new programs were associate degrees in Nursing, Criminal Justice, and Telecommunications. A new Nature Center and a nature trail facilitated environmental education, as well as providing recreational activities. In further outreach, an International Studies program was launched, and CCC offered college courses to prison inmates through New York State's Inmate Higher Education program.

In 1994, CCC took a major initiative by offering liberal arts classes in Oswego County. Quickly, the extension site in Fulton attracted significant enrollment, prompting SUNY to grant branch campus status in 2006. To accommodate further growth, the expanding branch campus moved to a new facility in 2012. With a subsidy by the Cayuga County Community College Foundation, a former industrial building was transformed into an 82,150-square-foot facility that now serves over one thousand students. The innovative concept and design of the Fulton River Glen campus was recognized by the American Institute of Architects' Eastern New York Chapter, which honored the project's architectural firm with a merit award for excellence in design.

In 2003, a partnership of federal, state, and local governments, as well as private contributors, funded the landmark Regional Economic Center. In addition to providing classrooms for Cayuga students, offices for several agencies providing employment services to area residents, and the college's Business and Industry Center workforce training complex, the center houses the college's NASA-sponsored Institute for the Application of Geospatial Technology, which provides hands-on training in space-based mapping and imaging.

To fulfill its enlarged mission to serve as the community college for Cayuga and Oswego counties, Cayuga Community College offers transfer and career-oriented curricula on a degree and certificate basis. A variety of certificate programs provide job seekers and working professionals an opportunity to learn new or enhance existing skills in fields such as Computer-Aided Design, Electronics, and Computer Information Systems.

Popular degree programs include Radio and Television Broadcasting, Studio Art and Design, Business, Nursing, and Criminal Justice. Students in the liberal arts degree programs choose from a wide range of concentrations in fields such as Film and Cinema Studies, Education, Psychology, Health Sciences, Game Design, Photography, Writing, Theater, and Wine Studies. Graduates of Cayuga's Nursing program con-

Geographic Information Systems students apply a global vision to regional projects.

Telecommunications students work on a broadcast in the television studio.

183

sistently score well above state and national average pass rates for the National Council Licensure Exam (NCLEX). Placement percentage for Nursing graduates is one hundred percent, with eighty-eight percent going directly into the workforce and twelve percent going on for advanced degrees in Nursing.

Flexibility is a hallmark of program delivery at Cayuga. More than forty percent of students are over the age of twenty-two, many with job and family responsibilities. Students can take courses in Auburn, Fulton, or both, and choose from weekday and evening classes. Many courses, and some complete degree programs, are also available online. With an average class size of eighteen, students are able to form lasting relationships with their instructors as well as with their peers.

For all students, campus life provides a number of interests. The Cayuga Collegian reports on campus events, the Harlequins offer theatrical experience, and WDWN broadcasts at three thousand watts. Ten Spartan teams compete in intercollegiate contests.

The college chorus sings for the college and community.

Cayuga's faculty are committed to innovative teaching methods that focus on student-centered learning. Some faculty have adapted their classes to distance-education formats, creating opportunities for continued direct student-faculty interaction and personalized instruction. Courses with modular content allow students to choose to work self-guided and complete the course at their own pace throughout the semester. Split-semester courses allow students to complete and earn credit for specific sequential courses during a single semester. Hybrid courses schedule class time both on campus and online, using the Blackboard learning management system. Experiential learning allows students to learn by doing and connects classroom content with real-world situations. Internships, field experiences, and practicums each offer students opportunities to gain career-related experience tied to their course of study by working in a professional environment while earning academic credit.

A focus on student engagement and successful completion of academic goals is evidenced in offerings designed specifically for underprepared students. Learning communities featuring college success courses, a mentoring support system, and additional developmental courses help students become active and successful learners. Advisement and counseling services help guide students through the processes of choosing an academic major, transferring to four-year colleges, and selecting an appropriate career path.

Cayuga Community College has certainly come a long way since its modest beginning in 1953. But it still seeks to fulfill the goal expressed in its first catalogue "to establish programs of study which will enable the students to more actively participate in community life as well as to enjoy more effective personal living."

STATE UNIVERSITY COLLEGE AT CORTLAND

Perched above the city of Cortland in the picturesque rolling hills of central New York is one of SUNY's older colleges. The State University College at Cortland traces its history back to 1868 when Cortland County convinced the New York State Legislature to select it as one of four new normal schools. The citizens raised nearly $100,000 to erect a grand three-story, mansard-style building on a five-acre campus in the middle of the town. Cortland Normal School welcomed its first students the following year, and for the next half century Cortland Normal School trained teachers on its increasingly crowded campus.

In 1919, fire struck and the campus building burned. The local citizenry again demonstrated its support, opening churches, civic buildings, and homes to rehouse the Cortland Normal School. Trag-

edy was converted into opportunity and the decision was made to move to the college's current hilltop location. With the completion of Old Main, the new campus opened its doors to students in 1923. Moving up the hill to the spacious new location meant further growth could be accommodated more comfortably and in more modern facilities.

Cortland Normal School's curriculum matured as teaching professionalized. In 1905 a program offering two years of postsecondary school instruction for the training of teachers was introduced. In 1921 it was extended to three years, and then in 1938 yet another year was added to the program. When the New York State Legislature approved baccalaureate status for normal schools, and Governor Lehman reluctantly signed the legislation in 1941, Cortland became a four-year college offering bachelor's degrees, a change reflected in a new name, Cortland State Teachers College. The Regents' postwar plan designated Cortland as one of the two state teachers' colleges to specialize in training health and physical education teachers, launching fields that continue to be signature programs. Master's programs further enhanced the curriculum in 1947.

When the SUNY system was created in 1948, Cortland joined as a founding member as a one-building campus serving just over one thousand students. For Cortland's first fifteen years in SUNY, all students promised to enter the teaching profession. Then, in 1963, Cortland's students were given the option of majoring in the humanities, social sciences, or sciences. The renamed SUNY College at Cortland was on its way to becoming a comprehensive college combining liberal education and professional training. Rapid growth followed, and by the mid-1980s over six thousand undergraduate and graduate students walked the campus.

Although the college's enrollments were soaring and its curricular offerings diversifying dramatically, teacher education remained a central focus. In 1982, in order to facilitate teacher preparation programs, the Center for Educational Exchange was established. This promoted networking with both elementary and secondary schools throughout central New York. In 2003 the School of Education was established, and one year later its program

Learning from the great poets.

received accreditation from the National Council for Accreditation of Teacher Education. With this, SUNY Cortland became the largest Teacher Education program in New York State to receive national accreditation.

In addition to Education, Cortland houses two other academic divisions, Arts and Sciences and Professional Studies. In total, the three divisions include twenty-eight academic departments with a faculty of more than six hundred educating over seven thousand students. Additionally, graduate students can pursue four certificates of advanced study and thirty-three graduate majors. The student body has been enriched by a $5 million bequest by alumnus John Fantauzzi that supports scholarships for first-generation college students and children of immigrants.

On campus student life took on new energy in the early 1950s. The first student union, Brockway Hall, became—and continues to be—a center of student activity. The construction of dormitories fundamentally changed campus life, making SUNY Cortland a home away from home for many.

The massive forty-thousand-square-foot Lusk Field House hosts indoor track meets, concerts, and provides facilities for recreational basketball, volleyball, and badminton. The football team, one of SUNY's oldest, concludes each season competing for the Cortaca Jug against Ithaca College in what is a most venerable rivalry.

Neoclassical Old Main remains the focal point of the campus.

Adjunct campuses for outdoor education and recreation are a Cortland specialty. In the same year that Cortland joined SUNY, the two-hundred-acre Huntington Memorial Camp at Raquette Lake in the Adirondacks was gifted to the college for outdoor education. The Hoxie Gorge Nature Preserve, acquired in 1966, provides 165 acres for science education and recreation. The thirty-three-acre Brauer Education Center, located near Albany, serves as a geological field research center. These facilities provide students with both academic and applied training for jobs in the regional tourism industry. And generations of Cortland students have fond memories of their recreational benefits.

Since its inception, Cortland has been an integral part of the larger community, working in many ways to improve the quality of life across the region. In 2006, for example, Cortland opened the Main Street SUNY Cortland facility, providing the college, once again, with a presence in downtown Cortland. It houses offices for the Institute of Civic Engagement, the Cortland Downtown Partnership, and the Center for Eco-

Another Red Dragons championship.

nomic Education, as well as the Beard Gallery that showcases local artists. Main Street also directly engages with the life of downtown Cortland by providing information about local businesses and public events. By hosting the New York Jets' training camp, the college provides late-summer entertainment for town and gown. And campus groups participate in the CROP Hunger Walk, raising significant funds to combat hunger, and other regional charities.

SUNY Cortland will continue to build on its traditional strengths in teacher education, physical education, and outdoor education. More broadly, it will continue offering a well-rounded education, giving students the basis for lifetime intellectual, professional, and civic development. The college's General Education statement promises that Cortland will provide "students with an intellectual and cultural basis for their development as informed individuals in our society," as well as an understanding of "the ideas that have formed our own civilization" and a "knowledge of the fundamental principles that govern the physical universe." Cortland graduates join nearly seventy thousand alumni taking their place as productive citizens of the region, the nation, and the world.

Enjoying downtown Cortland.

The outdoor campuses enhance indoor science education.

Residence halls provide a home away from home.

COLLEGE OF ENVIRONMENTAL SCIENCE AND FORESTRY

SUNY ESF emerged from late nineteenth-century concerns about the destruction of Adirondack forests by the logging, tanning, paper, and charcoal industries, which led to the creation of the Adirondack Park in 1892. A New York State College of Forestry began at Cornell University in 1898 to address these issues, but it soon encountered political turmoil by implementing a concept of "scientific forestry" that included a plan to clear-cut thirty thousand acres in the Adirondacks.

A group of wealthy "great camp" owners on Saranac Lake

Early College of Environmental Science and Forestry students participate in a tree-cutting competition.

brought a lawsuit against Cornell and in 1903 succeeded in having the College of Forestry closed. In the ensuing years Syracuse University trustee Louis Marshall, a constitutional lawyer who had been instrumental in the establishment of the Adirondack Forest preserve, campaigned to obtain New York State funding for a new college of forestry.

Marshall succeeded, resulting in the opening of a second New York State College of Forestry in partnership with Syracuse University in 1911. That first year, two faculty members, headed by Dean Hugh P. Baker, instructed fifty-

189

Today's ESF students are as at home in the lab as in nature.

two students in classes that met in the basement of Lyman Hall of Natural Sciences on the Syracuse University campus. The charter legislation directed the college "to educate people in the management and use of the forest resource for the benefit of man," and from these first years, college leadership responded to the broader needs of environmental professionalism. Over the years, programs were added in design, engineering, and life sciences, as well as natural resources management and other areas of study, to serve this larger mission. The college's commitment to research dates back to a 1912 study that identified firms using wood in New York State and the species and quantities of the lumber consumed. This foretold countless research projects conducted at the college over the years.

In 1912, the college opened its Ranger School in Wanakena, New York, on two thousand acres of land donated by the Rich Lumber Company. The announcement of the Ranger School noted, "Practical field work in Silviculture, Forest Surveying, Estimating and Mapping, Forest Protection, Methods of Lumbering, etc., would take precedence over classroom work in the courses but theoretical and practical instruction would go hand in hand." Students and faculty spent months blasting rocks and leveling ground for the first building.

New York State purchased twelve acres of land adjacent to Syracuse University in 1913 for a campus. Four years later, Bray Hall was completed and the college had a permanent home. When it became known that no state funds had been appropriated to move the books, furniture, and laboratory equipment from Syracuse University to the new building, faculty members and students volunteered their services and completed the move in just two days. Bray remained the only

Students ponder a hydrology problem.

In addition to accessing thousands of acres of outdoor campuses, students also study nature in controlled conditions.

building on the campus until Marshall Hall's completion in 1933.

Despite occupying a separate campus, the College of Forestry remained very much a part of campus life at Syracuse University. Forestry students took part in its activities, and their clubs appeared in Syracuse's yearbook, the *Onondagan*. Graduates of both schools have participated each year in a joint commencement ceremony. The legendary Syracuse University lacrosse team was founded in 1916 through the efforts of College of Forestry students. The first team was largely composed of forestry students coached by Laurie Cox, a landscape architecture professor.

In the late 1940s the first three women graduated from the college, one with a degree in landscape engineering and two others with degrees in pulp and paper. While these were the first women to complete their degrees, the college had enrolled women as early as 1915.

Over the years, name changes reflected shifting affiliations and curricular focus. With SUNY's formation in 1948, the college was designated as a specialized college and renamed the State University College of Forestry at Syracuse University. In 1972, the college's name changed yet again, to better reflect the tradition and grounding of forestry in the environmental studies. By act of the New York State Legislature, it became the State University of New York College of Environmental Science and Forestry.

SUNY ESF celebrated its one hundredth anniversary in 2011 as the oldest and largest college in the nation focused exclusively on the science, design, engineering, and management of natural resources and the environment. Its Syracuse campus covers only twelve acres, but its students have access to more than twenty-five thousand acres in regional campuses throughout central New York and the Adirondacks.

Students look to the stars from the Gateway Center.

ESF plays a leadership role in developing alternative energy, protecting endangered species, creating sustainable environments, and addressing a broad range of environmental issues. The college's more than 1,700 undergraduate and 450 graduate students can choose from twenty-four undergraduate and thirty graduate degree programs, including eight doctoral programs in the sciences, engineering, forestry,

and landscape architecture. Associate degrees are offered by ESF's Ranger School in the Adirondacks.

ESF continues its century-long partnership with Syracuse University as its students take classes there, use the library and computing facilities, join student clubs, and eat in the university dining halls. But in recent years ESF has also developed a distinct student life. The new Gateway Center, with LEED Platinum certification for its unique heat and power plants, now gives ESF students a hub. The opening of its first student residence has provided a full on-campus experience. Long overshadowed by Syracuse University's high-powered athletic program, ESF launched its first intercollegiate athletic teams in the early 2000s. Mighty Oaks teams compete in five traditional sports as well as timber sports. ESF students contribute more than seventy thousand hours of community service annually, earning the college a place on the President's Higher Education Community Service Honor Roll.

ESF alumni have played important roles in guarding and improving our environment. Among notable alumni is Robert Marshall, Class of 1924, who is credited with creating the wilderness preservation movement. Howard Ris, Class of 1975, served as president of the Union of Concerned Scientists and in that role did much to link issues of environmental safety and nuclear arms control. And Joseph Martens of the Class of 1982 served as Commissioner of the New York State Department of Environmental Conservation, coordinating all state programs designed to protect and enhance the environment.

These alumni exemplify the hard work and concern for the environment that typifies SUNY ESF's more than eighteen thousand graduates. With twenty-first-century challenges defined by complex environmental challenges, SUNY ESF will continue in its second century to provide environmental leadership by offering a small-campus education while tackling some of the largest, most defining issues of our time.

Oakie the Acorn encourages the Mighty Oaks cross-country team.

ONONDAGA COMMUNITY COLLEGE

Located in the heart of Onondaga County on a campus noted for its forested hills and lovely views of Onondaga Lake, Onondaga Community College has served its county and region for over a half century.

In the fall of 1962 SUNY's twenty-first two-year institution, the newly formed Onondaga Community College, first opened its doors to students. Located in the less-than-glamorous surroundings of a former typewriter factory in the Midtown Plaza in downtown Syracuse, few in that first class would have guessed how quickly the new college would grow. There

The college began in Syracuse's midtown on September 24, 1962.

was, however, among the students and the professors a strong sense of mission.

Growth has been one of the primary characteristics of Onondaga Community College. Enrollment has grown to nearly thirteen thousand students from the initial class of 1,294. Students in 1962 chose among four fields of study and two concentrations. Today, students can earn associate degrees in thirty-eight fields, certificates in eight, and minors in eighteen. That explosive growth necessitated a change in venue. Thus, in 1970 the school moved to its current 280-acre campus, and,

A future chef learns from the master.

in the succeeding years, sixteen buildings have been constructed to house a wide variety of certificate and degree programs.

One of OCC's primary goals is to produce graduates who are well prepared to take their place in the regional economy. Among the associate degree programs specifically designed to meet regional employment needs are Fire Protection Technology, Hospitality Management, and Computer Forensics. Other programs prepare OCC's graduates to transfer to four-year colleges, both in the SUNY system and beyond.

Keeping abreast of the latest in technology and making those insights available to students is vital to the Onondaga mission. This includes a commitment to online education. Today, OCC offers eight degrees and two certificates that students can complete wholly online. In addition, an associate degree in Electronic Media Communications prepares graduates to take an active role in the growing field of electronic media.

While continuing to serve thousands of commuting students, Onondaga Community College also offers a full residential college experience for those who want it. Since 2006, students have been accommodated in on-campus residence halls that provide housing for nearly nine hundred students. In addition, OCC students can choose from a wide variety of clubs and organizations that enrich campus life and allow students to engage in activities with others who share their interests.

The athletics program is especially vibrant, with many of the teams consistently earning national rankings. As befits a college only a few miles from the Onondaga Nation, the men's and women's lacrosse teams have been extraordinarily successful, winning eleven national championships between them. The men's team celebrated their 105th consecutive victory in May 2015.

Onondaga is known in the Syracuse community for its excellent arts programs. Its music program is particularly accomplished, with faculty who are also professional musicians with the Syracuse Symphoria and the Society for New Music. Among the more successful alumni is singer, songwriter, and cultural icon Grace Jones. Arts Across Campus, an innovative all-year arts and cultural program, brings the fine arts to every area of the campus. The Storer Auditorium and Ann Felton Multicultural Center host concerts, theater, lectures, art exhibits, and art installations. The college also partners with cutting-edge arts organizations such as Symphoria, the Society for New Music, and the Syracuse Jazz Fest.

Though most students hail from the state's Central Region, students come to Onondaga from across New York State and other states, as well as from twenty-two countries. Onondaga students can take advantage of the robust Study Abroad program the college offers. A variety of fields including Nursing, Spanish, Anthropology, History, and Art offer students the opportunity to complete part of their studies abroad.

Onondaga signed on to the American College and University Presidents' Climate Commitment in May 2007. This program led Onondaga Community College to embrace plans designed to reduce, and ultimately eliminate, carbon-based emissions as well as to provide education designed to promote sustainability. Each of these initiatives will help stabilize the earth's changing climate. A wide variety of programs from the relatively small—the use of compostable

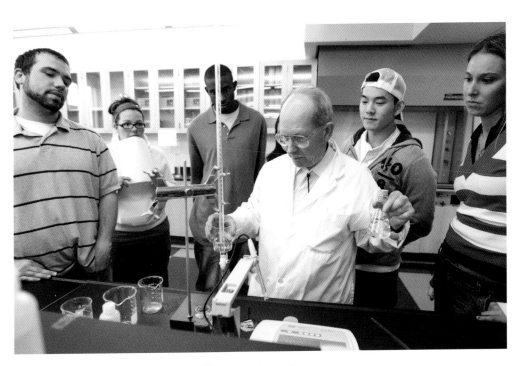

All eyes on the professor.

Excelling at a game with a special history in the region.

The campus basks in the autumnal splendor of the Onondaga Hill.

plates and cups—to the very large—the installation of a 21.16-kilowatt-powered solar array—have been undertaken since the college committed itself to the program.

As leaders in the community, Onondaga Community College and its forty thousand alumni continue to enhance the life of Onondaga County and central New York, a region it has served and helped shape for over half a century. The campus, with its five-decade record of excellence, looks forward to the work ahead, a time when education will become an ever-more crucial element in individual, community, and regional success.

Solar panels atop the Whitney Applied Technology Center give students hands-on training while reducing the college's greenhouse emissions.

STATE UNIVERSITY COLLEGE AT OSWEGO

Beautiful sunsets over Lake Ontario, a famous fort, the Oswego Method, and world-famous snowfall—these are a few of the things Oswego, New York, and SUNY Oswego are known for.

The college that began in a few borrowed rooms in a local hotel now covers about seven hundred acres with fifty-eight buildings offering degrees from Accounting to Zoology to eight thousand undergraduates and graduate students. Founded in 1861 by Edward Austin Sheldon as the Oswego Primary Teachers Training School, the school soon put Oswego on the educational

Students visit the creator of the Oswego Method at his home in the 1890s.

map as Dr. Sheldon worked to change the course of education in America. His "Oswego Method" of "object teaching," which used objects, graphics, and proactive learning instead of the traditional rote instruction, soon spread to other normal schools.

Sheldon's pedagogical theories drew attention from far beyond New York State. In 1893, for example, he was invited to present a symposium on the Oswego Method of Education at the Columbian World's Fair in Chicago. Oswego's methods were even implemented abroad, where alumni spread his method to South America, Mexico, and even as far as Japan, where

The Tin Shop.

Hideo Takamine, Class of 1878, became principal of two normal schools in Tokyo.

It was natural for Oswego to become a leader in Industrial Arts education, since Dr. Sheldon's use of objects that stimulated observation and perception transitioned easily to manual training, the basis of Industrial Arts education. The first shop was set up by the head janitor in 1886, where students learned about the assortment of tools in their spare time. In 1893 a trained, experienced instructor was secured, as well as an adequate space and proper tools. This laid the foundation for Industrial Arts education in Oswego. From 1916 to 1920 the Department of Industrial Arts expanded from one shop to five, tripled the number of faculty, and moved from a three-year training period to a four-year, degree-granting program. Between the wars, Oswego developed one of the best and most sought after programs for Industrial Arts, one that later became an integral aspect of the campus's General Education program.

Oswego received nationwide attention again in the 1940s—not just the college, but the city of Oswego, when 982 mostly Jewish refugees arrived from war-torn Europe in 1944. They were placed in America's only refugee camp for war victims at a recently decommissioned military base, Fort Ontario. While their movements were restricted, they were able to further their education in Oswego schools. Ten attended the college, while twenty-eight enrolled in the Campus School. The campus was soon honored by a visit from Eleanor Roosevelt, who had been instrumental in bringing the Jewish refugees to Fort Ontario.

As World War II was drawing to an end, President Roosevelt signed the Servicemen's Readjustment Bill of 1944, more commonly known as the GI Bill, which enabled millions of returning servicemen to enroll in college, including Oswego State Teachers College.

As the Regents had banned dormitories decades earlier, the influx created a housing crisis, which was reinforced by the heightened demand for elementary school teachers resulting from the postwar baby boom. Although the campus had a double residence hall in Lonis and Moreland halls in 1951, more room was needed for students. Oswego homeowners with spare rooms accommodated many students, while others were housed in temporary quarters provided by surplus military barracks. These modest new "homes" became lovingly known as Splinter Village and served as a home away from home for students until 1957, when permanent residence halls were constructed.

The influential First Lady visits the campus and refugees at Fort Ontario.

Joining the State University of New York as a founding member provided new direction and the funding that underwrote Oswego's educational boom in the 1960s. In that expansive decade, twenty-nine new buildings were designed to take advantage of views of Lake Ontario and to provide practical and aesthetically pleasing modern facilities. The curriculum also expanded dramatically. Oswego evolved into one of SUNY's comprehensive colleges, adding a full range of arts and sciences and professional training to its traditional commitment to teacher training.

The two decades that followed proved to be more challenging—years of energy crises, economic stagnation, and state budgetary cuts that led to unavoidable reductions in faculty and staff. Federal budget cuts reduced student aid and support for academic programs, especially in the humanities and the arts. Only by adopting the most stringent belt-tightening

efficiencies was Oswego able to weather the austere decades with its reputation intact.

By the 1990s Oswego had redefined its academic mission with greater use of online instruction, and it addressed globalization by offering experience with modern technology and an education designed to produce graduates who would have the tools necessary for successful participation in the evolving world of the twenty-first century. Private funding stepped in to provide scholarships, especially in the sciences. The Richard S. Shineman Center for Sciences, Engineering, and Innovation, opened in 2013, provides a state-of-the-art facility for future scientists, engineers, and teachers with the latest technology and inspires creative research. And the establishment of a global laboratory initiative that enables students to spend

Oswego's industrial arts tradition evolves.

Student housing has come a long way since the post-WWII converted barracks.

Another goal in the Lakers' signature sport.

time studying science in foreign countries illustrates the campus commitment to global instruction.

A vibrant campus life enriches the student experience. In stark contrast to the postwar housing crisis, today's campus houses over 4,300 students in modern dormitories and residential communities. Oswego students participate in nearly two hundred clubs and organizations, while its twenty-four inter-collegiate teams compete in the SUNY Athletic Conference and other conferences.

Dr. Sheldon's legacy of gently guiding students through their education continues with today's commitment to kindling lifelong learning and building life-long relationships on a modern campus that would astonish the founder. Far more than just an educational enterprise, SUNY Oswego today enriches the quality of life in central New York through its diverse cultural programs, research projects, and charitable contributions from faculty, staff, and students.

TOMPKINS CORTLAND COMMUNITY COLLEGE

Perched on a hill overlooking Dryden in the picturesque Finger Lakes region of central New York, Tompkins Cortland Community College is set on a stunning 220-acre campus. Most academic programs are housed in the 276,000-square-foot main campus building located against a dramatic backdrop of lakes and mountains. The college offers over fifty degrees and certificates in a wide array of fields designed to meet the needs of the students from sponsoring counties for transfer programs as well as vocational and technical education.

As a joint initiative of Cortland and Tompkins counties, the college was chartered by SUNY in 1967 and opened its doors in 1968 in a renovated high school building in Groton. The first class of 133 day students and forty-seven night students could choose from thirty-four courses in the liberal arts and sciences and business. By the time Tompkins Cortland moved to its current location in 1974,

The academic heart of the campus.

Students searching for knowledge.

enrollment had soared to 1,092 day students and 977 night students, and the curricular choices, both for transfer and immediate employment, were growing apace. The college was clearly fulfilling a deeply felt need. Enrollment continued to grow, reaching 3,500 by the mid-1980s. Since that time the main campus has undergone significant renovations and additions, which include the Student Center, a modernized library, cutting-edge instructional suites, and student tutorial areas. To reach out to more residents of the two counties, extension campuses have been established in Ithaca and Cortland.

About half of Tompkins Cortland graduates transfer to baccalaureate programs. Those planning to transfer can prepare by taking AA or AS degrees in over twenty-five programs ranging across the arts and sciences, as well as more applied studies, in

areas such as Biotechnology, Digital Cinema, Environmental Studies, and New Media.

In keeping with the environmental needs of the Finger Lakes region and the growing demand for graduates trained in sustainability, Tompkins Cortland offers innovative programs in Sustainable Farming and in Wine Marketing. The degree in Sustainable Farming and Food Systems prepares students to manage small farms that operate according to the economic and ecological demands for truly sustainable food production. The Wine Marketing degree and certificate programs prepare students for employment in the rapidly expanding wine industry in the Finger Lakes and beyond. It is possible to earn a sustainability designation with every degree from Tompkins Cortland, which fosters a Sustainability Literacy program that offers an interdisciplinary approach to

The arts and sciences, such as Chemistry, are strong presences in both transfer and professional programs.

the degree in New Media uses the liberal arts as a foundation for the students' education in the growing fields of animation and interactivity. Technology is also utilized to provide a wide array of online programs offered through Open SUNY.

The 220-acre Dryden campus offers students a full residential college life. Tompkins Cortland was one of the first community colleges in New York State to offer on-campus housing. Today, over eight hundred students take advantage of seven apartment-style dormitories less than a five-minute walk from the main building on campus. Over twenty-five student clubs offer a home for students with virtually any interest. The Panthers compete in ten intercollegiate sports in the Mid-State Athletic Conference.

Tompkins Cortland Community College invests in its students' success. Students can find the academic and financial support they need through the Vector Scholars program. This program, which provides individual peer and faculty mentoring, assists students in identifying a clear academic path and developing the skills they need in order to successfully follow that path to completion. Another program utilizes

understanding the complexities of sustainability in many areas.

As the tourism and hospitality industries are major drivers of the Finger Lakes economy, it is appropriate that Tompkins Cortland offers programs that enable graduates to enter those fields and to help build the regional economy. Thus the college offers degrees in Culinary Arts as well as Hotel and Restaurant Management.

The agricultural and hospitality programs contribute to Tompkins Cortland's Farm to Bistro concept, introduced in 2013, in which participants gain real-world, hands-on experience in the college's restaurant, Coltivare, in downtown Ithaca. The Tompkins County Chamber of Commerce honored this new venture with its 2015 Distinguished Business of the Year award.

Tompkins Cortland Community College also designs curricula to prepare students for our rapidly changing technological world. For instance,

Personalized computer instruction.

Over eight hundred students experience residential life.

of New York State, more than a dozen other states, and more than fifty foreign nations. While connecting the area to the broader world, the college has fulfilled its fundamental mission to serve the residents of Cortland and Tompkins counties with traditional educational programs as well as innovative responses to needs and opportunities no one could have predicted when Tompkins Cortland opened its doors a half a century ago.

a network of peer mentors to provide academic and social support for first-generation college students and those from historically underrepresented groups. The program aims to assist these students in making a successful transition to college life and to successfully navigate the academic experience.

The college reaches out across both counties. In 2011, Tompkins Cortland opened the ten-thousand-square-foot extension center in Cortland to make its services more accessible to Cortland County residents, especially adult students. The $1,800,000 center provides classrooms for a wide variety of courses and houses computer labs. The new center also offers meeting spaces and training facilities for local businesses and nonprofit organizations. As the college's business development and training center, Biz at Tompkins Cortland Community College assists local and regional businesses' and organizations' design training programs and offers noncredit professional development programs. The college has brought significant funding to the area through grants from the SUNY Community College Workforce Development Training program. These highly competitive grants provide workforce training and program development to local businesses and organizations.

Since its modest beginning, Tompkins Cortland Community College has grown dramatically; its more than 3,800 students come from all regions

A Panther shoots.

STATE UNIVERSITY OF NEW YORK HEALTH SCIENCE CENTER AT SYRACUSE

One of the oldest medical schools in the country, Upstate Medical University traces its history back to 1834. Founded as the Medical Institute of Geneva (today Hobart) College, it was the brainchild of some leading New York City medical educators who designed it to train doctors to serve the booming population along the recently opened Erie Canal. Classes began in February 1835 and its first MDs graduated later that year.

Geneva Medical College, as it came to be known, soon gained national distinction as the first medical school in the United States to grant the MD to a woman. Elizabeth Blackwell,

Elizabeth Blackwell, MD.

who graduated first in the Class of 1849, went on to found the New York Infirmary for Women and Children and, during the Civil War, the Union Army Nursing Corps. When she returned to her native England, she became the first woman to be listed on the UK Medical Register.

After several successful decades in which it graduated more than eight hundred doctors, enrollment declined. The small-town setting, aging facilities, and competition from new upstate medical schools took their toll after the Civil War. In 1871 the college disbanded. But it would live on in Syracuse. When several faculty approached newly founded Syracuse

University about absorbing Geneva's defunct medical department, the university agreed. Geneva's faculty became the core of the new Syracuse University College of Physicians and Surgeons. A Geneva faculty member, Dr. John Towler, purchased the library and anatomical museum and donated them to Syracuse.

In 1872 classes began in a renovated blacksmith's shop while a permanent home, in a former carriage factory, was being readied. Classes moved to the permanent facility in 1875, the same year the college instituted a three-year graded curriculum, becoming one of the first four medical schools—with Harvard, the University of Pennsylvania, and the University of Michigan—to create medical programs comprised of distinct preclinical and clinical years. Fortuitously, that was the year that St. Joseph's Hospital on the North Side and the Hospital of the Good Shepherd on University Hill opened, providing students with excellent clinical training.

Syracuse University was founded as a coeducational institution, and the Medical College graduated eleven women in its first six years. In 1876, Sarah Loguen Fraser, the daughter of a prominent abolitionist, became the fourth African American woman to earn an MD in the United States, the second in New York.

Soon, the education offered at Syracuse University College of Medicine was being compared favorably with that in leading medical schools. Its reputation was further enhanced when Henry Elsner joined the faculty in 1882. Elsner brought a deep familiarity with the German approach to medical education to Syracuse and guided it to become the second American medical school to update its laboratory facilities to meet German standards.

Growth and rising standards in medical education necessitated building a new campus, which opened in 1895. The following year the faculty voted unanimously to extend the graded program of study to four years. Continued improvements to area hospitals allowed for excellent student clinical training, including the introduction of bedside teaching during rounds.

Syracuse's commitment to high quality enabled it to survive the 1910 Flexner Report, which led to

President Roosevelt enjoying the occasion of laying the cornerstone for Weiskotten Hall.

Students doing the rounds with faculty is a long tradition at Upstate Medical University.

The new century saw two additions. The Center for Bioethics and Humanities was founded in 2000 to encourage patient-centered, just, and compassionate health care. The same year the Institute for Human Performance opened as an incubator for millions of dollars' worth of biomedical research aimed at vastly improving the range of human performance and reducing the limitations created by disability, disease, and aging.

The College of Medicine introduced a new medical curriculum in 2001 that included a Practice of Medicine course designed to better inculcate clinical skills by giving students patient contact in their first year. The emphasis is on a nontraditional approach to education, fewer lectures, and fewer contact hours, allowing more time for study and hands-on experiences.

closing about half of the country's medical schools. In 1915 the university acquired the Hospital of the Good Shepherd, thus incorporating a convenient source of firsthand experience for students. Between the wars the college built a larger complex on University Hill, on the grounds of the fourteen-acre Yates Castle estate. President Franklin Delano Roosevelt laid the cornerstone on September 29, 1936, for today's Weiskotten Hall.

Despite continued innovations in education, the Medical College never received the financial support it needed from Syracuse University, which was itself struggling financially. Thus, in 1950, Syracuse University sold the medical school to SUNY, renamed as the SUNY College of Medicine at Syracuse. The name changed again in 1953 to SUNY Upstate Medical Center to reflect plans to offer degrees other than the MD. The year 1961 saw completion of the new University Hospital. The School of Allied Health Professions (today's College of Health Professions) and a Nursing program were soon added to the curriculum, and by the end of the twentieth century, the growing mission required another name change, this time to SUNY Upstate Medical University.

Helping children to a healthy future.

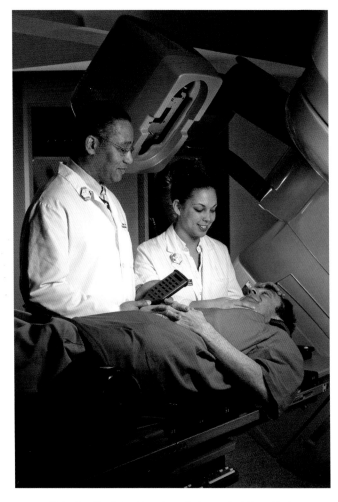

Bringing the latest treatments to central New York.

Upstate Cancer Center is home to one of only three VERO Stereotactic Body Radiotherapy systems in the nation. This tool combines treatment and imaging capabilities to provide advanced treatment of cancers such as lung, spine, liver, and prostate.

Upstate Medical University is the only public academic medical center in the region and has an estimated $2.3 billion impact on the central New York economy. It is the area's largest employer with a faculty and staff of nearly nine thousand who hail from nearly thirty counties. Upstate continues to combine its roles as an educational and research institution with that of being a healthcare provider for central New York in ways that fulfill the needs of today while anticipating those of tomorrow.

Upstate combines the functions of a cutting-edge research and teaching institution with that of a healthcare provider that serves almost two million people in a region that reaches from the Canadian border in the north to Pennsylvania in the south. Centrally located, the Golisano Children's Hospital has the only dedicated pediatric emergency operation between Rochester and Vermont and has the only pediatric intensive care unit in the seventeen surrounding counties.

The research program at Upstate Medical University emphasizes the most common human diseases, including heart disease, diabetes, cancer, nervous system disorders, and infectious diseases. The

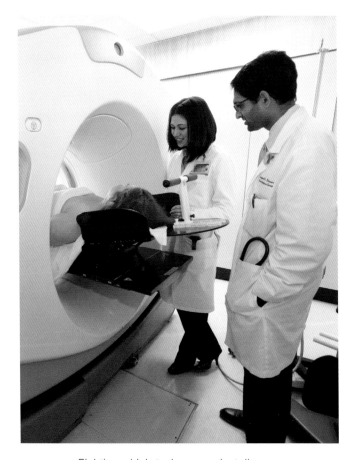

Fighting a high-tech war against disease.

FINGER LAKES AND GENESEE VALLEY

State University College at Brockport

Finger Lakes Community College

Genesee Community College

State University College at Geneseo

Monroe Community College

Like the charming cobblestone structures that are one of the defining features of this region, the strength of the Finger Lakes and Genesee Valley region comes from its individual parts combining together to create something distinct. From the Finger Lakes in the east westward to Genesee County sits the seedbed for many of the reform movements of the nineteenth century. Known as the "Burned-Over District" for its role as progenitor of the early nineteenth century's Second Great Awakening, the region was a center of the abolitionist move-

ment, the home to Frederick Douglass, Harriet Tubman, Susan B. Anthony and Elizabeth Cady Stanton, and one northern terminus of the Underground Railroad. In 1848, Seneca Falls was the site of the first Women's Rights Convention.

The Finger Lakes, a defining natural feature of the region, historically framed a central part of the Iroquois territory. The loosely confederated Native groups maintained their power until the American Revolution, when they found themselves caught between the clashing European authorities, the

Elizabeth Cady Stanton House, Seneca Falls.

ever, the industry went into decline in the first half of the twentieth century, until it was revived in the early 1960s by Dr. Konstantin Frank, a Ukrainian immigrant with a PhD in Plant Science. Since that time, the number of wineries has grown to more than a hundred.

The region is also home to the city of Rochester, long a center of innovative industry. In the early nineteenth century Colonel Nathaniel Rochester, Colonel William Fitzhugh, and Major Charles Carroll bought the land that created the village of Rochesterville. In 1823, the name was shortened to Rochester and the eight-hundred-foot Erie Canal Aqueduct was finished over the Genesee River, an innovation that utterly transformed the fortunes of the city. Two years later the canal was opened from Buffalo to the Hudson River, and Rochester became the first boomtown in the United States, known as the "Flour City" for the vast amounts of flour shipped from the city's flourmills to New York City and Albany.

The wealth that the canal brought to the city provided the foundation for the creation of important industries, some of which still play an important role in the national economy. In 1853, John Jacob Bausch and Henry Lomb founded the Bausch and Lomb Company, one of the world's largest suppliers of eye health products.

In 1892, George Eastman established the Eastman Kodak Corporation, which long dominated the region's economic and cultural life. In 1904, the R. T. French Company introduced the now ubiquitous French's yellow mustard to the world. In the past thirty years Kodak and other major industries, such as Stromberg-Carlson and Xerox, have struggled, almost all leaving the city in whole or

British, and the embattled Americans. In the end, many chose to side with the British, and the colonists responded with a reprisal campaign in 1779, defeating the Iroquois Confederacy, breaking their power in the region.

The new nation, and particularly its Empire State, soon transformed the region, as migrants followed the main road that paralleled the southern shore of Lake Ontario west. And then in 1817, Governor DeWitt Clinton convinced New York's legislature to allocate $7 million to build the 360-mile Erie Canal, a project that quickly led to land acquisition all along the Genesee frontier.

Even today, agriculture remains a major source of the regional economy, especially the fruit farms and vineyards that line the eleven glacial lakes. The first recorded wine maker in the Finger Lakes was William Warner Bostwick, an Episcopal minister who planted wine grapes in his rectory garden in 1829. Commercial winemaking officially began in 1862, and the area became famous for sparkling wines. How-part. But, in their wake, the region has adapted and continues to thrive, capitalizing on its history with optics at the center of a high-tech cluster of firms and businesses. The economic plan for the region centers on the creation of a knowledge-based economy built on an educated workforce, a commitment to innovation, and the use of renewable natural resources. The Atlantic recently named the Finger Lakes and Genesee Valley region one of thirty-five national "Innovation Hubs."

Unfortunately, the innovative traditions are not the whole story, especially for Rochester over the past half century, during which it has exhibited so many of the problems of America's older cities: declining population, declining social services, declining tax base, rising unemployment, rising health issues for poorer residents, and deepening poverty. In the midst of one of the more prosperous counties in New York State, the city of Rochester, according to the 2010 Census, has the fifth highest poverty rate among the nation's top seventy-five metropolitan areas, and ranked third for highest concentration of extremely poor neighborhoods among cities in the top one hundred metro areas. Most dramatically stated, Rochester has a poverty rate four times greater—

One of many vineyards along Seneca Lake.

Postcard of the Eastman Kodak Corporation headquarters.

211

and a significantly lower level of educational attainment—than immediately neighboring towns. In fact, it has one of the highest child poverty rates in the country.

The growth and innovation that has so long characterized life in the larger Genesee region has been made possible in large part by the colleges that are located there. Both The College at Brockport and SUNY Geneseo began as nineteenth-century teacher training schools, and both were among the initial institutions to join the SUNY system when it was created in 1948. Today, these campuses with their forty thousand graduates residing in the region, along with tens of thousands of others from Monroe Community College, Genesee Community College, and Finger Lakes Community College, are deeply engaged in breaking the cycle of poverty and its accompanying lack of educational attainment. The region's community colleges have been particularly innovative in their approaches to these issues, working closely with area governments and employers.

Since the 1960s, SUNY's schools in the Genesee region have worked to meet a variety of postsecondary educational needs, in industry, in service agencies, in education, and in every area of community economic, social, and cultural life. Each of these campuses has prospered by providing accessible education of the highest quality and workforce development to the region's residents; all of these institutions are integral to sustaining the innovative spirit that has characterized the Finger Lakes and Genesee Valley region.

Sunset in the Finger Lakes.

STATE UNIVERSITY
COLLEGE AT BROCKPORT

SUNY's third oldest institution, The College at Brockport was founded in 1835 as a Baptist college in a booming Erie Canal village twenty miles west of Rochester. Bankrupted by the Panic of 1837, it quickly reopened as an academy, financed by local boosters. After several near-death experiences, it achieved stability in 1866 when New York State incorporated it into its growing network of normal schools.

Brockport Normal School was encouraged by the state to slowly tilt its curriculum away from academic subjects toward pedagogical courses, and the old academy tradition of a rounded education withered. By World War I, the school was offering one- and two-year professional teacher training curricula. Consistent with John Dewey's educational philosophy, a "laboratory school" was added where students

could practice their emerging teaching skills on three hundred young pupils. Despite the Regents' ban on residential halls at normal schools, campus life developed recognizable contemporary "collegiate" events,

The campus lab school initiated students in the art of teaching.

A tense moment as postwar Brockport partakes in an autumnal collegiate ritual—football.

such as Color Day, musical performances, and athletic teams for both males and females.

In 1942 Brockport, along with other New York normal schools, gained collegiate status with a four-year degree program. The Regents' post-war plan added a specialization to each of the newly minted state teachers' colleges. Brockport's was Health and Physical Education, which attracted veterans using the GI Bill, doubling the enrollment between 1946 and 1950.

The post-WWII generation left an indelible mark on Brockport student life. Although few of their parents had experienced higher education, postwar students brought definite images of collegiate culture and

thirsted for the full range of activities they associated with college life, including on-campus residences and intercollegiate athletics, especially football and a revived soccer team destined for national glory in the 1950s. Other college traditions were born. Homecoming began in 1947, providing an annual autumn renewal of alumni connections. Christmas pageants, the Winter Carnival, and formal dances all enhanced social life. *The Stylus*, the student newspaper founded in 1914 as a monthly, became a weekly, and an expansive yearbook chronicled flourishing new religious, musical, dramatic, and academic organizations.

The educational panic induced by Sputnik, the election of Nelson A. Rockefeller in 1958, and the approaching tidal wave of baby boomers demanding collegiate education created the necessity for change. Brockport—along with the other teachers' colleges—was transformed into a college of liberal arts and sciences, with a full range of programs in the traditional arts and sciences along with a growing range of professional, pre-professional, and graduate programs. Enrollments soared once again, from 3,353 students in 1965 to 11,696 in 1975. To accommodate this exploding enrollment, classroom buildings and residence halls were constructed at a hectic pace, creating the built environment that would last for the next four decades.

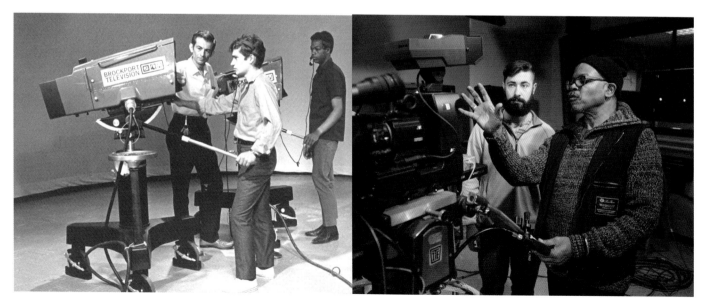

More than 40 years of Brockport educational television.

Student volunteers and famous athletes assist at the International Special Olympics, 1979.

rich tradition of intellectual leadership, as demonstrated by Brockport's sponsorship of SUNY's first Undergraduate Research Conference, which drew more than 800 participants in 2014.

In the midst of a calamitous enrollment decline—nearly one-third of the student body between 1975 and 1982—an extraordinary event occurred in the summer of 1979, when the college hosted the International Special Olympics. It attracted tens of thousands of visitors, including some of the world's most famous athletes—Muhammad Ali and Rafer Johnson (the 1960 Olympic decathalon champion), among others—and reaffirmed the college's relationship with teacher education, especially physical education, and its tradition of social service. More than memories, the event left an indelible mark on the campus. An innovative adaptive physical education program remains one of the college's hallmarks, providing programs for the community and national leadership in the field. And the campus received a gift from the people of the Soviet Union, two monu-

The turmoil caused by the constant construction was mirrored in the intellectual ferment across the campus. The newly hired faculty members joined with those who had hired them to create an extraordinary series of academic initiatives. Curricular alternatives abounded, such as the unique Peace Corps program that included an academic major and training for subsequent placements and the Alternate College, funded by the Carnegie Corporation, which offered students an opportunity to earn a baccalaureate degree in three full-time years. One illustration of the ambitions borne by dramatic growth was a Psychology Department request for the authority to develop three doctoral programs.

Departments sponsored events that drew national attention; the history department sponsored a series of conferences that led to the organization of the Social Science Historical Association, while the English department organized the Writers Forum, which featured interviews with leading writers, a program that continues today. As does the

An enthusiastic professor directing students of the renowned Sankofa African dance group.

Special Olympics Park at night.

the changing campus culture was the replacement of "Spring-In," a bacchanalia with beer trucks and bands, with "Scholars' Day," during which students have presented their work to the college community for more than thirty years.

In recent years, the college has expanded its electronically mediated instruction capability in order to serve students who live, work, and study at a distance from the campus. In addition, the completion of a long-awaited Special Events and Recreation Center provided a conducive environment for concerts, indoor athletics, and academic ceremonies. The new Liberal Arts Building, the first new classroom/office building constructed on campus since the early 1970s, represented the college's continued commitment to the humanities as it provides a venue for conference and lecture series.

mental sculptures, the larger of which, affectionately called the "Lollipop Men," serves as the centerpiece for Special Olympics Park.

Toward the end of the century, enrollments stabilized, desperately needed renovations of older buildings began, a physical presence in downtown Rochester became permanent, and the curriculum matured, reflecting the modern comprehensive college's distinctive blend of undergraduate programs in the liberal arts and sciences as well as the professions with a broad array of graduate programs. Brockport made special efforts to serve the needs of mature students who brought an exceptional work ethic to the classrooms and captured many academic prizes.

In the late 1990s a new administration reorganized admissions and attracted greater numbers of highly qualified students through an extensive scholarship program and increased funding for the Honors program. Academic ceremonies, both traditional and new, such as an Opening of School Convocation, an annual Diversity Conference, and a spring Honors Convocation, became regular events on the college's annual calendar. One reflection of

Among the traditions that have enlivened campus life over the past half century are the extensive arts presentations, especially the dance programs, as well as a full range of intercollegiate—and intramural—athletics. Nearly six hundred men and women compete on college teams annually, while nine hundred others engage in organized intramural sports. Men's wrestling has long been a national powerhouse, as has women's gymnastics.

Today's college, with an enrollment of more than eight thousand students, mostly from western New York and especially the greater Rochester region, continues to develop the human capital necessary for successful communities. More than thirty thousand college alumni work and reside in the greater Rochester area. Clustered particularly in the service professions, they provide daily evidence of the value of the educational opportunities The College at Brockport has provided to the Genesee Valley and beyond, with the promise of building on their success for the future.

FINGER LAKES COMMUNITY COLLEGE

Many of the alumni of Finger Lakes Community College still know their alma mater by another name: Community College of the Finger Lakes. It was fitting that the word "community" came first because it was hard to tell the difference between the city of Canandaigua and the college in those early days. Seven full-time faculty members and a few administrators opened CCFL in January 1968 in whatever spaces they could find—often in rooms above downtown Canandaigua storefronts—for the 85 full-time and 125 part-time students. The Admissions Office occupied an unassuming house on one end of town, while nurses learned their craft in the VA Medical Center on the other. An old auto repair shop became a science lab, while science classes were held above a JC Penney store on Main Street.

As vacant storefronts filled with students, so did the odd spare bedroom. The dean of students kept a list of residents willing to rent rooms and apartments to students who, along with their professors, would later become known as FLCC's "storefront pioneers."

And the city seemed happy to have them, too, according to Anthony Capozzi, one of the college's first students and—courtesy of a last name that started with "C"—its first graduate. "The city of Canandaigua, I think, opened its arms to the institution," he said, noting that officials seemed to "look the other way" on parking laws as students arrived from out of town to go to class.

The storefront college thrived. Enrollment nearly tripled by fall 1968 to 612 students. In 1969, the college's sponsor, Ontario County, purchased 235 acres just outside the city for a permanent campus.

The college offered degree programs that met obvious regional needs, such as transfer programs and Nursing, and one in particular that met a less-than-obvious need for the times, Natural Resources Conservation. William Banaszewski and his colleagues recognized the importance of protecting the region's deep, glacier-carved lakes and the fragile hills that rose above them. Banaszewski, now a professor emeritus, recalls the skepticism that greeted the initial plans for a conservation degree. Local officials told him conservation was volunteer work. "I remember going to a meeting and saying, 'My goodness, if we follow that concept, maybe people should volunteer to plow our roads and take care of us in our hospitals. Why is ensuring that we have clean water and healthy forests less important than that?'"

The State University of New York approved the Natural Resources Conservation degree in 1970, and today the college confers the second-largest number of two-year conservation degrees in the nation. After the FLCC main campus opened in 1975, conservation faculty and students had some room to apply classroom knowledge. The arboretum they planted in 1977 gives the campus the park-like ambiance it has today with oaks, maples, birches, willows, and towering evergreens. Students and their instructors also built trails through the wooded areas, adding an outdoor classroom and boardwalks to give access to marshes.

College offerings continued to expand to meet the emerging needs of students and the community. In 1976, Mechanical Technology and Graphic Arts were among a series of new degrees. Other changes in the late 1970s and early 1980s included the first two-plus-two programs to smooth the transfer path to baccalaureate institutions. The college adopted the Educational Opportunity Program for disadvan-

Two members of the champion FLCC Woodsmen Team.

taged students and developmental studies classes for those who needed to improve academic skills. As the college approached its twentieth anniversary, more than three thousand students were enrolled in twenty degree-granting programs and attended classes at the main campus and at eight off-campus sites.

The main campus continued to expand in the 1990s with a forty-thousand-square-foot addition to provide improved nursing and music facilities. A 1995 project to add a third floor to the library and new classrooms followed. This was also the decade when the college changed its name to the more conventional Finger Lakes Community College.

By the mid-2000s, the college was bursting at the seams again with approximately five thousand students. As FLCC began planning the largest expansion in its forty-year history, college leaders sought to balance the need for more construction with care for the environment. The college adopted a policy that the seventy-eight-thousand-square-foot Student Center and all future new buildings be certified by the US Green Building Council's Leadership in Energy and Environmental Design (LEED) program. Opened in 2012, the Student Center's green features include low-flow plumbing, occupancy sensors and high-efficiency heating, ventilation and air conditioning. Outside, rain and snowmelt are channeled into three linked marshes that filter the increased runoff, allowing the landscape to help maintain equilibrium with a busy campus.

These less noticeable features are overshadowed by the sustainably harvested wood paneling, regionally quarried stonework, and extensive use of natural light, making for a bright, airy building that has become a popular location for community arts and cultural programming. Chief among these is the Canandaigua Lake Music Festival, a celebration of chamber music that the college now hosts in the Student Center's state-of-the-art auditorium. Choral concerts, faculty recitals, and the Spring Arts Festival, an FLCC tradition, are now attracting greater audiences as well.

The college continues to build new community connections with academic programming, most recently in response to the spectacular growth of the wine and grape industry. FLCC asked grape growers and winemakers for their help developing a curriculum for the next generation of Finger Lakes vintners. The first students of the new FLCC Viticulture degree program enrolled in 2011, and the college now counts winemakers at some of the region's most well-known wineries among its alumni.

Attractive meeting spaces for college and community events.

FLCC and Canandaigua are the center of a vibrant musical scene.

Learning about grapes from vine to table for the thriving Finger Lakes wine industry.

Today, Finger Lakes Community College serves about 6,300 full- and part-time students at the main campus in Canandaigua and campus centers in Victor, Newark, and Geneva. FLCC welcomes everyone from adults seeking a new career to high schoolers trying to get ahead on college credits. In 2015, the college opened a teaching winery for the viticulture students, and in 2016 celebrated the redevelopment of the Geneva Campus Center, still close to the heart of the city. Both will be green buildings as the college maintains the commitments it made nearly fifty years ago to the people of the Finger Lakes region and the natural surroundings they call home.

Long jumping for the Lakers.

GENESEE COMMUNITY COLLEGE

The founding of Genesee Community College exemplifies the importance of community action and the long-term impact of civic responsibility. In the early 1960s, the Genesee County Board of Supervisors conducted a study of the regional need for—and viability of—a locally established community college, which concluded that student enrollment would never exceed seventy-five students. The Batavia Jaycees, however, prevailed with their own study that reached a different conclusion. In February 1964, the Jaycees reported that not only was there a need for a community college, but also that the community with its favorable economic climate and growing population had the financial ability to support a successful college. The Board of Supervisors decided that a public referendum was the best way to make this important decision.

Through the next year, community-wide debate ensued. The proponents of the community college organized a "Citizens Committee" and led a vigorous and well-planned campaign that in November 1965 succeeded by a margin of over 1,400. Genesee Community College thus became one of only two voter-established community colleges in New York State, and in May 1966 SUNY appointed a Board of Trustees for the college. The board's first task was to hire an energetic, experienced president who would have the vision to help secure the college's future. From a large pool of applicants, the board appointed Dr. Alfred C. O'Connell, who left his position as the president of Harford Junior College in Bel Air, Maryland.

Under President O'Connell's leadership, the dream became reality. After securing fifty-six thousand square feet of the former Valu Discount Store on

West Main Street in Batavia, which construction crews renovated throughout the summer of 1967, the college welcomed its first class of 378 full-time and 243 part-time students in September 1967. This initial group was approximately two hundred more students than had been projected and five hundred more than the Board of Supervisors had anticipated. President O'Connell's first dean of students, Stuart Steiner, would eventually become president of the college in 1975 and serve in this capacity for thirty-seven years, one of the longest-serving college presidents in America.

A modest beginning in a renovated former retail store.

Growth and innovation have long characterized Genesee Community College. Academic programs, enrollment, faculty, staff, and facilities have all experienced steady growth and development. In January 1972, the college moved into a new, permanent facility at One College Road, overlooking the scenic hillsides and farmland of Genesee County, just east of Batavia. Twenty years later, in 1991, the Stuart Steiner Theatre opened, featuring a complete fine arts center with a 328-seat theater, box office, gallery, scene shop, costume shop, dance and music studios, labs for Digital Art and Drafting, and a ceramics suite offering two kilns and more than a dozen potter's wheels.

Genesee Community College expanded once again in 2000, with the renovation of the library and the opening of the Conable Technology Building, named after the region's long-term US congressman and World Bank president Barber Conable and his wife Charlotte. The two-story wing offers state-of-the-art computer labs, a media production suite, online learning offices, "smart" classrooms, and a 150-seat tiered lecture hall.

In January 2006, Genesee opened the Wolcott J. Humphrey III Student Union. The 10,500-square-foot student activity center provides multipurpose meeting rooms, offices for the Student Government Association, a dedicated Veterans Lounge, and a large recreation area featuring a spectacular view of the countryside and a cozy fireplace. The Rosalie Steiner Art Gallery was added in 2011, rounding out the Genesee Center for the Arts with a dedicated, museum-

Building the set for a Steiner Theatre production.

Reaching across four counties, GCC provides instruction in previously underserved areas.

quality exhibit space for both students and professional artists.

GCC was among the first community colleges in New York State to recognize students' interest in living on or near its campus. In 2001, the Genesee Community College Foundation acquired an apartment complex adjacent to the campus and established College Village, a residence community just for GCC's full-time students. Since that time, College Village has expanded, adding four more buildings and Village Hall, the centrally located meeting, study, and office facility. Today, College Village accommodates more than 450 students and enjoys a multicultural population that includes many international residents.

While supporting the steady growth on the Batavia campus, college leaders realized that plenty of deserving students in the

The Conable Technology Building makes up-to-date technology accessible.

The College Village residences were among the first to provide on-campus living for community college students.

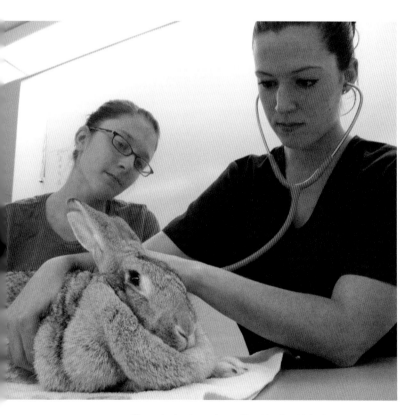

Two students and a patient in the Veterinary Technology program.

adjacent counties could not commute or move to Batavia. Since 1990 GCC has substantially increased accessibility to students in neighboring counties by establishing six satellite campus centers, two each in the three adjacent counties, Orleans, Wyoming, and Livingston. Four of these campus centers have either been extensively renovated or relocated to accommodate better teaching and learning capabilities.

Today, Genesee has nearly seventy associate degree and certificate programs and continues to develop and implement new academic programs aimed at tomorrow's careers. Food Processing Technology, Supply Chain Management, E-Commerce, Event Planning, Fashion Design, Biotechnology, Veterinary Technology, Polysomnographic Technology (the study of sleep disorders), and Technical Theatre are among the newest programs the college offers its students.

In addition, GCC remains at the forefront of the creation of a wide array of online learning opportunities. Each semester, well over one hundred online courses are offered, and fifteen degrees or certificates can be earned exclusively online. The college is continuing to explore, expand, and introduce new online modalities, such as its 360-degree learning option, currently in development.

The Business and Employee Skills Training Center (BEST) is another college service. It works with businesses throughout the region by providing customized training; personal, professional, leadership, and small business development; as well as assistance with grant writing, noncredit coursework, certification, driver education, rural police training, and more.

As GCC approaches its fiftieth anniversary and reflects on its history, there is one common denominator—a consistent passion for and commitment to student success that has remained its strategic priority for decades. It is witnessed in classrooms and laboratories, on athletic fields and courts, in the award-winning library, the state-of-the-art language and math labs, and in students' everyday experience.

STATE UNIVERSITY COLLEGE AT GENESEO

On a hill overlooking the Genesee River valley, in a National Historic Landmark Village, sits State University of New York College at Geneseo, which means "beautiful valley" in the Seneca language. Founded as the Geneseo Normal School in 1871, the college blends long traditions of teacher training with an emphasis on the liberal arts and sciences. "Old Main," the college's original and, for sixty years, sole building, was built near the heart of the village, just one block from Main Street.

Since joining SUNY in 1948 as one of the system's

Geneseo Normal School's original home.

smaller state teachers' colleges, Geneseo in recent decades has evolved into a premier public liberal arts and sciences college, earning national acclaim for its academic quality and value. Geneseo is New York's sole member on the Council of Public Liberal Arts Colleges, an illustration that the college's reputation that extends well beyond its idyllic setting in western New York.

The college comprises twenty academic departments as well as the School of Business and the Ella Cline Shear School of Education. Together, they offer forty undergraduate degree programs as well as two master's programs and twenty-three interdisciplinary majors. Geneseo also offers an array of international study programs, including courses taught in England, Europe, Central America, and, most recently, China.

The college maintains a beautifully landscaped 220-acre campus that evokes a touch of New England in western New York. The village provides a comfortable home for the college. Students and alumni share memories when they see Emmeline, the bronze bear, perched atop the Wadsworth Fountain on Main Street, a town-gown fixture since 1888. The well-preserved Main Street offers a variety of shops, restaurants, and college buildings, as well as the Big Tree Inn and the Lockhart Gallery. Just thirty minutes south of Rochester and one hour east of Buffalo, Geneseo offers the pleasures of rural living with the appeal of urban access.

A walking tour of Geneseo's campus reveals its rich history, from the iconic Sturges Hall with its clock tower to the newly renovated Doty Hall (the original Geneseo High School) to Brodie Hall, whose unique design reflects the architectural brilliance of Edgar Tafel, a Frank Lloyd Wright protégé. Tafel also

Welles Hall (1932) named for James B. Welles, the last principal (1934–1946), who led the college's transformation from Normal School to State Teachers College.

designed Geneseo's gazebo, a destination landmark where students, alumni, and visitors have long gathered to enjoy the panoramic view of signature sunsets over the Genesee Valley.

Building updates reflect Geneseo's evolving curriculum. The Integrated Science Center, opened in 2006, houses the Biology, Chemistry, Geological Sciences, and Physics departments, with a Foucault pendulum in the lobby demonstrating Earth's rotation.

The center also houses a Pelletron particle accelerator for physics research—among the nation's very few operating at a baccalaureate college and the only one in western New York—as well as a state-of-the-art Molecular Structure Laboratory. In addition, a twenty-inch reflector telescope with state-of-the-art instrumentation is housed in a dome on top of the roof. The center supports undergraduate research at Geneseo as well as scientific study in the region. Among the nation's baccalaureate institutions, Geneseo ranks highly in the number of alumni with doctorates in STEM fields.

Recently renovated Bailey Hall houses the Geography, Anthropology, Sociology, and Psychology departments. And Monroe Residence Hall, a model "green" building, is the first at Geneseo to earn Leadership in Energy and Environmental Design Gold certification, reflecting Geneseo's commitment to environmental responsibility and sustainability.

Geneseo's innovative Digital Thoreau project enables English Department students and faculty to employ technology and digital communications to study multiple manuscript versions of Thoreau's *Walden*. Beyond virtual recreations, the project includes plans to construct a replica of nineteenth-century American transcendentalist Henry David Thoreau's famous cabin in the woods.

Students who, like Thoreau, desire time in the woods are just minutes away from the soothing silence of nature at the Spencer J. Roemer Arboretum. The twenty-acre sanctuary, used for both recreation and instruction, contains more than seventy species of trees, shrubs, and wildflowers, including stately two-hundred-year-old oak trees.

Within a short drive, students and faculty can enjoy the spectacular scenery and natural wonder of Letchworth State Park—the "Grand Canyon of the East." Geneseo partners with Letchworth to provide programming and support for its recently opened Humphrey Nature Center, a $4.8 million project serving as a natural laboratory for Geneseo's geography and biology students.

In fulfilling its mission to develop socially responsible citizens, Geneseo offers award-winning programs in student leadership (Geneseo Opportunities for Leadership Development) and a community/college collaboration, Livingston CARES, which has been dedicated to rebuilding areas devastated by storms such as Hurricane Katrina and, most recently, Superstorm Sandy. As evidence of its dedication to civic engagement, the college has been named multiple times to the President's Higher Education Community Service Honor Roll.

Campus programs and Main Street happenings enhance town-gown relations. The college supports four art galleries that exhibit work by students, faculty, and artists and hosts over forty concerts, recitals, and theater and dance performances each year,

The Pelletron particle accelerator—a key asset for scientific research in western New York.

The Finger Lakes provide opportunities for hands-on science.

Professional opera comes to Geneseo.

enhancing the quality of life and increasing access to the arts for surrounding communities. The Finger Lakes Opera at Geneseo brings professional summer operatic productions to the Genesee Valley. Geneseo also sponsors a number of distinguished speakers

MacVittie Union is a gathering point for the annual GREAT Day celebration of scholarly and creative endeavors.

and lectureships open to the public on the leading issues of the day.

In addition, the college promotes student internships through its Department of Career Development, a Small Business Development Center, and an entrepreneurship program called VentureWorks that connects the college's expertise and students with regional organizations and businesses.

Geneseo's athletic program—with twenty-one intercollegiate sports—brings students and community residents together to cheer on the Knights. The women's cross-country team has won the national championship, and the Knights have garnered over 120 SUNY Athletic Conference championships. MacVittie College Union, named for President Robert MacVittie (1963–1979), provides a center for student life.

Approaching its sesquicentennial in 2021, Geneseo cherishes its proud history that has shaped today's college—and embraces the challenges and opportunities to prepare future generations for leadership and success in the twenty-first century.

MONROE COMMUNITY COLLEGE

Anticipating the baby boom's impact on the number of local high school graduates and the local economy's growing need for educated workers to support growing high-tech industries, the SUNY Master Plan of 1950 identified Rochester, home to Eastman Kodak, Bausch and Lomb, and Stromberg-Carlson, as a place in need of a community college. Local educators, business and community leaders, and elected officials all shared a vision to make higher education more accessible and

The first campus was housed in the former East High School.

more responsive to the needs of the local community.

A decade later, Gordon Howe, chairman of the Monroe County Board of Supervisors, initiated the authorization for a new college. He appointed Dr. Samuel J. Stabins to chair the first Monroe Community College Board of Trustees, which included leading Rochester professionals in business, health care, education, and law. In early 1962, the board hired an experienced community college president, Dr. LeRoy V. Good, and selected the former East High School in Rochester as the college's

MCC students in the Atrium of the Damon City Campus in central Rochester.

enrollment shot up by more than forty-one percent, an increase that has continued to this day, when the Brighton campus serves over fourteen thousand students.

Such relentless growth soon led to the creation of a second campus, giving a renewed presence in downtown Rochester. In the early 1990s plans were developed for what became known as the Damon City Campus, honoring longtime trustee E. Kent Damon. It opened in 1992 on the fourth and fifth floors of the Sibley Building, once home to Rochester's first and finest department store. The college offered a varied curriculum at the site, including popular majors, such as Criminal Justice, Human Services, Law, and Kin-

initial location. Given the building's age (it had been Rochester's first public high school) extensive renovations had to be carried out before the first students arrived in September 1962.

The 720 students who enrolled that fall were well beyond the initial projection of 550. The evidence of early success extended beyond enrollment. In 1965, for example, MCC became the first US community college to earn accreditation within three years of its founding, a remarkable achievement.

The determination to build a thriving college extended far beyond accreditation. It resulted in swift enrollment and program growth. By 1968, Monroe Community College had clearly outgrown the East High School site, and the board moved the campus to a new location on East Henrietta Road in suburban Brighton. Situated on a former farm, the new campus was designed to meet the needs of four thousand students as MCC had become New York State's fastest growing community college. During the 1980s

EMS training at the Public Safety Training Facility.

dergarten through Secondary Education, while demonstrating its ongoing commitment to serving Rochester's residents by making educational opportunity more accessible.

In keeping with its mission to provide practical education to fill regional economic needs, MCC's Applied Technologies Center opened in 1997 on West Henrietta Road. This center provides hands-on training to about one thousand students, many of whom are later employed by local industry. It's the site for up-to-date instruction in Automotive Technology; Precision Machining; Optical Fabrication; and Heating, Ventilation, and Air Conditioning.

MCC is committed to offering students broad curricular choices. Its more than ninety degree and certificate programs range from those leading to the Associate of Arts and Associate of Science degrees that prepare students for successful transfer to baccalaureate degree colleges (seventy percent of MCC students arrive intending to transfer) to an incredible array of more technical programs. Among the recent innovations are the Public Safety Training Facility designed in collaboration with Monroe County and regional emergency response organizations, which became available in 2002, and the Agriculture and Life Sciences Institute that opened in 2007.

Today, MCC educates future nurses in its state-of-the-art Nursing lab, where students work for either—or both—immediate employment and further education. The employment record of MCC graduates demonstrates the contribution of the career degree and certificate programs to the local economy and quality of life; approximately eighty-seven percent of nursing alumni are employed full-time in local business, companies, and agencies.

When MCC opened the Alice Holloway Young Residence Halls on the Brighton Campus in 2003, it joined several other community colleges in New York to provide on-campus housing. Since then, four more residences have followed, each equipped with modern technology services. The presence of on-campus residential students has considerably enhanced a growing sense of campus community. For example, a

dozen NCAA intercollegiate teams provide opportunities for students to express college spirit in support of their Tribunes, while many other MCC students participate in more than sixty campus clubs and organizations.

Since its founding in the 1960s, Monroe Community College has continually expanded, both in enrollment and curricular offerings, ensuring that the students of the region have access to an education that prepares them to participate fully in their changing economy and society. This is no less true today than it was fifty years ago. MCC's first graduates, the Class of 1964, numbered only eighty-three. Today, MCC serves over nineteen thousand students and is

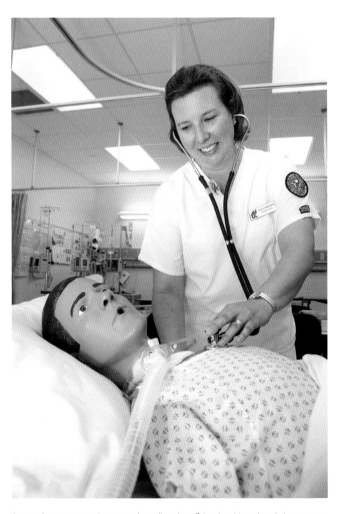

Learning to care for a patient "patient" in the Nursing laboratory.

231

Student resident assistants oversee life in the new residential halls.

Graduation.

among the top twenty-five community colleges in the nation in the number of associate degrees awarded.

Building on its heritage of success, MCC is poised to continue to provide the region with educated graduates who are ready to fulfill the area's needs. It has become an access point to the best education possible, whether that involves providing a more skilled workforce, aiding economic innovation, or preparing students for further studies.

SOUTHERN TIER

Binghamton University

Broome Community College

Cornell University and Its Four SUNY Contract Colleges

Corning Community College

College of Technology at Delhi

Beautifully scenic, New York State's Southern Tier provides a cornerstone of New York State's traditions and cultural heritage. Located among the Southern Tier's ten state parks, Binghamton, the region's industrial center, and the several dozen towns and villages that dot the primarily rural landscape form a cohesive community that takes advantage of some of New York State's most impressive natural resources, productive agricultural land, and profitable industry. The cities of Elmira, Hornell, and Corning also provide the region with an increasingly diverse population and serve as cultural centers. Located along Pennsylvania's northern border, the Southern Tier continues to act not only as a residential and tourist destination but also as a nucleus of higher education.

Comprised of Broome, Chenango, Delaware, Schuyler, Steuben, Tioga, and Tompkins counties, the Southern Tier attracts investment from industrial and commercial concerns as well as tourists. Primarily acclaimed for its landscape of lushly forested rolling hills and picturesque waterways, the region also serves as the location for several major industrial and manufacturing enterprises. In addition to being home to Corning Incorporated, a Fortune 500 company, the region also supports several high-tech firms, including Lockheed Martin and BAE Systems. Both the central and southwest sections of the Finger Lakes attract tourists who come for the wineries, the museums, the National Parks, and the scenic travel from one location to the next.

In the seventeenth and eighteenth centuries, the Iroquois Confederacy had large settlements in the region, to which the colonies of New York, Massachusetts, and Pennsylvania laid claim, even though they made little, if any, attempt to settle there. Not until during and after the Revolutionary War did European settlers make significant inroads into the area. The soldiers of the Sullivan Expedition who marched into the area of the modern city of Binghamton in 1779 destroyed the existing Oneida and Onondaga villages.

The area struggled economically in the beginning of the nineteenth century because the hilly terrain meant that it was ideal neither for major canal nor railroad building. On a smaller scale the Chenango Canal, finished in 1837, linked Binghamton and the Susquehanna River to the Erie Canal and provided the initial impetus for commercial development. The Erie Railroad followed the canal in 1849, fostering further development. Shortly after mid-century, the Delaware, Lackawanna and Western Railroad began consolidating the rail system that within thirty years ran from Hoboken, New Jersey, through Binghamton west to Buffalo.

In 1834, settlers organized a village government at Chenango Point. Renamed Binghamton in 1867, the village's strategic location on the Susquehanna and Chenango Rivers provided the community with commercial and industrial opportunities. Binghamton provided the region with a centralized focal point of commerce and contributed to the region's increasing prominence as a living destination. By the late nineteenth century, Binghamton supported a thriving cigar industry and was home to the regional leader in shoe manufacturing, Endicott-Johnson Shoes, and to the world-renowned International Time Recording and Tabulating Company, which later became International Business Machines (IBM).

Binghamton continues to serve as the Southern Tier's most populated city and contains a diverse, professional community continually engaged in supporting higher education. Yet, like so many older industrial cities, it lost significant employment during

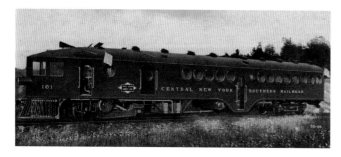

Central New York Southern Railroad McKeen car.

Iron Foot Bridge, Watkins Glen State Park.

Chenango Canal Prism and Lock 107, Chenango Forks.

the last half of the twentieth century, particularly as IBM closed its plants and the region's defense industries became casualties of the end the Cold War. Manufacturing employment in the Binghamton area fell by more than fifty percent between 1990 and 2005.

Two recent New York State programs seek to assist the Southern Tier's communities and industries. The Rural Initiative program reduces financial risk and increases the sustainability of the agriculture and forestry ventures so characteristic of the region by supporting the renewable energy initiatives that protect the region's scenic environment. And, the Community Revitalization program facilitates the redevelopment of downtowns and community centers in the region's cities, towns, and villages. In conjunction with the SUNY colleges located in the Southern Tier, this program reinforces communal bonds by engaging community members in the process.

Community engagement and protection of the natural environment became essential elements in the recent debates, some quite fierce, about the possibility of widespread hydrofracturing (fracking) across the length of the Marcellus Shale Formation, which is rich in difficult to extract oil and natural gas deposits. The issue has been settled by Governor Cuomo's decision to ban the practice on environmental grounds, leaving many disappointed that the hoped-for oil boom was not going to occur.

Hydraulic Fracturing at a Marcellus Shale well, 2013.

In the debate over the best route for economic development, the five SUNY institutions in the Southern Tier have played—and will continue to play—active roles. By educating the region's population, by their innovative research initiatives, by working in collaboration with the major employers of the region on advanced manufacturing techniques, and by connecting students to employment opportunities that support the area's businesses and industries, the colleges and universities are in the forefront of the efforts to revitalize the region's economy.

As one of SUNY's four research universities, Binghamton University serves as a major focus for academic research and continues to earn its high reputation for undergraduate education within a research university setting. In addition, the four contract colleges at Cornell University—the College of Agriculture and Life Sciences, the College of Veterinary Medicine, the College of Human Ecology, and the School of Industrial Relations—provide research

and educational opportunities that span the region's many needs, from agriculture to tourism to biomedical breakthroughs.

Originally one of the New York State Schools of Agriculture and Domestic Sciences, SUNY Delhi today offers superb postsecondary education with an emphasis on community service. Indeed, in 1997, the campus won an AmeriCorps Community Service Grant to develop a fifty-acre outdoor recreation park for the community. Dedicated to supporting businesses in the region, Corning Community College's Workforce Development Center works directly with local industries to provide consulting, workforce training, and professional development services to foster economic growth. So too does Broome Community College, located just north of Binghamton, offering a thriving campus life as well as dramatic plays, musicals, and other performances for the area's population.

The Southern Tier of New York has, since the last part of the eighteenth century, utilized its rich natural resources and scenic landscape to facilitate economic growth. With industries ranging from high-tech, in both manufacturing and agriculture, to tourism, the area provides a wide range of employment opportunities, each demanding a more educated workforce. The five SUNY colleges and universities in the region have been important partners in growing the Southern Tier's economy and enhancing its quality of life.

Village of Delhi Riverwalk, 2014.

Ansco Company, Binghamton, 1909.

BINGHAMTON UNIVERSITY

Today's university began modestly after World War II as Triple Cities College, an extension of the private Syracuse University. It was designed to meet the immediate educational needs of returning servicemen from the Binghamton, Endicott, and Johnson City area without creating a demand for a state university system. The GI Bill funded most of Triple Cities' early students.

Located in Endicott, the college opened in September 1946 with fifty-three faculty members and enrolling 957 students who could pursue

Colonial Hall mansion, donated in 1946 by IBM chairman Thomas Watson, housed Triple Cities College.

bachelor's degrees in liberal arts and business administration. The campus consisted of a former mansion known as Colonial Hall, which housed administrative offices, student organizations, and the bookstore, and military-surplus prefabricated buildings, which served as classrooms, laboratories, the library, faculty offices, and the cafeteria. Nearby facilities were utilized for athletic and campus activities.

After separating from Syracuse University, Triple Cities College survived to join the newly established State University of New York system in 1950. The school, renamed Harpur College in honor of Robert Harpur, a colonial educator and patriot from the nearby community of Harpursville, was the only public liberal arts college in New York.

In 1951, an innovative liberal arts program was implemented to allow students to move "from breadth, through depth, to perspective." Students began with broadly based general education courses in the humanities, social sciences, and the physical sciences and mathematics before specializing in specific academic areas such as history or biology. All faculty members shared responsibility for teaching the general education courses.

The institution earned national recognition through the development of this program, and by the 1960s, Harpur College had emerged as a leader in American higher education. Graduate coursework was first offered in Master of Arts programs in English and Mathematics in 1961, and the college was on the path to becoming a research university.

Harpur College had quickly outgrown its original location and purchased land in Binghamton for a new campus. Construction began in 1954, and the move to the new campus consisting of a gymnasium, residence halls, a classroom and administration building, a student union, a library, and a science building was completed in February 1961.

In 1965 Harpur College was selected to be one of SUNY's four newly designated graduate centers and was renamed the State University of New York at Binghamton (in 1992, Binghamton University

Governor Thomas Dewey and SUNY's second president, William Carlson, break ground for the new campus.

was adopted as an informal name). This designation enhanced faculty research opportunities, and SUNY Binghamton was on its way to be a respected research university. The university began forming research centers to promote interdisciplinary research activities supported through external funding; seven centers were in operation by 1979.

With the shifting emphasis to graduate programs in the late 1960s, the focus on a broader education in many disciplines was replaced by specialized training beyond the liberal arts and sciences, making it necessary for the university to broaden its mission. To meet these challenges, four professional schools were established over the next two decades, with Harpur College remaining as the university's liberal arts school. Yet, the reframed mission enhanced, rather than compromised, Binghamton's well-deserved reputation as a campus committed to superb undergraduate education.

The School of Advanced Technology was founded in 1967 to offer graduate instruction in computer science, applied mathematics, and general systems theory. In 1983, this school became part of the new Thomas J. Watson School of Engineering and Applied Science, designed to meet the increasing need for education in mechanical, industrial, and electrical engineering.

The School of Education and Human Development evolved from three separate programs: Professional Education, a Technical Service Center, and the School of General Studies. These three components were merged in 1979 to form the School of General

Science has thrived as part of the liberal arts and science curricula and at the graduate level.

The arts have a strong presence.

Studies and Professional Education, later renamed the School of Education and Human Development in 1987. In 2006, the school was again reorganized to create the School of Education (now Graduate School of Education) and the College of Community and Public Affairs.

The School of Nursing was established in 1969 in response to a critical shortage of college-educated nurses. Upon receipt of a $1 million endowment from the Dr. G. Clifford and Florence B. Decker Foundation in 1989, the school was renamed the Decker School of Nursing. The fourth school, the School of Management, traces its history to the business enterprise and accounting courses offered through the Harpur College Division of Social Sciences during the 1950s. This school opened in 1970, originally called the School of Business.

During the 1970s, major budget cuts curtailed the university's growth. New construction ceased, public funding was cut, and several academic programs had to be eliminated. But by the late 1980s, the university once again began inaugurating new undergraduate programs and strengthening its doctoral programs through SUNY's Graduate Education and Research Initiative, which allocated funds to enhance SUNY's University Centers' graduate program reputation. Soon new doctoral programs in Management, Philosophy, and Engineering were launched, and the university was receiving national recognition for the quality and breadth of its curricula.

A 1991 comprehensive review of campus facilities led to construction of a residential complex; a childcare facility; and an academic complex housing the Decker School of Nursing, the School of Education, the School of Management, and the Undergraduate Admissions Office. Campus growth has continued with the completion of several residential communities; the University Downtown Center, which houses the College of Community and Public Affairs; two additional science buildings; a renovated University Union and dining halls; a multi-purpose Events Center; and the Innovative Technologies Complex that is home to the Biotechnology Building, the Engineering and Science Building, and the Center of Excellence Building. In 2018 a facility designed specifically for the new School of Pharmacy and Pharmaceutical Sciences will open in nearby Johnson City.

In 1969, after students protested plans to turn the area into athletic fields, President Dearing set it aside as an expansive nature preserve.

Life for the more than thirteen thousand undergraduates, centered in six residential communities, is modeled on Oxford University, complete with faculty masters. The Anderson Center for the Performing Arts and the Binghamton University Art Museum enhance students' cultural life. Twenty-one Bearcat intercollegiate teams compete in NCAA Division athletics, while students participate in a wide variety of indoor and outdoor activities. The 190-acre Nature Preserve gives student access to forest, woodland, and a six-acre pond on the campus.

The university has built and maintained strong partnerships with local businesses, industry, and community agencies through its economic outreach programs, the Small Business Development Center, Trade Adjustment Assistance Center, and Strategic Partnership for Industrial Resurgence.

From an almost-accidental outgrowth of the GI Bill, Binghamton has grown into a widely recognized leader in American public higher education. Its undergraduate program continues the Harpur College liberal arts tradition in a public college setting, while its reputation as a research university has steadily grown.

The university celebrates its national and international reputation at graduation.

BROOME COMMUNITY COLLEGE

SUNY Broome Community College owes its existence, like several other SUNY campuses, to the World War II veterans' unexpected demand for higher education. In 1946 the New York State Legislature responded by establishing five institutes of arts and sciences—in Binghamton, Buffalo, Utica, White Plans, and New York City—for an experimental five-year period.

The Institute of Applied Arts and Sciences opened a year later in the State Armory in downtown Binghamton with sixty-three World War II veterans among the 215 students. Plans to convert the institute into a two-year community college took shape when Governor Thomas Dewey approved the 1950 Master Plan for New York's education facilities.

Then disaster struck in the early morning hours of Labor Day in 1951. The State Armory was destroyed

But like a phoenix . . .

in the worst property damage fire in the city's history. Despite the massive loss, college officials were determined to rebuild. "We'll never have a better opportunity to plan for the campus that we all know we'll need someday," Director Cecil Tyrrell told his fellow administrators while surveying the smoldering ruins. "We'll start planning tomorrow morning."

In a show of support, other colleges sent trucks labeled "Bundles for Binghamton," bearing books and other materials to help the college, and one month later, the Institute reopened in the Kalurah Temple next door and in several other downtown sites. Renamed the Broome County Technical Institute, it became a SUNY community college in 1953. Over the following year, the county's planning board considered more than twenty sites for the college's new home before choosing the former County Poor Farm—giving SUNY Broome the honor of becoming the first community college in SUNY to construct a completely new campus.

The first building opened in 1956, the same year the name changed yet again, to Broome Technical Community College. Five buildings were complete when the college celebrated its first on-site graduation in 1958.

Paul F. Titchener Hall opened in 1961 and eventually became home to the college's Liberal Arts program, which was established in 1962 to award the Associate in Arts degree, making it possible for students to complete the first two years of their bachelor's degree. This initiative paved the way in 1973 for a joint degree program between the college and Binghamton University—and the fifty articulation agreements SUNY Broome has with four-year institutions today.

The campus continued to grow in the following decades. The library building opened in 1968, followed by the business building in 1971, the same year the college's name changed yet again, this time to Broome Community College. The Applied Technology Building, a new Campus Services Building, and the state-of-the-art Decker Health Science Center fol-

Music plays an important role in the liberal arts program.

Training a new generation of nurses.

A Hornet prepares to strike.

horizons of its local students, who can study abroad in Italy, Ecuador, Dominican Republic, Haiti, and London—or, if they choose, stay close to home, with satellite classrooms in their own communities.

While the college plays a crucial role in training workers for employment, it has continued to develop its academic programs and reach out to different populations. Since the 1980s, high school students have been able to complete their first year of college while still enrolled in high school. The Pipeline Initiative connects regional high school students with SUNY Broome, Binghamton University, and local industries. Academically gifted high school students can earn their Associate in Arts degree in a single year, saving both time and money before transferring to a baccalaureate college.

In 2013, the college's name changed once more, to SUNY Broome Community College, a name that highlights its long history as a member of the State University of New York. That fall also marked a renewed emphasis on the college's technical and scientific roots as well as recognition of the increasing importance of science, technology, engineering, and math (STEM) education with the opening of the $21 million Natural Science Center, which brings all of the college's high-tech laboratories and science classrooms under one roof.

The original campus is undergoing extensive renovations after six decades of good service. The Darwin R. Wales Center—one of the oldest buildings on campus—has been converted into a handicap-accessible and energy efficient welcome center and campus hub. Transformation of the rest of the original campus is proceeding. And the college plans to return to its roots in downtown Binghamton

lowed—the latter housing the largest health science division among SUNY's community colleges.

The college's student life also matured. SUNY Broome's sports program quickly entered the national athletics spotlight in 1961, when the Hornets' basketball game against New York City Tech became the first junior college game televised in the country. Coach Dick Baldwin eventually became the winningest active college coach at either two- or four-year colleges. A long-awaited dream came true in fall 2014, when the Student Village housing opened for 360 students, making SUNY Broome a residential campus. This project has added a new dimension to the student culture on campus, offering SUNY Broome students access to a full residential collegiate life.

The college has become increasingly global with growing numbers of international students. Already by 1982 there were 130 international students at SUNY Broome. Today, the college hosts over two hundred students from Central America, the Caribbean, and Mexico as part of its Scholarship for Education and Economic Development (SEED) program and offers online courses for international students. In turn, the college also broadens the geographic

Completion of the Natural Science Center in 2013 began a wave of campus modernization.

by converting historic Carnegie Library into a center where students will train for careers in the hospitality industry.

Reaching further afield, SUNY Broome has long offered off-campus courses. The college first offered off-campus courses in the late 1970s and 1980s via the technology of the day: local newspapers and video cassettes. The 1990s brought online courses, and today students can complete a degree without setting foot in a campus classroom.

SUNY Broome Community College has served the Broome County region for over six decades. Today, its campus offers twenty-first-century facilities for classes and extracurricular campus life, while extending its reach in both the virtual world and across the globe.

Technology has always been a SUNY Broome specialty, but today's equipment would have confounded the founders.

CORNELL UNIVERSITY AND ITS FOUR SUNY CONTRACT COLLEGES

"Far above Cayuga's Waters..." stands Cornell University, set in the gorgeous hills above Cayuga Lake, a setting immortalized by one of America's most familiar collegiate alma maters. Cornell University evolved from a meeting in the New York State Senate in 1864 between Andrew Dickson White of Syracuse and Ezra Cornell of Ithaca. They both chaired committees that would influence the allocation of New York's share of the federal Morrill Land-Grant Act funds, which were designated to create colleges that taught agriculture and the mechanical arts. Cornell, who had risen from poverty to amass a great fortune, wanted to support the creation of a new college that emphasized practical skills, while White, a Yale alumnus and later a professor of history at the University of Michigan, proved to be a willing partner in his desire to reform American higher education.

Cornell offered to donate hundreds of thousands of dollars if part of New York's federal land grant proceeds were used to locate a college in Ithaca. When White opposed dividing the Morrill Act funds, the two began working together to create a new university with the entire allocation. Despite opposition that argued for existing colleges' claims, a bill finally passed in April 1865, resulting in the founding of an extraordinary educational experiment, with Cornell as benefactor and White as its first president. The campus in Ithaca was readied and welcomed its first students in 1967.

From its inception, Cornell differed from most of the colleges that dotted the rural American landscape. It was nonsectarian, its curriculum featured an elective system that permitted students to choose their own courses of study, it fostered students working to help pay for their educations, and it strived to fulfill Ezra Cornell's commitment to "found an institution where any person can find instruction in any study." The university was open to all students, welcoming students of all races and nationalities. Only two years after it opened, the college became one of the first in the nation to admit women, and in 1873, the cornerstone for the home of the Sage College for Women was laid. The college even pioneered financial aid designed specifically for women. In addition, African American students began to enroll, albeit in very low numbers, in the mid-1880s; twenty years later, Cornell's first African American fraternity was founded.

Cornell University was, and remains, distinctive in yet another way. Unlike the great public land-grant universities in other states, Ivied Cornell, a private university, is New York's land-grant institution. And in time it became the home for four state-supported contract colleges, each sharing a unique history, each administered by the university, and each a member of SUNY.

With the founding of SUNY in 1948, Cornell University administrators saw dangers, which never materialized, if the new SUNY Board of Trustees sought tighter control over the contract colleges than that exercised historically by the State Education Department. A forty-year battle over annual budget appropriations ensued, with Cornell University arguing that SUNY's fundamental campus budget mechanism, which relied heavily on enrollments, provided inadequate funding levels for the contract colleges, especially for the extension programs. In the 1980s, the issue was temporarily settled by an agreement that authorized Cornell to make its budget case to the legislature directly and, finally, in 2009 SUNY was prohibited from shifting any funds designated for one of Cornell's contract colleges to other campuses.

Student and veterinarian with their patient.

The College of Veterinary Medicine

From the beginning, one of Ezra Cornell's primary interests was veterinary medicine, and in 1865 he insisted that the college create a chair in the field. The department created in those early years adhered to more rigorous standards than were customary, offering a bachelor's degree, and by 1871, a Doctor of Veterinary Medicine, the first such degree in the nation. In 1894, the department became the New York State Veterinary College, the first state-supported college at Cornell. The college continued to grow and has remained in the forefront of innovations in the field, including the education of women veterinarians. Today it is a world leader in veterinary medical education, biomedical research, and public health.

The College of Agriculture and Life Sciences

Befitting its land-grant origins, the university initially offered programs that focused on agriculture and forestry. In time, Morrill Act funding proved to be insufficient for these programs, and in 1904 the Veterinary College model was adopted to create the New York State College of Agriculture, the second publically supported contract college at Cornell. In addition, the Forestry School moved to Syracuse, in time becoming SUNY's College of Environmental Science and Forestry.

Today the College of Agriculture and Life Sciences ,the second largest undergraduate college at Cornell, houses a variety of programs focused on agriculture, food and nutrition, applied economics, life sciences, community and rural development, communication, environmental sciences, and natural resources as well as international programs that are recognized as being among the best in the world.

Students from the School of Agriculture measuring crops.

It operates two agricultural experiment stations—one in Ithaca and the second in Geneva, New York—and serves the communities throughout the state through extension offices shared with the College of Human Ecology.

College of Human Ecology

In 1900 the university authorized a Home Economics program to serve both the women who attended Cornell and the farmwomen whose communities were served by Cornell Cooperative Extension. By 1907, the program had become the Department of Home Economics within the College of Agriculture, and four years later the women who taught in the program were accorded faculty status.

Over the next two decades, the program grew rapidly, achieving "school" status in 1919 and becoming the New York State College of Home Economics in 1925. The college became a welcome home to thousands of New York women seeking a college education, and their degrees led to careers in a broad range of professions, in education, research, govern-

ment and hospitality. In 1969, the name changed to the College of Human Ecology, which more accurately reflected the interdisciplinary nature of its mission.

Today the college strives to connect human life to natural, social, and built environments by continuing to explore the human dimensions of social and natural sciences, design, nutrition and health, public policy, society, family, and community. Using Cor-

The College of Human Ecology's new home.

nell's far-reaching extension network, it delivers findings directly to New York communities and families.

The School of Industrial and Labor Relations

While each of the three state colleges mentioned earlier have achieved no small measure of distinction, the most unique is the New York State School of Industrial and Labor Relations (ILR) at Cornell. The brainchild of a liberal Republican, Irving M. Ives, who had served as both Speaker of the New York State Assembly and chair of the Cornell Board of Trustees, the school opened in 1945 in temporary war-surplus Quonset huts. While some trustees balked, suspicious that the school would tilt toward organized labor, the president and Ives succeeded in getting the necessary authorization and funding from the state.

Dedicated to bringing both labor and business leaders—present and future—together at the same place and time to work through common problems, the school sought to create a healthier labor-management environment in American workplaces. Beyond creating degree-granting curricula, the school established its own extension service with sites across the state and offered classes that were scheduled for working adults.

To this day, the ILR School continues to help improve labor-management relations. Through teaching, research and outreach, ILR advances the world of work by preparing leaders, informing national and international employment and labor policy, and improving working lives around the world

These, then, are the four contract SUNY colleges at Cornell, each distinctive by history and disciplines but united in their educational purpose. Out of the federal Morrill Land-Grant Act, the cauldron of nineteenth-century New York politics, and New York State's traditional preference for private colleges and universities has come a unique model that has benefited the state and beyond. To have four renowned publically supported colleges operating within one of the world's leading private universities demonstrates both the adaptability of Ezra Cornell's vision of a uni-

Instructor working with an ILR class.

versity governed by democratic principles, focused on the personal and social benefits of practical education designed to solve real-world problems, and the ability of SUNY, a state-supported system, to serve as an umbrella for an extraordinary variety of postsecondary institutions. In this sense, Cornell and SUNY's uniqueness mirror one another within the larger mission of public higher education for New York State.

Sun setting far above Cayuga's waters.

CORNING COMMUNITY COLLEGE

orning Community College has grown exponentially from its humble beginning. Initially, little more than a hope of community leaders in the mid-1950s, it soon became more concrete after a consulting group from the Harvard Graduate School issued its report, "A Valley and a Decision." The report endorsed the need for an institution of higher education in the Corning area.

Corning Community College opened in September 1958, with its first classes convening in a recently closed Corning elementary school. Soon two private homes were donated and the school was refurbished. The classes were taught by ten faculty members to a student body of 120 under the sponsorship of the Corning–Painted Post School District.

By 1960, college enrollment had increased to 350 full-time students and 210 part-time students,

with the faculty doubling to thirty-five. This growth spawned a search for a permanent home. With a generous gift of land by Arthur A. Houghton Jr. and a $2,250,000 donation from the Corning Glass Works Foundation, the college began planning of a new campus on Spencer Hill in October.

Classes began on "the hill" in the fall of 1963. Situated on three hundred acres of rolling hills, the campus of six architecturally integrated buildings was formally dedicated in May 1964. The next month it received Middle States accreditation.

The college celebrated its tenth birthday in 1968 with a graduating class of 459—nearly ten times the size of the first graduating class in 1960. In 1970, the college added the Nursing Building, increasing classroom capacity by twenty-five percent. By 1975, the number of full-time faculty had risen to eighty-four

Nursing is one of Corning's most venerable programs.

organized into eight academic divisions, and the student body had grown to 1,952 full-time and 832 part-time students.

Corning Community College's identity and sponsorship changed dramatically in 1985. It had become clear that the Corning-Painted Post School District could not afford to finance further expansion. The solution was to become the first regional community college in New York, with support from three counties: Steuben, Chemung, and Schuyler.

As was the case with many other colleges, the 1990s proved particularly challenging, with budget cutbacks, enrollment declines, and a permanent change in the student body makeup. Full-time enrollments declined to about 1,700, while part-time enrollment soared to 2,200 students, a student mix that continues to the present. Despite fiscal restraints, the college continued to reach out to the community and added the Airport Corporate Park, which houses automotive and machine tool technology programs. Completion of the Eileen Collins Observatory, with its

sixteen- and twenty-inch telescopes for astronomy classes and weekly open houses for the public, added a facility matched by few community colleges.

The new century brought renewed growth and increased optimism. In 2007, the Academic and

Corning students don't just reach for the stars, they see them up close.

Workforce Development Center in Elmira opened with three major goals: to meet the need for skilled employees, to attract new jobs to the region, and to assist both entrepreneurs with start-ups and those with established businesses. By the fall of 2009, the college enrolled 2,559 full-time and 3,113 part-time students, a far cry from 120 students in 1958. Off-campus enrollments grew rapidly, including a near doubling of students in its high school concurrent enrollment program.

In an important departure, in 2012 Corning's Regional Board of Trustees unanimously approved student housing on the hill. The $17.7 million building initiative was entirely financed by the Corning Community College Development Foundation, using private funds and named for Corning's founding president, William Perry. Perry Hall welcomed its first residential students in fall 2013—nearly fifty years to the day from when President Perry oversaw the first classes on the hill.

Full-time students participate in a wide range of social and cultural activities. Red Barons teams compete against other community colleges, and intramural athletics provide for more relaxed activity. The combination of the Observatory, Planetarium, and Spencer Crest Nature Center provide a unique set of educational facilities for both the campus and the

Music is an important part of campus life.

Students enjoy modern suite accommodations.

community. The Nature Center features 250 acres and seven miles of trails with two ponds, a stream, a museum of natural systems, and an apiary within an environmentally sensitive design.

The library is the cornerstone project of the $23.3 million transformational investment in student-centered learning funded by the sponsoring counties, SUNY, USDA Rural Development, Corning Incorporated Foundation, and private gifts. The Student Commons Building was transformed in 2015, as was the gymnasium, which now has an adjacent turf field.

Corning provides a varied curriculum serving a variety of constituent needs. Those who wish to

Corning students can get out into nature.

move directly into employment, or just upgrade existing skills, can choose from the campus's fifteen AAS degree programs and seven certificates. For those wishing to transfer to a baccalaureate college or university, there are degrees in the liberal arts and sciences and an additional nine applied transfer programs. All academic programs are enriched by the reimagined Arthur A. Houghton Jr. Library. The technology rich library includes climate-controlled spaces to protect rare resources; centralized academic support services, including tutoring and mentoring; and dynamic spaces for IT help, access and reference services, and faculty professional development.

Corning Community College remains a strong and vibrant institution dedicated to serving the educational and cultural needs of its students, almost all of whom are drawn from the region surrounding its lovely 550-acre campus. As a guest lecturer, Vincent Price, the famous ghoulish actor, once told the faculty, "I envy you teaching in such a setting." The visual beauty of the campus reflects the natural riches of Steuben, Chemung, and Schuyler counties, a bounty the college seeks to enhance through its work with its residents, its businesses, and through its communities.

An idyllic learning scene.

COLLEGE OF TECHNOLOGY AT DELHI

S itting among the northern foothills of the Catskill Mountains on a 625-acre campus, SUNY Delhi traces its roots to early 1900s concerns about rural life. Rapid population growth and urbanization were simultaneously depop- ulating rural areas and threatening food production. Agricultural education was seen as one way to stem the migration of the rural young and bolster the rural econo- mies. In Delhi Elizabeth and Amelia MacDonald drove a community-based effort to bring agricultural education to the area. The campaign culminated successfully on

A first home for man and beast.

May 24, 1913, when Governor William Sulzer signed the bill establishing the State School for Agriculture and Domestic Science at Delhi.

The college opened its doors with nine students in one cold, half-furnished building where, as one wrote: "Red noses were in vogue." But the Delhi spirit had been established, since, as the student newspaper observed, "What was lack- ing in equipment was made up for in enthusiasm."

Later, the college dem- onstrated evidence of Delhi's important role in economic development. When World War I left Delaware County

Building Construction has a long history at Delhi.

and string beans. We also packed dozens of boxes of carrots in sand and picked bushels of potatoes to be used in the cafeteria."

Specialized agriculture courses were offered to more than two hundred individuals who took advantage of the training and subsequent job opportunities on local dairy farms. Those students included nearly one hundred men recruited by the federal government from Newfoundland to bolster the wartime labor force.

The 1940s also brought permanent changes. In 1943, a new Practical Nursing program responded to a national call for nurses. Recruitment announcements in twenty-five upstate New York newspapers proclaimed: "Women who have been seeking ways to help the war effort will find that this program offers good opportunities." Applications far exceeded openings. Food Technology was added to the curriculum in 1945, beginning Delhi's nationally recognized Hospitality Management program offerings. Three years later, Delhi became a founding member of SUNY.

facing an acute farmworker shortage, Delhi moved quickly to fill the gap. Intensive training programs were created to prepare students from the New York City region for immediate employment on area farms.

SUNY Delhi responded to other needs throughout its history. A building construction program, the first in the United States, was introduced in 1933 to meet the demand for trained carpenters and builders in rural New York. Other nonagricultural courses were added, and the college's expanded mission was formally recognized in 1941 by its new name, the New York State Agricultural and Technical Institute at Delhi.

But this new era in Delhi history was quickly overshadowed by American involvement in World War II, during which a majority of male students and faculty members enlisted. Students and staff who remained behind rallied on the home front to support the war effort. One student recalled, "We planted a huge victory garden, harvested crops and helped the home economics students fill hundreds of glass jars with tomatoes

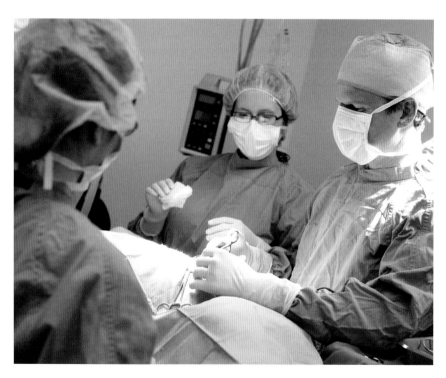
A surgical suite is part of the extensive learning facility that houses SUNY Delhi's Veterinary Science Technology program.

254

Golf and Sports Turf Management—the often-forgotten ingredient of successful athletic events.

Delhi shared in SUNY's 1960s expansion. A massive construction project modernized the campus, which Governor Nelson A. Rockefeller visited in 1965 to dedicate the new buildings. Academic innovation accompanied physical growth. The Veterinary Science Technology program, established in 1961, was the first in the United States and is fully accredited by the American Veterinary Medical Association. Support from Delhi alumni and New York State led to the construction of a golf course that today serves both as a laboratory for the Golf and Sports Turf Management and the Golf Course Management majors and an attraction for tourists. The course is one of only three college courses nationwide to be recognized as an Audubon International Cooperative Sanctuary.

The growing role of technology in New York State commerce and the college's curriculum was recognized in 1987 by adopting its current name, the State University College of Technology at Delhi. One example of its innovative approach to technology education was demonstrated in the construction of an Applied Technologies complex. Contractors erected the outer shell of the building while students gained practical experience by completing the inside finishing work. In recent years, Delhi has earned a national reputation for the excellence of its online programs, which have enabled the campus to meet the educational needs of students who live and work throughout New York and beyond.

Delhi has become a leader in hospitality education. Alumni played a prominent role in raising funds to convert Alumni Hall into a modern hospitality education and conference center. In 1989, the National Restaurant Association honored Delhi as the best two-year Hospitality program in New York State. The Culinary Arts program began in 1994, and four years later the SUNY Board of Trustees approved the college's first baccalaureate degree—a Bachelor of

Food preparation and presentation are a fine art at Delhi.

Business Administration in Hospitality Management. Delhi culinary students won the American Culinary Federation National Championship in 2010 and 2012.

Today, Delhi's over 3,600 students can choose among thirty associate degree programs, which can lead to immediate employment, continuation in Delhi's bachelor degree programs, or transfer to other baccalaureate institutions. The fifteen bachelor degree programs feature hands-on or applied training that builds on a strong base in the liberal arts and sciences.

While many students commute and some enroll in Delhi's online programs, others participate in a residential college experience. Six residential halls provide a home away from home. The campus supports a wide range of cultural and social organizations, and seventeen Broncos teams compete at the intercollegiate level.

The college's commitment to community service was formalized in 1999 with a grant from the A. Lindsay and Olive B. O'Connor Foundation to create the O'Connor Center for Community Engagement. The center matches the needs of area nonprofit organizations with student, faculty, and staff volunteers.

Today, nearly eighty percent of Delhi students participate in community service, and faculty have incorporated service learning throughout the curriculum.

Delhi began celebrating its centennial in 2012, adopting the theme "Celebrating 100 years of Inspiring Minds, Changing Lives." The yearlong celebration became the largest fundraising campaign in Delhi history. Alumni, faculty, staff, and friends responded enthusiastically, raising more than $3.4 million, half of it for student scholarships. As SUNY Delhi enters its second century, the college has clearly fulfilled the vision of the MacDonald sisters to enrich the life of this beautiful rural area. Delhi is an educational leader that serves as a vital economic engine for the larger community that brought it to life, while training young people to contribute to its quality of life.

The fine and liberal arts enrich the Delhi experience.

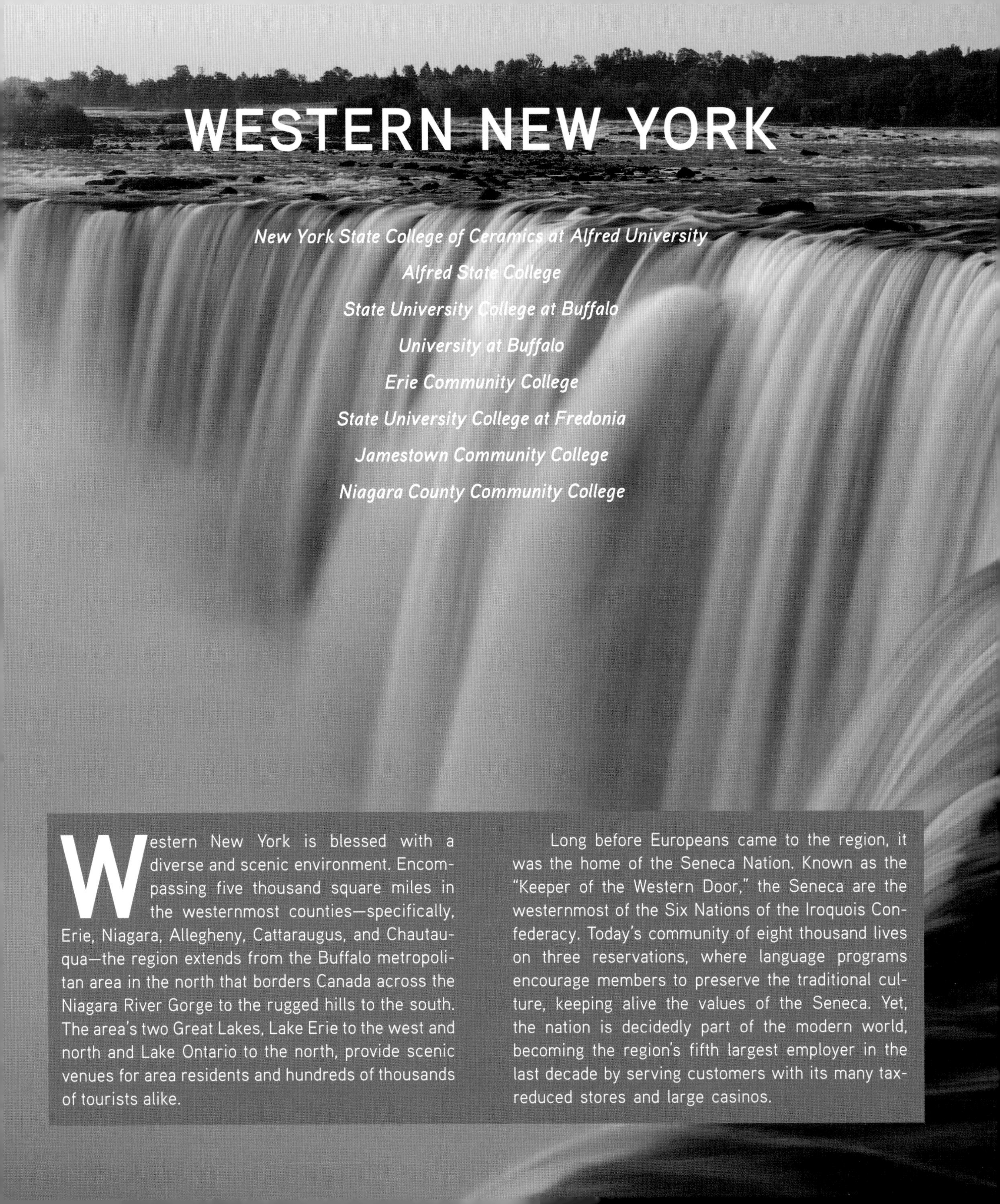

WESTERN NEW YORK

New York State College of Ceramics at Alfred University

Alfred State College

State University College at Buffalo

University at Buffalo

Erie Community College

State University College at Fredonia

Jamestown Community College

Niagara County Community College

Western New York is blessed with a diverse and scenic environment. Encompassing five thousand square miles in the westernmost counties—specifically, Erie, Niagara, Allegheny, Cattaraugus, and Chautauqua—the region extends from the Buffalo metropolitan area in the north that borders Canada across the Niagara River Gorge to the rugged hills to the south. The area's two Great Lakes, Lake Erie to the west and north and Lake Ontario to the north, provide scenic venues for area residents and hundreds of thousands of tourists alike.

Long before Europeans came to the region, it was the home of the Seneca Nation. Known as the "Keeper of the Western Door," the Seneca are the westernmost of the Six Nations of the Iroquois Confederacy. Today's community of eight thousand lives on three reservations, where language programs encourage members to preserve the traditional culture, keeping alive the values of the Seneca. Yet, the nation is decidedly part of the modern world, becoming the region's fifth largest employer in the last decade by serving customers with its many tax-reduced stores and large casinos.

Buffalo and Niagara Falls have contributed greatly to the region's history. Originally settled in the late eighteenth century, the city of Buffalo soon became a commercial center. In 1825, the completion of the Erie Canal further stimulated Buffalo's commercial activity by connecting it through a series of locks and waterways across the state to the Hudson River, to other parts of New York State's burgeoning canal system, and to New York City. As its population grew, Buffalo developed into a leading industrial center, broadcast to the world by its 1901 Pan-American Exposition. In the succeeding decades, as aircraft, automobile, and steel factories lined the shores of Lake Erie, Buffalo and the region boomed, especially during World War II, but as with so many other cities in the Northeast and Midwest, the postwar industrial base slowly eroded. Lost employment led to flight, with fifty percent of the city's residents leaving by 2000. Left behind were unoccupied houses and the city's severely diminished tax base.

The city that had entered the twentieth century with so much optimism, then, seemed to leave it with little else to offer other than the ubiquitous "Buffalo Wings" from the storied Anchor Bar, a string of beautiful, but inadequately tended, Frederick Law Olmsted

1901 Pan-American Exposition.

parks and parkways, and a well-deserved reputation for wonderfully moderate summers, followed by harsh, snowy, dark winters. To many, it appeared that Buffalo approached the twenty-first century with prospects as dim as those of the post-1990s Buffalo Bills.

But the city, like cleaned up Lake Erie, revived. Recent construction in downtown Buffalo has renewed optimism. New buildings on Buffalo's Canal Side and the establishment of local events and concert series in Buffalo's Inner and Outer Harbor forge a new cultural landscape for the city's population. The development of the new Buffalo–Niagara medical complex near downtown, with the SUNY Buffalo School of Medicine as an anchor, and the plans for "Buffalo Billion," which will use a billion dollars in public funding to induce private investment of billions more—has restored confidence.

Twenty miles to the north, the city of Niagara Falls' population has followed an arc resembling Buffalo's, rising steadily through the first half of the twentieth century, peaking in 1960, and then declining by fifty percent over the rest of the century. Many residents worked in local industries that had been drawn to the area by the cheap electricity and waterpower provided by the Niagara River as it ran its thirty-six-mile course from Lake Erie northward to Lake Ontario. One of those industries, many of which fled the region after 1960, was the infamous Hooker Chemical. It sold its "Love Canal" site to the Niagara Falls School District for $1 in 1953, but development in the next two decades revealed toxic industrial pollutants that posed serious dangers to public health. The resulting furor added fuel to the environmental movement of the 1970s and changed the corporate liability laws in the United States.

By 2000, many of the old industrial concerns had been replaced, in part, by tourists drawn to the Falls, which now had one of the largest casinos—owned and operated by the Seneca—in New York. The river continued to flow, serving more than tourists, with the Niagara Power Plant that was constructed in 1961 remaining the greatest single source of electricity in the state. To the east of the river, vineyards,

Albright-Knox Art Gallery.

fruit orchards, and truck farms abound, maintaining the essentially rural character of much of the area.

South of the Buffalo metropolitan area, rolling hills extend into Pennsylvania, providing elevation to blanket the region with snow, lots of snow, every winter. This natural annual cycle has created a number of successful ski resorts that today cater to a wide range of winter outdoor enthusiasts. Since the late nineteenth century, the western end of New York's Southern Tier has been a destination for vacationers who sought to escape the noise, congestion, and hubbub of northeastern cities for a week or more along the shores of Chautauqua Lake. There they found the Chautauqua Institute, which offered a natural setting, educational lectures from some of the most readily recognized public figures of the day, and live entertainment, much of which carried a decidedly Christian message. The combination of education and entertainment had such broad appeal to turn-of-the-century Americans that touring troupes roamed the country under the Chautauqua banner, lecturing and performing to small-town audiences from one coast

to the other before they were displaced by the more modern media, radio and movies. The entertainment traditions of the area extended into the twentieth century through Lucille Ball, who hailed from Jamestown, the small industrial city at the southern end of the lake.

The eight SUNY campuses of western New York offer a range of educational opportunities and unique histories. SUNY Buffalo was founded as a private school in 1846 and then incorporated into the SUNY system in 1962 as one of the four SUNY research universities. It has become one of the most important linchpins in the economic revival underway, providing irreplaceable intellectual capital and a core of technological and scientific knowledge and skills. Buffalo State College has grown from its nineteenth-century roots as a normal school, as did SUNY Fredonia fifty miles to the southeast along the shore of Lake Erie. Both comprehensive colleges maintain their traditions by continuing to offer programs to prepare teachers and school leaders, and each has developed distinctive programs such as the visual arts for Buffalo State and music for SUNY Fredonia.

Southward in "Happy Valley," deep in the Southern Tier, are two SUNY institutions, the New York State College of Ceramics at Alfred University and Alfred State College, that evolved from state-funded specialized schools that were legislatively authorized at the turn of the twentieth century as state-supported units of Alfred University. The College of Ceramics has maintained its status as a contract college within Alfred, becoming one of the world's leading schools of ceramic engineering and the fine arts. It and neighboring Alfred State College were incorporated into the SUNY system in 1948, the same year that the then-named School of Agriculture achieved its independence from Alfred University. Today, its technology-centered programs prepare students for either immediate employment in western New York businesses and service agencies or continued study in baccalaureate programs at either Alfred State College or another college.

Western New York communities strongly support three community colleges—Niagara County Community College in the north, Erie Community College with its three campuses around Buffalo, and Jamestown Community College to the south—that serve both students and their communities in extraordinary and distinctive ways. Niagara County Community College, for example, recently created the Niagara Falls Culinary Institute, designed to support the tourist industry of the region.

In looking to the future, community leaders throughout the region seek to attract even more advanced manufacturing businesses by a combination of cutting-edge technological research, a highly educated workforce, low housing costs, and generous public programs that leverage private investment with public resources. In each of these areas, SUNY's campuses are positioned to play a central role, one they embrace as part of their public missions.

Downtown Buffalo.

NEW YORK STATE COLLEGE OF CERAMICS AT ALFRED UNIVERSITY

Exemplifying SUNY's extraordinary variety is its statutory college operated by the private Alfred University. The College of Ceramics is an internationally acclaimed institution nestled in the foothills of the Allegheny Mountains that shares a small village with SUNY's "Alfred State College" on the other side of the valley.

Alfred University was founded in 1832 by Seventh Day Baptists, a small Protestant denomination that worshiped on Saturdays and maintained an unusual commitment to gender equality. Thus, it was one of the first coeducational institutions in the nation and a fervent supporter of women's rights and other reform movements in an unlikely small village setting. With both an academy and a college, the early university offered courses crossing the lines that today are defined as secondary and higher education. By the end of the nineteenth century it was becoming more truly collegiate.

In the late 1800s, Alfred University president Boothe C. Davis and local businessman John Jake Merrill seized a unique opportunity to offer industrial training in clay working to support the region's brick and roofing tile industry. In 1900, Governor Theodore Roosevelt signed legislation creating the New York State School of Clayworking and Ceramics at Alfred University. A separate building was completed the following year, and Charles F. Binns, a prominent figure in the ceramic and glass industries, was appointed the first director. With the help of art educator Lillie W. Tourtellotte and chemist Edward S. Babcock, Binns began working to fulfill the mandate "to give scientific, technical, art and practical training for the manufacture of all kinds of ceramic products and to

Founding director Binns working in his studio in the 1920s.

Students removing their fired pieces from the kiln circa 1900.

conduct experiments in reference to the value for commercial purposes of the clays and shales of New York State." By 1913, the school offered two distinct degree programs—a Bachelor of Science in Ceramic Engineering and a Bachelor of Science in Applied Arts—a clear precursor of the college's present organization into a School of Engineering and a School of Art and Design.

In 1932, the School of Clayworking and Ceramics was renamed the New York State College of Ceramics, and the following years were characterized by curricular diversification. A new Glass Technology Department provided specialized science training. An expanding faculty and new facilities enabled the college to venture into graduate education, beginning with master's degrees in Ceramic Engineering and Applied Arts. New applications of ceramics led

to the growth of advanced materials research fueled by federal funding. The Department of Applied Art increased its focus on design and played a critical role in the success of Glidden Pottery stoneware that was produced in Alfred from 1940 until 1957.

Transforming clay into art.

Temperatures go ever higher.

The College of Ceramics Glass Science degree stands alone in American higher education.

As a result of the GI Bill, enrollment increased by one-third, and the campus facilities—both temporary and permanent—were expanded to accommodate the students and their families. Then, in 1948, the college joined the newly formed SUNY system. Since joining SUNY, the international reputation of the College of Ceramics as a center for education, research, and creativity has continued to grow, as has its curriculum. The School of Art and Design now offers the BFA degree, the BS degree in Art History, the MFA degrees in Ceramic Art, in Sculpture/Dimensional Studies, and in Electronic Integrated Art.

In 2005 the Engineering program was endowed by the Kyocera Corporation to honor its founder, Dr. Kazuo Inamori. The Inamori School of Engineering offers undergraduate and graduate degrees in Biomaterials Engineering (BS and MS), Ceramic Engineering (BS through PhD), Glass Engineering Science (BS through PhD), and Materials Science and Engineering (BS through PhD). The Inamori School is one of only two institutions in the United States that offers a BS in Ceramic Engineering, and it is the only American college that offers degrees in glass science.

The Hall of Glass Science and Engineering was built by the State University of New York Construction Fund with additional contributions from General Electric and the Keck Foundation. Dedicated in April 1999, it contains glass science laboratories—including a glass fiber-drawing unit—a specially equipped biomaterials laboratory, and office space for graduate students and faculty members.

The Inamori School of Engineering has a vibrant research program sponsored by federal, state, and industry funding. The university's Center for Advanced Ceramic Technology facilitates collaboration between academic researchers and New York State's advanced materials industries. Recently, the state invested over $6 million in a Center for High Temperature Characterization to provide advanced characterization services to the state's industry.

A specialized library emerged under the leadership of Dean Samuel Scholes in the late 1940s. Today, the appropriately named Scholes Library, built in 1990, holds internationally significant collections on the art, science, engineering, technology, and history of ceramics and glass as well as valuable holdings in art history, electronic media, glass art, photography, and sculpture.

True to its original mission, the College of Ceramics benefits New York State through its unique combination of expertise in the areas of engineering, science, the visual arts, and design. The School of Art and Design serves as a cultural focal point for rural western New York. Each year, the school hosts dozens of exhibitions featuring emerging and established artists in three galleries. The annual senior show, which features the artwork of every graduating senior, is a cherished community event that attracts over a thousand visitors.

The Alfred Ceramic Art Museum is a teaching and research facility housing nearly eight thousand ceramic and glass objects ranging from ancient pieces of anthropological interest to advanced ceramics created by utilizing advanced ceramic engineering technology. A $10 million private donation has underwritten construction of a new building that will permit bringing much of the extensive collection out of storage and into display.

Students learn fine arts techniques and display the results to the community.

In addition, the Inamori Kyocera Fine Ceramics Museum in Binns-Merrill Hall, which opened in 2011, features the history of the technological progression of fine ceramics (also known as advanced or engineered ceramics) and displays cutting-edge applications. The museum is the first of its kind in the United States to provide a comprehensive overview of fine ceramics history and technology.

The second smallest of SUNY's colleges and universities, the New York State College of Ceramics at Alfred University is truly a hidden gem that draws international attention to a small village in western New York.

ALFRED STATE COLLEGE

On May 6, 1908, a stroke of Governor Charles Evans Hughes's pen launched the "New York State School of Agriculture at Alfred University." This initiative responded to both the pressure from granges and other agrarian organizations concerned about the future of western New York agriculture and the lobbying efforts of Alfred University President Boothe Davis. The New York State Legislature had already created agricultural colleges at Cornell University and St. Lawrence

A muddy beginning—President Davis leads the parade celebrating the founding in 1908.

University (now State University of New York College of Technology at Canton), and Alfred University already served as the host campus for the New York State College of Clayworking and Ceramics (today's New York State College of Ceramics at Alfred University), making it a perfect candidate to house the state's third college of agriculture.

A year later, four faculty welcomed forty-six students for the first classes, thirty-six men and ten women, and no tuition was charged. By 1912 enrollment had swelled to over two hundred. The curriculum also expanded, offering courses not only in agriculture but also in cement work, cooking, drafting and shop work, English, farm accounts, farm surveying, home nursing, landscaping, veterinary studies, and woodworking. The school also undertook agricultural extension work, sponsoring speakers to bring modern methods to local farmers.

After the promising beginning, the school went through uncertain times. In the decade following World War I, enrollment declined to a low of only forty-eight students by 1925. Two years later, Alfred University gave up administrative oversight of the school when the New York State Legislature placed the agriculture schools at Alfred and St. Lawrence universities under the supervision of the State Education Department.

In 1937 a radical shift in mission started Alfred on the path to its modern role as one of SUNY's Colleges of Technology. In that year the State Education Department authorized the agricultural schools at Alfred, Canton, Delhi, and Morrisville to offer technical courses to bring technical vocational training to rural areas of the state. Accordingly, the school was renamed the New York State Agricultural and Technical Institute at Alfred University in 1941.

With the creation of the State University of New York in 1948, the Agricultural and Technical Institute at Alfred became fully independent of Alfred University, although its main buildings were surrounded by university property. Throughout the 1950s Alfred University pressured SUNY to either move the institute or integrate it into the host university. By 1955 the institute's enrollment had surpassed the university's by several hundred students. Finally, land on a largely undeveloped hill across the valley on the other side of the village was purchased for a new campus for the newly named State University of New York College of Agriculture and Technology at Alfred.

Construction began and the supportive Governor Nelson A. Rockefeller made an impromptu visit to the campus on February 11, 1965, to check on progress. The Huntington Administration Building and the Hinkle Memorial Library were both completed later that

The governor always enjoyed new construction.

year. In November, SUNY chancellor Samuel Gould (who was then called "president") led a procession of students and faculty transferring the library books to their new home. The Orvis Activities Center was completed soon after, and 214 acres near the Alfred campus were deeded over by the US Department of Agriculture for the Agriculture program.

In addition, Alfred State College created a Vocational Division (now the School of Applied Technology) by renovating eight buildings at the deactivated Sinclair oil refinery in Wellsville, and classes began there in October of 1966. The physical plant has continued to expand, featuring a Workforce Development Center. Reflecting the Wellsville campus's intersection of traditional skills and innovation, the building trades program students constructed the Green Home Project, a net-zero energy showcase home. The Wellsville campus also offers programs in fields such as the electrical trades, heavy equipment operation, automotive mechanics, and the culinary arts.

Construction continued at the Alfred campus as well, with the completion of the Hunter Student Development Center and the recently constructed Student Leadership Center, a comprehensive con-

The trademark bell tower arrives.

nection point for students, staff, and faculty to access leadership and civic engagement opportunities on campus.

Alfred State College students can pursue associate degrees in either applied fields or those designed to prepare students for a bachelor's degree program. SUNY authorized Alfred to award AAS degrees in 1951 and expanded its charge to include AA and AS degrees in 1967. A major mission expansion began in 1985 when the college offered its first baccalaureate degree, in engineering technology, in conjunction with the State University of New York at Binghamton. Soon after, Alfred was authorized to develop its own programs, and today's students can work toward more than twenty bachelor degrees awarded by the college. Some reflect the college's origins, such as the Nursing and Mechanical Engineering Technology programs, while others are in the arts and science disciplines, and still others are in areas that the founders could not have imagined, such as Information Technology.

Campus life has evolved along with the expanding curriculum. Increasingly, Alfred students seek a full collegiate experience. The inauguration of annual homecoming celebrations in 2008 added a taste of traditional college life. Another indication of that maturation is the recent move of Alfred State College's Pioneers athletic teams from community college competition to NCAA Division III status. And a vibrant intramural program even includes a very competitive polo team. Residential options include over twenty lifestyle and affinity group choices.

The village of Alfred offers students a true "college town." Just down the hill from the campus is an attractive village with a classic Main Street and two thousand residents that welcomes over six thousand

Building the home of the future on the Wellsville campus.

The center of student life.

students at the university, the College of Ceramics, and Alfred State College. An annual town-gown feature is Hot Dog Day, a charity festival begun by two Alfred State College students in 1972.

Alfred State College has come a long way since President Davis led a team of oxen in celebration of Governor Hughes's signing the enabling legislation for the school and a $75,000 authorization for construction and equipment. A half century later, Rockefeller-era construction amounted to $75,000,000—one thousand times that first appropriation. Today 275 faculty and staff support more than seventy programs in agriculture, health, business, and engineering technologies, the liberal arts and sciences, and in applied technology. The campus's 3,700 students benefit from a 108-year history of building a college that continues its founding commitments to agriculture while offering other programs that were unimagined in 1908.

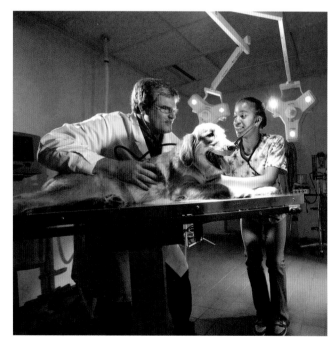

Veterinary Technology students learn to care for their future patients.

STATE UNIVERSITY COLLEGE
AT BUFFALO

I n 1871, Buffalo's dramatic growth led to the need for many more public school teachers, which in turn led to the opening of the State Normal School. Fifteen faculty provided instruction for the eighty-six students (seventy-five of whom were women) and a School of Practice with 195 children. All activity—learning and teaching—occurred in a three-story building on the West Side of the city.

Over the years, the curriculum and the campus grew to meet the changing requirements of its student body. In 1888 a science building, connected to the original building by a second-story bridge,

A 1928 sketch of the campus's five buildings.

was built. Since Buffalo was more industrialized than Albany and in greater need of vocational training teachers, the Industrial Arts Department of the State Teachers College at Albany was transferred to Buffalo in 1906. The Household Arts Department, later known as Home Economics, was established in 1910; its students spent extended periods living at the "Practice House." In 1919 the Home Economics program was lengthened to four years, resulting in a Bachelor of Science degree.

The State Normal School began granting four-year degrees in education in 1925 for its rapidly growing student

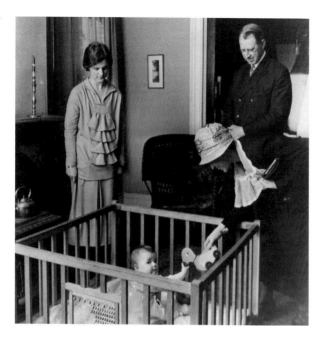

Practice House, where students learned the art of child care.

body. Striving to offer the most useful and innovative curriculum, the school established the Art Education program in 1930, becoming the only such state-supported program in the nation. The administration added special education to the offerings in 1944; the Exceptional Education Department focused primarily on the education of physically challenged children.

Not surprisingly, enrollment continued to grow, necessitating major expansions of the physical campus. In 1946 the state granted the newly renamed New York State College for Teachers at Buffalo a million-dollar allotment to add three new buildings, including a library, and undertake major renovations on two others. In 1948, the college joined the SUNY system, and shortly thereafter again changed its name, this time to the State University College for Teachers at Buffalo. With 1,971 full-time students, it was the largest teachers' college in New York. During the next six decades, buildings continued to be added to the campus at a steady rate, culminating in 2011's groundbreaking for the $36.5 million, 87,000-square-foot Technology Building, which houses Engineering Technology, Computer Information Systems, and Fashion and Textile Technology.

Under SUNY, the college continued to thrive and innovate, allowing students to expand their educational experience well beyond the borders of western New York. In 1961 it became the first SUNY school to offer a study-abroad program, a semester in Siena, Italy. The Center for China Studies, which opened in 2000, works to encourage international research and collaborative opportunities with universities in China. In 2013, the Fashion and Textile Technology department began an exchange program with Beijing University. Today, the International Education Office facilitates student study in Australia, England, Italy, the Netherlands, Quebec, and Spain.

In the 1960s, following the recommendations of the Heald Commission, the college instituted a new curriculum, featuring traditional liberal arts and science programs. In 1963, the college received permission to offer Bachelor of Arts degrees in twelve dis-

The new Technology Building, a major part of the building program in the last decade.

Campus House, the learning lab for the hospitality program.

celebrate its sesquicentennial, underscoring its vital place in the city's life. The rich ethnic and racial diversity of the city is today reflected on the campus, both in programs and in the campus community. The Educational Opportunity program, for example, was organized in the mid-1960s to provide opportunities to disadvantaged students, and the college was an early and eager participant. The Bulger Lifelong Learning Center, designed to meet the needs of nontraditional students, opened in 1983. And, in 1998, with the opening of the Frank C. Moore Student Apartment Complex, the college provided on-campus housing for students with children.

ciplines, and by the end of the decade it had added Bachelor of Science degrees in Industrial Technology and Home Economics. Disciplinary graduate degrees soon followed with Master of Arts programs in Chemistry, Biology, and Philosophy, and Master of Science degree programs in Creative Studies, Criminal Justice, and Clinical Dietetics.

Buffalo State has deep ties to the city and the region, and it strives to prepare students for regional employment. In 1995, the college created a multidisciplinary degree in Great Lakes Environmental Studies, and the Great Lakes Center today coordinates research on Lakes Erie and Ontario and works with other colleges and universities to both understand and protect the vast Great Lakes ecosystem. And, the hospitality program is the largest in SUNY. In 2001 the program moved into Campus House, the former president's residence, which was renovated to serve as a social club for the campus and a teaching laboratory that provides students with hands-on experience in food preparation, service, and management.

Buffalo State works hard to maintain a strong relationship with the community and to provide learning opportunities beyond the traditional college student. In 1982, Buffalo State helped the city of Buffalo

The college has often reflected the larger social and political issues of the time. For example, while student enrollment had always included a large number of women, the college administration was exclusively male until, in response to the agitation for increased roles for women, Catherine Reed was appointed the first dean of women in 1926. In the post–World War II era, enrollment exploded, particularly that of male veterans, and then two decades later, Buffalo State experienced the antiwar student protests of the late 1960s and early 1970s. While much less controversial, the campus has hosted important figures such as Colin Powell, Hillary Rodham Clinton, and Julian Bond over the past several decades.

Buffalo State College's consistent support for the arts has been a distinctive feature of the campus. The graduate program in Art Conservation, one of only three such departments in the country, moved to Buffalo State from its previous home at the State University College at Oneonta in 1983. In 2014, the department received a $1.25 million grant from the Mellon Foundation to enhance its highly regarded, unique curriculum. Highly competitive, it only admits ten students a year. And across the street from the campus are the Buffalo History Museum and the renowned Albright-Knox Art Gallery, while the

The Community Academic Center, where the college's commitment to the Westside community and cradle-to-career education meet.

magnificent Burchfield Penney Art Center, the only museum dedicated to the art and artists of western New York, is on the campus.

From the perspective of 1871, today's Buffalo State would be unrecognizable. With its more than eleven thousand students, it dwarfs those humble beginnings. But, not all would be unfamiliar. From the beginning, its mission to serve the society of which it is so vital a part has been constant. While that mission in 1871 had a singular programmatic focus, the education and training of teachers, it is much more complex today, offering 160 programs in more than sixty disciplines. Proud of its heritage, the college declared 2013–2014 as the "Year of the Teacher."

Teaching art conservation.

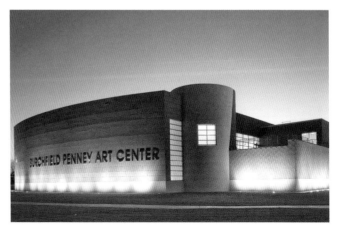

The Burchfield Penney Art Center at night.

STATE UNIVERSITY OF NEW YORK AT BUFFALO

SUNY's largest institution and one of its four university centers, the University at Buffalo has traveled a unique path to its current configuration. A private university until 1962, it has emerged as a major research university, a member of the prestigious Association of American Universities, and in recent decades a leader in the Buffalo area's resurgent economy.

The school's roots reach back to 1846 when the New York State Legislature incorporated the University of Buffalo with a broad mandate to create "academic, theological, legal and medical" departments. But the com-

World War II veterans swelled enrollment and shaped a collegiate culture.

munity leaders who were raising funds to launch the institution were mainly interested in the latter. The Medical Department remained the only branch for four decades despite the efforts of the university chancellor, former United States president Millard Fillmore, to broaden the university's mission. Then, in the 1880s and 1890s a flurry of professional schools, for Pharmacy, Law, and Dentistry, were added.

In 1909 the university purchased 106 acres and buildings that had served as the Erie County almshouse with the intention of creating a college of arts and sciences. The next year the famous and powerful

The team that said *no*.

Flexner Report on North American medical education was published, demanding that medical students have several years of liberal education. Buffalo had no choice but to strengthen those offerings. Building proceeded, and slowly the "Main Street campus" took shape, housing all divisions except Law.

Samuel Capen, chancellor from 1922 to 1950, oversaw the development of a complete university. He promoted the development of a full undergraduate arts and sciences program as well as graduate degrees in the academic disciplines. Additional professional schools were also developed, including Business, Education, Engineering, Social Work, and Nursing.

The influx of veterans sponsored by the GI Bill and then the construction of dormitories created the basis for a more traditional student life, including serious intercollegiate athletics. Most famously, the 1958 Bulls football team went 8–1 and won the Lambert Cup but declined a bid to the Tangerine Bowl in Orlando, Florida, when the team discovered the invitation was dependent upon leaving its two African American players behind.

In 1962, the private University of Buffalo made a dramatic transition when it joined SUNY. The transition was not always smooth as the many stakeholders sought to ensure that their own requirements were met. However, joining SUNY meant that the university no longer depended on tuition, and, in fact, tuition and fees were lowered. The relatively deep pockets of the state in the Rockefeller years ensured that faculty and staff salaries increased and there were plentiful funds for expansion of the physical plant.

The visible manifestation of the new revenue stream was the construction of the North campus. In 1964 land was purchased for a new campus in Amherst, three miles from the Main Street campus. Four years later, plans were unveiled for a massive $650,000,000 campus potentially boosting university enrollment to forty thousand. But such expansive dreams were shattered by a declining Northeastern economy and a changing political climate, especially after major student unrest at Buffalo led to SUNY chancellor Gould's resignation and undercut public support. New enrollment goals were still ambitious, but with a target of twenty-five thousand.

Despite the turmoil and setbacks, the 1960s and early 1970s were years of dynamic, if sometimes traumatic, growth. Martin Meyerson, former acting chancellor of University of California, Berkeley, was chosen as the University at Buffalo's first president after the university joined the SUNY system. His administration was tasked with converting a modest regional university into a major research university. Under Meyerson, UB began the challenging process of recruiting top-flight students, faculty, and staff. He took advantage of his extensive network within elite higher education to attract nationally important figures and national attention to the university.

Meyerson's presidency and the optimism that

accompanied his appointment were casualties of student unrest, but construction of the new North campus and expansion continued. The first building opened in 1973, and by 1977 it was officially designated the central campus. Today, it covers more than one thousand acres and has 128 buildings, while the Main Street (or South) campus houses fifty-one buildings on 154 acres. Today, nearly 30,000S students are taught by over 1,750 faculty. Students are able to pursue more than one hundred undergraduate degrees, 205 master's degrees, and ninety-four doctoral and professional degrees in eleven professional schools and the College of the Arts and Sciences, leading to about 7,500 degrees awarded annually.

From the time of its merger with the SUNY system, the University at Buffalo has worked to maintain close and cooperative ties to its community. President Meyerson stated that the school "must

The Bull does double duty as athletic mascot and guard of the Center for the Arts.

have a close and dynamic relationship with the community . . ." This mission is exemplified by the UB Downtown Gateway Complex in a transformed abandoned factory that facilitates community outreach, service, and research programs. At the same complex, the Arthur O. Eve Educational Opportunity Center opened in spring 2013. Another example is the Center for the Arts, established in 1994, which sponsors high-quality visual and performing arts for the university and the wider community.

As befitting SUNY's western-most university center, UB has worked consistently to support the economy of western New York through research initiatives. With approximately $388 million in annual research expenditures, UB's economic impact on New York State is $2.18 billion. For instance, the formation

A time of campus unrest.

The Gateway Center brings the university into the heart of the city.

of the Calspan–University at Buffalo Research Corporation has supported wind tunnel research in the aeronautics field and other engineering activities. UB maintains an active program of business engagement and outreach in which the university works with businesses to ensure students are being prepared to take advantage of the jobs available in the region and that businesses are assisted in the utilization of the latest technological innovations.

In keeping with its nineteenth-century roots, UB's Jacobs School of Medicine and Biomedical Sciences remains a leader in medical education and innovation. Located adjacent to the site of the 1849 medical building, the university's new Downtown Campus is integrated into the Buffalo Niagara Medical Campus, facilitating collaboration with local research hospitals to make strides in emerging fields such as medical instrumentation. UB's New York State Center of Excellence in Bioinformatics and Life Sciences provides facilities and R&D to both scientists and industry engaged in biomedical research.

UB's reach extends well beyond western New York State. More than ten percent of its students participate in study abroad, five times the national average. The University at Buffalo has a higher proportion of international students, nearly twenty percent, than any other comprehensive public research university in the nation, a tradition that dates back to 1847 when two Canadian students became the University at Buffalo's first international students. Today, they come to western New York from 115 different countries. In turn, UB students can take advantage of international exchange programs with more than seventy-five universities.

After the turmoil of the late 1960s and early 1970s, SUNY Buffalo has emerged as one of the nation's rising research universities. Regionally, its production of human capital and cutting-edge research has made the university a linchpin of Buffalo's future.

Jacobs School of Medicine and Biomedical Sciences.

ERIE COMMUNITY COLLEGE

Serving Erie County and communities in western New York for more than six decades, Erie Community College welcomes students to any one of its three campuses: in Williamsville in the north; in downtown Buffalo; and in Orchard Park, the home of the Buffalo Bills, in the south. Its historic goal has been to provide students of the region with an education that equips them for jobs in the regional workforce, a mission that has become much more complex over time.

Unlike most New York community colleges, ECC's history began immediately after World War II, when the New York State Legislature established the New York State Institute of Applied Arts and Sciences at Buffalo in April 1946. The school was one of five such two-year schools offering technical-vocational education tuition free to high school graduates; the others were in Binghamton, New York City, Utica, and White Plains. A small team developed the plans for the school while operating out of an office building that once housed the Pierce-Arrow Motor Car Company, the luxury car company that fell victim to the Great Depression in 1938.

Buffalo's institute offered eight programs, admitting sixty students to each: Construction Technology, Dental Hygiene, Electrical Technology, Mechanical Technology, Food Service Administration, Chemical Technology, Metallurgical Technology, and Optical Technology. The technology programs participated in a unique cooperative education program in which students divided their time between the classroom and the job site. Ironically, it was phased out in the mid-1960s, a half century before SUNY's current push for cooperative and experiential education.

The open atrium of the downtown campus. A place for refreshment, rest, or contemplation between classes.

In 1948, the school joined the new SUNY system. Two years later, the state passed the Community College Law that required two-year schools to have local, usually county, sponsorship. In 1953, Erie County reluctantly assumed a share of the financial responsibility for the college under the original state funding model for community colleges: one-third

The stairs to the library at the Williamsville campus.

each by the state, local government, and students. This led to very modest tuition charges for the first time in 1953. Although it was technically a community college, its name, the Erie County Technical Institute, conveyed the reality that the school did not offer liberal arts programs.

In the mid-1960s, the school faced increasing pressure to offer a liberal arts curriculum designed to prepare students for transfer to baccalaureate degree programs. A vice chancellor of the SUNY system noted that only two community colleges did not offer liberal arts: Erie County Tech and the Fashion Institute of Technology in New York City. Since FIT was never intended to operate as a traditional college, Erie was identified as the lone holdout.

Despite strong feelings among the faculty and administration at Erie that the college should remain true to its vocational-education roots, the school began offering programs based in the liberal arts in 1969, with Nursing, Engineering Science, and Inhalation Therapy also finding places in the curriculum that year. The new name, Erie Community College, reflected the changes that added new programs without supplanting the strength and breadth of the college's technical and vocational programs.

Like many other community colleges across the state and nation, ECC appealed to nontraditional students, adults who had family and/or work responsibilities. To accommodate their schedules, the college established an Evening Division, which proved to be very popular, enrolling several thousand. At the time of its creation, the Evening Division was entirely self-supporting.

As the total number of students at the college increased, the physical structure needed to grow as well. In 1960 the Erie County Technical Institute moved to Williamsville, north and east of the city

The South Courtyard in Orchard Park.

A lighter moment in a class for police officers, one of the many groups who use the expertise available at ECC.

of Buffalo, to the site of ECC's current North campus. The downtown Buffalo campus, which was housed in the former Bishop O'Hern High School, opened in 1971. The addition of this facility made ECC one of the first multicampus colleges in New York State. In January 1982, the downtown campus relocated to its present site, the renovated Old Post Office, a magnificent setting. The need to offer greater accessibility to students from the "Southtowns" of the county was recognized in the early 1970s, leading to the opening of a third site, the South campus in Orchard Park in 1974.

Since opening the Buffalo campus, ECC has maintained strong ties with the downtown Buffalo community. For example, the school recently partnered with the Buffalo City Mission, enabling nearly thirty of the mission's residents to study subjects such as welding, website design, and culinary arts, which prepare them to take up living-wage jobs upon graduation.

Over the decades, the number of programs offered at ECC has grown dramatically, as has its impact on the economy of western New York. From its inception as the New York State Institute of Applied Arts and Sciences at Buffalo until the present, ECC has tailored its curriculum to the needs of employers in western New York. In 1965, for example, Data Processing, Secretarial Science, and Business Administration were added. In 2011 it became possible for students to receive degrees in Criminal Justice and Homeland Security.

In 2014, ECC became the first New York State community college to offer a degree in Nanotechnology. The college developed this program as it became clear that the Buffalo Billion startups at the newly created Buffalo Niagara Medical campus and the Riverbend Commerce Park would create a significant num-

Happy students between classes.

ber of jobs for graduates in the field. That same year, the college submitted a proposal to the State Education Department to offer a certificate program in Brewing Science and Service, designed to train students in the growing field of craft beer production in a one-year program that includes interning with a local brewer.

Today, ECC has partnerships with more than two hundred local and regional businesses and has an estimated $668 million impact on the economy of western New York.

From its roots as a technical school serving local industries, ECC has grown into one of the largest colleges in western New York, today serving over fourteen thousand students on its three campuses. And, the original eight-program curriculum has mushroomed into the more than ninety associate degree, certificate, and online programs that ECC offers its diverse student body and community. The college is committed to providing the county's residents with the educational resources necessary to prepare them for success, whether they seek immediate employment, transfer to a four-year institution, or personal enrichment.

A student intently concentrating on his work in a science lab.

STATE UNIVERSITY COLLEGE
AT FREDONIA

On its striking 256-acre campus, the State University College at Fredonia embodies in its architecture the varied nature of its historic development. An outer ring of traditional brick buildings encircles a central complex of strikingly modern architecture. Over its nearly two-hundred-year history, Fredonia has strived to retain the best of its traditions while continuing to embrace the new.

Like many SUNY colleges, Fredonia traces its history back to a nineteenth-century academy and normal school, both of which struggled financially. In 1826, Fredonia Academy opened under the leadership of Principal Austin Smith,

The clocktower.

built on a lot donated for that purpose by Hezekiah Barker in 1821. Five years of fundraising finally garnered sufficient funds from the state and the local community for the project to proceed. Within a year fifty-five girls and eighty-one boys were enrolled, reaching a peak enrollment of 217 in 1856.

But the academy ran into serious financial problems during the Civil War and temporarily shut down. Providentially, a lifeline was thrown when New York decided to create four new normal schools. The community rallied behind Fredonia's candidacy, raising $100,000 to fund a new building, an amazing sum for a community of less than 2,500. Fredonia's chances were probably not hurt by

Home of Fredonia Normal School from 1868 until the disastrous 1900 fire.

the fact that Governor Reuben Fenton was a Fredonia Academy alumnus. The bid was successful, and in December 1867 classes resumed in the newly designated New York State Normal School, with an initial enrollment of eighty-five women and sixty-two men.

Fredonia operated as a normal school for eighty-two years. For much of that time, it teetered on the edge of closing its doors due to unsteady enrollment and erratic state funding. Further trouble ensued when on December 14, 1900, a fire broke out, killing six students and the janitor as well as destroying most of the school building. This tragedy led the Regents to ban dormitories from all of its normal schools.

Fortunately, the New York State Legislature stepped in and funded reconstruction. Classes continued in temporary quarters until completion of the new building, later dubbed "Old Main," two years later. Although enrollments remained unpredictable, sufficient growth ensued to justify purchasing fifty-eight acres on the other side of the village and begin planning a new campus. The first building was completed in 1938. In 1942, like other New York normal schools, Fredonia became a state teachers' college, adding a fourth year of instruction that led to a baccalaureate degree. And in 1948 Fredonia joined the newly created SUNY system, thus ending the school's long history of uncertainty.

As a part of the larger system, Fredonia began to expand. The 1950s marked a period of growth and innovation at the college. Study abroad began with a junior semester in Antwerp. A College Preview program targeted talented high school seniors, faculty created more challenging courses, and admission criteria became more selective. Offerings in the liberal arts were strengthened when the Division of the Humanities was created in 1958. Two years later Fredonia received authorization from SUNY to grant the BA degree in addition to its degree in education.

The growth that began in the 1950s escalated in the 1960s. Enrollment more than doubled from 1,368 in 1961 to 3,226 in 1968, while the teaching faculty tripled. The drive was on to create a multipurpose college with broad academic offerings. Both the Science and Social Science departments were subdivided into more focused departments such as Biology, Chemistry, History, and Sociology. And, teacher education was revised in 1964 as the school implemented the Conant Plan, resulting in broader and more theoretical course offerings. In order to keep pace with the changes, the college administration invested heavily in the library.

As the campus grew, more physical space was urgently needed. In 1968, the college engaged the leading architectural firm of I. M. Pei to design a complex of ten interconnected buildings within

Carrying on Fredonia's long history of training teachers.

The prize-winning Reed Library.

a circular perimeter, Ring Road. It has become a famous exemplar of modern architecture, and the Reed Library earned the 1969 Prestressed Concrete Institute Award. Included in the complex were the Michael Rockefeller Arts Center; Maytum Hall, the administration building; and the Williams Center student union. The plan also included some of the earliest suite-style residence halls.

In addition to teacher training, Fredonia is renowned for its music program, the origins of which date back to the 1880s. Mason Hall, built for the music program, was the first building completed on the new campus in the late 1930s. The program's reputation and breadth has grown since them. In addition to training performers, the program trains students in music education, performance, composition, music theater, music therapy, and sound recording.

Today, the college's nearly five thousand undergraduate and graduate students enjoy a vibrant cam-

Building Fredonia's musical tradition.

Raising money for a good cause.

Bringing drama to western New York.

pus life in a rural and village environment. Fourteen residence halls provide a home away from home for most students. The Blue Devils compete in seventeen intercollegiate sports. Fredonia sponsors WCVF-FM, a National Public Radio affiliate, and has its own television station, WNYF, both of which rely on student participation. Budding journalists contribute to *The Leader*, the venerable campus newspaper founded in 1899. The Volunteer and Community Services Office coordinates a number of outreach programs and the annual Pink the Rink hockey game that raises money for cancer research at Roswell Park.

Fredonia's musical tradition extends beyond the campus. Through the Musical Journeys program founded in 2005, Fredonia students and faculty offer a broad range of individual instrumental and vocal instruction to all ages across western New York. Its activities include summer music programs, the New Horizons Band of Western New York, the Chautauqua Children's Chorale, and other ensem-

bles. Through music, theater, and dance programs, Fredonia enhances the western New York cultural scene.

The college plays a growing role in the region's economy. Through the Community Partners program, public relations students and faculty help local programs, such as Chautauqua Rails to Trails and Greystone Nature Preserve, promote their activities. The Fredonia Technology Incubator, founded in 2007 and located near the Dunkirk waterfront just north of the campus on the shores of Lake Erie, works with other Chautauqua County agencies to encourage and assist business startups.

The college has anchored the economy of the village of Fredonia for most of the past century, and mindful of its special role as a public college, it looks forward to continuing its contributions to the economic and cultural life of both the immediate area—Chautauqua County and western New York— and the state.

JAMESTOWN COMMUNITY COLLEGE

I n 1948 interested citizens and the Jamestown Chamber of Commerce petitioned the new State University of New York for a community college. The City of Jamestown agreed to sponsor what became Jamestown Community College, New York State's first locally sponsored public two-year college, when the SUNY Board of Trustees granted final authorization in February 1950. Unlike many other New York State community colleges, Jamestown's first programs focused on the liberal arts and sciences and were designed to prepare students for successful transfer to baccalaureate programs.

A 1950s science class in the original campus building.

Using classrooms and science laboratories at the Jamestown High School, the college registered its first students in September 1950. It soon moved into a mansion, but by the late 1950s, expansion required larger facilities. Thus, in 1959, JCC acquired 107 acres on the eastern edge of Jamestown for a permanent campus. In 1962, the college opened the doors of Hamilton Collegiate Center, the first building on the new campus.

Today, the Jamestown campus features eight academic buildings, including the recently opened Science Center, three residential living halls, and athletic facilities. Opened in the fall of 2011, the

The Jamestown campus, in a parklike setting.

Science Center was designed to meet LEED (Leadership in Energy and Environmental Design) silver standards and is a showplace for sustainability in building design and operation, featuring a number of "green" features to promote energy conservation and environmentally conscious thinking.

Housed within the Science Center are Jamestown's associate degree programs in Math/Sciences, Sciences, Environmental Science, and Biotechnology. The center features state-of-the-art classrooms, labs, and prep rooms for courses in biology, biotechnology, chemistry, and geology as well as

Biotechnology students working in the new facilities with modern equipment in the Science Center.

a student study area, loft lounge, greenhouse, and vegetative roof.

The college has expanded over the years, adding another campus in Olean, fifty miles east of Jamestown in neighboring Cattaraugus County, and two extension sites—in Dunkirk in the north on Lake Erie, and Warren, Pennsylvania, in the south—to provide needed postsecondary education for the whole western portion of New York's Southern Tier and Pennsylvania's northwestern region.

The Cattaraugus County campus has served Cattaraugus and Allegany counties in New York and McKean and Potter counties in northern Pennsylvania since 1976. Initially housed in a former elementary school, it moved to the center of the city in 1983, enhancing the college's visibility while providing an economic stimulus for downtown Olean. In 2002, with strong support from area businesses and civic leaders, the college invested $31 million in campus improvements.

Credit and noncredit courses and training services for business and industry are offered at the North County Center, located thirty miles north of Jamestown in Dunkirk.

The college has created distinct programs to serve a number of different groups. For example, while maintaining an open admissions policy, the college has assured itself of high quality in its student body by means of its Unified Student Assistance program, which guarantees a full resident tuition scholarship to students in the college's service area who graduate in the top twenty percent of their high school classes. Many of the scholarship students enroll in the honors program once they arrive at JCC. And College Connections, JCC's concurrent enrollment program that began in 1998, enrolls high school students to better prepare them for collegiate success. It is one of only eighty-four US collegiate programs fully accredited by the National Alliance of Concurrent Enrollment Partnerships and it serves nearly 2,000 students annually in nearly forty school districts.

JCC engages in major community outreach programs that focus on economic development, personal

Several buildings have been upgraded or constructed in the past decade.

enrichment, and cultural awareness. An example of its commitment to workforce development in the Chautauqua-Cattaraugus region is the Manufacturing Technology Institute on the Jamestown campus. In response to a call for customized technical training and pre-employment skill development, the Institute opened in 2001, co-sponsored by the Manufacturers Association of the Southern Tier. A similar facility has opened on the Cattaraugus County campus, providing instruction in advanced manufacturing skills.

JCC is renowned throughout the region for providing theater and music programming for students as well as community members. Its galleries feature an active exhibition schedule and a permanent col-

The college theater group presenting *Anything Goes*.

Soccer, one of the many sports JCC students play at both
intercollegiate and intramural levels.

lection reflecting a broad perspective of genres. In addition, the famous Roger Tory Peterson Institute of Natural History is housed on the Jamestown campus.

Athletics play a significant role in developing students' skills and talents, and JCC benefits from the contributions its scholar athletes have made in several intercollegiate sports. JCC has competed with pride at regional and national levels as a member of Region III of the National Junior College Athletic Association.

Many of JCC's programs, such as Nursing and Occupational Therapy Assistant, have been accredited by national disciplinary organizations. JCC is especially proud of the recognition it received from the New York State Division of Veterans' Affairs for the training it offers veterans and other eligible persons.

Today's JCC enrolls nearly five thousand students and residents who have come to one of the college's four sites to meet their particular educational needs: to qualify for immediate employment in the region, to fulfill one of the college's associate degree programs designed for seamless transfer, to develop improved job skills, or simply to acquire greater knowledge. The college offers students AA, AS, and AAS degrees in thirty-four areas as well as eighteen certificate programs. Over forty percent of graduates transfer to four-year colleges and universities throughout the nation, and JCC currently has transfer agreements with more than forty colleges and universities. It is in the rich diversity of its programs, including residence halls that accommodate 340 students in apartment suites, that JCC meets the many needs of its regional communities, a record of service that it has proudly built during the past six decades.

NIAGARA COUNTY COMMUNITY COLLEGE

In 1959, Edward Pawenski, a member of the Niagara County Board of Supervisors from North Tonawanda, conducted a study of New York State's community colleges that convinced him of the need for a community college in Niagara County. But his colleagues were reluctant. In response, community members organized a series of meetings to discuss the issue and convince the Board of Supervisors to begin formal discussions about creating a school to educate students in the liberal arts, technology, and vocational trades. Following considerable debate, the board voted to create a school in Niagara County.

The newly created institution encountered a series of challenges that it addressed in 1962; the college required staff, faculty, a president, a budget, and, most importantly, a central location. First, the trustees selected Dr. Ernest Notar, then dean of the Erie County Technical Institute, as president. Dr. Notar brought with him both invaluable expertise and experience in the region.

Then the college purchased the Union Carbide Metals building in Niagara Falls to house the new school. Formerly the office of the old Shredded Wheat plant, the building served as the primary location in the first years of the college. As a result of the

The new campus's Lewis Library and Notar Administration buildings.

289

building's past, the college quickly earned the nickname "Nabisco Tech." Local businesses and industries donated materials, such as books for the library, laboratory equipment, and office furnishings to ease the formation process.

On September 30, 1963, Dr. Notar symbolically unlocked the front door of the new campus center and classes commenced. Initially, Niagara County Community College offered a variety of programs that prepared students for either further higher education or vocational trades in local businesses and industries including Accounting, Electrical Technology, Liberal Arts and Sciences, and Secretarial Sciences. Increasing enrollment necessitated the acquisition of several more buildings: the former Third Street School, rooms at the Parkway Inn, and a house on Buffalo Avenue, later nicknamed "Moose Hall" because of a large moose head found there.

The college soon outgrew its site in Niagara Falls, and in 1964 the Board of Trustees began searching for a permanent, more centrally located site. Within two years, the board decided on a prime location in Sanborn, ten miles to the east, halfway between the two major cities in the county, Niagara Falls and Lockport. Attended by Governor Nelson A. Rockefeller, the groundbreaking ceremonies for a planned eight-building campus took place in September 1970. In spring 1973, classes began at the new campus with an expanded curriculum, including Criminal Justice, Surgical Technology, and Computer-Aided Drafting. To meet the needs of nontraditional students, the board authorized an Evening and Extension Division to provide more accessible class schedules for working adults.

Over the next several decades, NCCC's educational and outreach programs increasingly connected the college to the community. In an effort to stimulate regional economies, in 1981 the New York State Legislature authorized special aid to colleges that provided programs related to local businesses. In response, NCCC instituted the Corporate Training program that directly connected students to employment opportunities in Niagara County. By 1985, a total of four thousand workers in local industries were being assisted by college programs, including

The college's Theatre Arts program offers plays to the campus and regional community.

The college's Horticulture and Enology programs teach students skills needed throughout the largely rural region.

the manufacturing leader in the county, the Harrison Radiator Division of General Motors. Established in 1985, the college's Small Business Development Center provided management, marketing, and technical assistance to existing local businesses and entrepreneurs. By making tutoring available and opening classes to the public, the college continued to meet the diverse educational needs of county residents.

Continued growth prompted additional construction. In 2001, ground was broken for a new addition to the Ernest Notar Building. In 2004 the college opened the Mathematics Engineering Science Achievement (MESA) Center to provide academic enrichment to underprepared students in career programs that require mathematics. Further encouraging the community to engage in education, NCCC constructed the Student Village College Suites to accommodate students who lived further from the college and who wanted to experience collegiate life. And the college's seven-hundred-seat theater is the venue for a wide variety of musical and theatrical performances.

Today, NCCC offers more than seventy degree and certificate programs that prepare students for further higher education and connect them to local, national, and international employment opportunities. NCCC directly supports the area's largest current economic ventures through its programs in Engineering Studies, as well as a range of different aspects of the hospitality industry, such as Baking and Pastry Arts, Culinary Arts, the Craft Beverage Industry, and Hospitality.

To enhance the hospitality programs, NCCC opened the Niagara Falls Culinary Institute in downtown Niagara Falls to 350 students in 2012. This is where students learn to master the culinary arts and other hospitality and tourism–related disciplines. The facility boasts state-of-the-art teaching kitchens/laboratories and features a student-run exhibition kitchen, restaurant, pastry shop, and delicatessen. The dining facilities showcase the students' cooking techniques

State-of-the-art kitchens in the Niagara Falls Culinary Institute.

with elegant presentations. Other highlights include a culinary theater with a full demonstration kitchen for faculty and visiting guest chefs/speakers, a culinary-themed Barnes & Noble college bookstore, a wine boutique, and exhibition space.

Additionally, NFCI houses a community kitchen that offers noncredit classes as well as entertainment

The Village College Suites, a 308-bed complex opened in 2008.

and continuing education programs. The Wegmans Community Kitchen includes professional cookware and equipment. A kids' corner is attached to the kitchen, allowing families to participate in classes, prepare a meal together, and share their meal in the attached dining room. In addition, there is a Small Business Development Center and incubator on the second floor that provides outreach and support to area businesses.

In 2012, Niagara County Community College celebrated its fiftieth anniversary. From its inception, it has offered education and training that meets the needs of Niagara County by the timely creation of new programs, each marked by a constancy of excellence. This record of service to both the regional economy and the area's community life constitutes the foundation upon which the college confidently looks to build in the future.

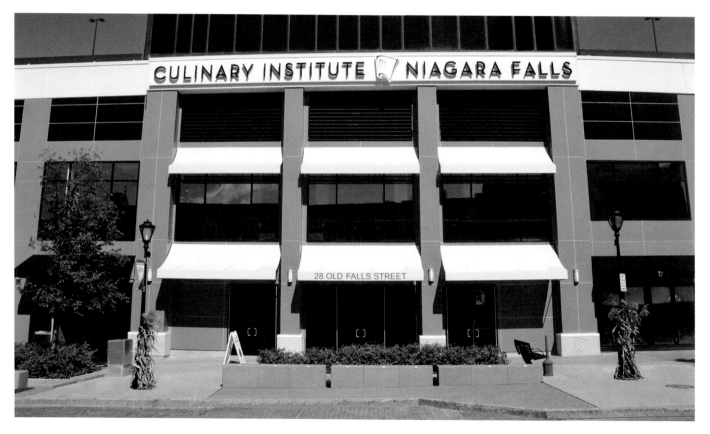

The Culinary Institute in downtown Niagara Falls, with its restaurant that is open to the public.

CONCLUDING THOUGHTS

W. Bruce Leslie and Kenneth P. O'Brien

The coeditors of this volume came to SUNY straight from doctoral programs in the fall of 1970, when the system was in the midst of its historic expansion, and we have been privileged to be participant-observers of the past forty-six years of the evolution of America's largest comprehensive system of higher education. Our professional careers have been conjoined for more than a half century, beginning one fall afternoon in 1964 when we shared the same football field at halftime, members of the marching bands of rival colleges.

As modern American historians in the same department, we have codesigned and cotaught courses together and supported one another professionally and personally as colleagues and friends. We have each written about the history of American higher education and served, with former interim chancellor John Clark, as coeditors of *SUNY at Sixty*. For those reasons, and others, we are deeply grateful to our faculty and professional staff colleagues, our students, and our fellow New York taxpayers who have supported SUNY and have provided so rich an educational environment in which we, and so many others, have been able to hone the skills necessary to

help fulfill the mission of this great experiment that is American public higher education.

Our understanding, then, of SUNY's history is both deeply personal and intensely professional. What we hope this volume provides, in parts and in sum, is an introduction to one of the most complex organizations of the last half century, the State University of New York. As we indicated in the introduction, the early SUNY was a pastiche formed from what was New York's state-supported educational institutional parts bin: teachers' colleges, technical institutes, specialized colleges, and contract colleges, which together enrolled no more than thirty thousand students.

SUNY was forged in the immediate post-WWII era, under intense pressure from a coalition of groups that had faced discrimination in admissions from New York's private colleges and professional schools and from veterans who, funded by the GI Bill, were storming the campus gates only to find that New York State offered little readily available public higher education. Once established, SUNY grew far beyond the compromises its proponents were forced to make at its creation. From that fractious birth has evolved a system of sixty-four campuses, a bewilder-

ing variety of institutions, created over the decades to meet almost every possible need residents of New York State might have for postsecondary education.

By its sixtieth anniversary SUNY as a system had achieved a large degree of stability, with campuses spread across the state, a growing presence online, millions of alumni, and tens of thousands of employees who helped educate over 450,000 students a year. Its research grants totaled almost a billion dollars annually, and the national reputation of several campuses indicated an increase in the quality of teaching, research productivity, and service that was the envy of many other state-supported systems.

But if SUNY had achieved a large degree of structural stability by 2009, it had done so with an unenviable record of central administrative instability, with seven chancellors (including interim appointments) in the preceding fifteen years. Without strong chancellors, the lines between policy and implementation blurred for several activist members of the Board of Trustees; campuses too often seized a larger share of control over the decisions that affected them; and system initiatives, such as Mission Review I and II, each designed to bring systemwide coordination with specific targets set for each campus, became the occasion for almost endless rounds of negotiation. At times SUNY seemed to be a collection of campuses united only by annual budget requests to New York State. By the turn of the twenty-first century, educational politics, at least on the system level, appeared to reflect the cultural politics of the larger culture, driven by mandates that sought to graft a business model onto public higher education. Whether that was the business model followed by Enron or Apple was rarely made clear and, if Apple, whether it was the corporation's vaunted reputation for innovation or its East Asian employment practices that provided the model.

SUNY was hardly the only public university system that faced new challenges to its legitimacy. By the end of the first decade of the twenty-first century, many state politicians had redirected their ire from public schools to public higher education. Usually, but not exclusively, articulated by more conservative politicians, they demanded greater accountability, greater evidence of success, and in some cases, greater control over the collegiate curricula that was funded, to a decreasing extent, by public tax dollars.

Academic expertise became suspect, often dismissed as driven by bias and self-interest. The accusations directed at the academy knew few disciplinary bounds: literature was losing sight of the great books; history was too biased toward multicultural readings of the past; biology was suspect since its foundation had been laid by nineteenth-century evolutionary biologists; and climatologists were obviously lying about human agency for global warming. Most humanities and social science disciplines were assumed to be dominated by liberals who, it was charged, excluded conservative intellectuals from their midst.

It was a time when belief was all too easily substituted for knowledge, and, in the fallout, what many regarded as one of the greatest contributions of nineteenth-century American society, the public land-grant university, was increasingly under sustained attack. So too were all public colleges, with little regard for the variety of their teaching, research, and service environments. Politicians slashed public higher education budgets, claiming that the benefits offered to students were solely private, and hence the students and their families should bear greater shares of the cost. While the details, and the extent, of the resulting disinvestment in public higher education varied state by state, the general pattern was nationwide. Fortunately, SUNY was not one of the worst cases, and, even more fortunately, New York's leadership protected SUNY students from the steeper tuition increases their counterparts suffered elsewhere.

We must remember that SUNY was—and remains—a product of state politics. Even during the "glory days," it was Governor Nelson A. Rockefeller who had almost single-handedly committed the state to build and support a great state university, a political act of both courage and vision. Twenty years later, Chancellor Wharton engineered a series of reforms designed to free the system from many of the rules governing all state agencies. SUNY had competed with every other state agency in the annual budget cycle for ever more precious public dollars, especially in years of economic slowdowns. And twenty years after the reform legislation had passed, Chancellor Robert King, who had been New York State's director of the budget immediately before his appointment as chancellor, once noted that his major budget objective was to move the State University of New York up the ladder of state budget priorities until it was securely ensconced one rung above the Department of Motor Vehicles.

The long-term process of state "disinvestment" in public higher education that began in the 1980s accelerated markedly in the first decade of the new century with, first, the economic downturn in 2001, then the Great Recession of 2008. New York's reliance on Wall Street bonuses for an unusually high portion of its personal income tax base meant that the fiscal impact of these events, particularly the latter, were especially brutal for SUNY and CUNY budgets, as the state budgets with reduced funding that passed in the spring often were cut again during the same budget year.

Strategic planning.

This then was the state of SUNY when Nancy L. Zimpher accepted the offer to serve as its twelfth chancellor and began her tenure in June 2009. She found SUNY beleaguered by a flurry of recent state budget reductions, out of favor with some of the state's political leadership, occasionally the subject of very public criticism by several members of the Board of Trustees, and searching for leadership. To begin to combat both the external and the internal issues, Chancellor Zimpher launched a three-month whirlwind tour of the state, visiting each of SUNY's sixty-four campuses, and at each stop she met both with members of the campus community and with regional political, business, and economic leaders. With extensive notes in hand, she and her staff then created a process for developing a new strategic plan for the university.

While strategic planning in the first year of a presidency, or, in this case, a chancellery, may be found on page one in the "new administrator" handbook, the approach adopted in this case was distinct. First, approximately two hundred participants, drawn from both SUNY campuses and the larger community, volunteered to meet six times

over six months in locations spread across the state, from Stony Brook on Long Island to Plattsburgh near the Canadian border, from New York City on the Hudson to Buffalo on Lake Erie. Each of the meetings focused on a specific issue facing the larger society.

The final plan, "The Power of SUNY," should be read as a reboot of SUNY's relationship with the

STRATEGIC PLAN
2010 & BEYOND

the Power of SUNY
The State University of New York

public. Adopting the spirit of the "Wisconsin Plan" and the service ethic of land-grant universities, SUNY committed itself to developing and using knowledge that addressed the critical issues facing society: providing more adequate high-quality health care, generating and using energy more efficiently, enhancing entrepreneurial abilities, supporting vibrant community life, stemming the leaks in the educational pipeline, and working effectively in a globalizing world. Each of the "Six Big Ideas" contained a special note termed "Diversity Counts," a fitting commitment for a system founded to combat discrimination, and each had a working group pursuing its goals, with a senior administrator responsible for progress. Together they formed the overarching commitment: "to revitalize New York's economy and enhance the quality of life for all its citizens."

This became the model for SUNY, the public university, as it requested the financial and other supports necessary to fulfill its promise. The focused commitment to economic development helps explain the organization of our book, which follows the pattern of New York's ten economic development regions, each with a guiding council, often with SUNY leaders at the helm. The academic communities across SUNY have become energized in seeking new ways to provide the expertise, the educational opportunities, and the leadership necessary for a more competitive New York in the next decades of the century.

This commitment to serving society's needs is apparent for each of SUNY's campus sectors. The research centers—the four university centers, the medical schools and associated health science centers, and the College of Environmental Science and Forestry—received additional funding through a variety of grants, tuition increases, and state-sponsored

programs, such as STARTUP New York, to support the new economic development initiatives. The university colleges, which had grown from their educator preparation roots, as is evident in this book, began to reach back into the communities to work even more closely with the educators in their region to help stem the tragic loss of human capital that resulted from the leaky educational pipeline. SUNY's colleges of technology began to work even more closely with regional businesses and organizations, as did the thirty community colleges that expanded their close ties to the businesses and agencies of

Chancellor Nancy L. Zimpher

their immediate regions. Every SUNY campus sought to work more closely with organizations and institutions in their area to provide the education and training demanded for a more effective workforce and by more engaged communities.

In addition, the system also looked inward; another element of the strategic plan was titled "Building a Better SUNY." It committed SUNY to carefully examining how well it managed its resources and delivered on its promises, both implicit and explicit, to students and other constituencies and, most pointedly, to reporting its shortcomings and successes publicly in an easily accessible format. As the relationship with the state and external constituencies became more transactional (i.e., providing something

tangible in return for the investment in public higher education), SUNY undertook a number of system-wide initiatives that promised to make the system more efficient, more flexible, and more effective in its operations. While we don't have the space here to discuss them all, the long list of initiatives created after 2009 includes Seamless Transfer, SUNY Report Card, SUNY Excels, SUNY Works, local Cradle to Career networks, Early College High Schools, Open SUNY, Shared Services, Investment Fund with performance-based budgeting, Access to Completion, Smart Track, TeachNY, Networks of Excellence, and Degree Works, among others.

In 2010, a new word appeared as these initiatives were rolled out, "systemness." Newly minted, it spoke to the possibility of leveraging the strength of the individual campuses to a larger common purpose, and to common system policies and procedures where appropriate. How has it worked? The "Seamless Transfer" of students between SUNY institutions provides an excellent example. Although this had been system policy since 1972 and the subject of seven Board of Trustees resolutions, practice had failed to follow policy, too often resulting in students being caught between conflicting demands of parallel programs as they moved from one campus to another. In December 2012, the board returned to the issue, but this time the SUNY provost and his staff had developed a process that drove curricular revisions for many SUNY degree programs and academic majors.

To implement the policy, the Provost's Office began by calling together faculty groups, discipline by discipline, to identify the material in the discipline that students needed to master in the first two years of a program in order to succeed—and finish on time—in the last two. Face-to-face meetings characterized the first process, which involved four hundred faculty from the campuses who created more than thirty disciplinary transfer paths. But, as many faculty felt that their programs had not been represented in this process, new technologies to conduct electronic meetings were employed to involve more than nine hundred disciplinary faculty from every campus in subsequent discussions. Working during the spring semester, faculty groups recommended more than fifty disciplinary transfer paths, which became embedded in each of the programs SUNY offers in that discipline and which applied to more than ninety-five percent of the students who transfer annually across SUNY.

The development of these paths to foster the Seamless Transfer policy illustrates "systemness" at work. Instead of leaving decisions regarding transfer credit to disciplinary faculty on each campus, as tradition dictated, the systemwide faculty groups had created what amounted to core curricula for each of the disciplines. While none of this has been accomplished without pushback from a number of faculty, in the end systemwide practice is now aligned with system policy.

In sum, SUNY has undergone significant changes since 2009, both in its outreach to external constituencies and in the way that it conducts its traditional business, the education of almost a half million students annually, the creation of new knowledge and ways of understanding both human and natural phenomena, and the provider of services to its regional communities.

One result of these initiatives has been the passage of NYSUNY 2020, which provided a predictable

Construction at the Jacobs School of Medicine and Biomedical Sciences in downtown Buffalo, funded by the NYSUNY 2020 Challenge Grant program and other sources, including private philanthropy.

funding pattern from New York State. In the past, state political leaders had been reluctant to raise SUNY and CUNY tuition charges, except in periods of economic downturns when state tax revenues fell. At such times, tuition could increase suddenly and dramatically to make up for the most recent cut in state support. The effect of this pattern, although more muted in New York than in most other states, had been to shift the burden of instructional costs for SUNY from the state to the students and their families. This privatization of the cost of public higher education has been increasingly financed through loans. Even so, SUNY tuition charges in 2009 (other than those for community colleges, which were funded differently) were among the lowest in the Northeast for public colleges and universities.

NYSUNY 2020 reframed the budget model by allowing modest tuition increases in each of the next five years. Additionally, the state committed to a "maintenance of effort," which meant that state support would not be decreased. Even with the tuition increases since 2011, SUNY's tuition and fees (again, except for those charged by the community colleges) remained among the lowest in the region. Equally important, the neediest students in New York received significant financial support through New York's Tuition Assistance Program, which provided over a billion dollars a year to students in both the state's public and private colleges based solely on financial need and the expansion of the federal Pell Grant program, which funneled another $2 billion of direct aid to a half million New York students. In short, college access had been guaranteed for the neediest students despite higher tuition rates. While NYSUNY 2020 was not renewed in the 2016 state budget, there was a commitment to increase SUNY's allocation instead.

⸙

The rule for assessing real estate value is "location, location, location." Much the same could be said for SUNY, a system created with the express intention of placing a campus within thirty miles of every New York resident. This volume has featured the stories of SUNY's sixty-four campuses and their historic relationship to their surrounding regions and, in some cases, far beyond. While each of these historical sketches is able to stand alone, they are also chapters in a larger story, the history of the State University of New York. Our reading of that recent history centers on two critical relationships: first, SUNY's relationship to external communities, a relationship that has been refocused with greater attention paid to undertaking research, providing services, creating knowledge, and generating the human capital necessary for economic health and vibrant communities; and second, SUNY's internal negotiation between system goals and individual campus needs and ambitions. Each of these relationships is fraught with inevitable tensions, but resolution through healthy debate has generated the initiatives that further fostered change. And, not so incidentally, it has provided a new system of public accountability.

"Systemness" is the catchword that captures much of this dynamic. It means, according to Chancellor Zimpher's 2012 State of the University Address, "the coordination of multiple components that when working together create a network of activity that is more powerful than any action of individual parts on their own," or as the chancellor has termed it more succinctly elsewhere, SUNY's "collective impact." By its commitment to meet the varied public needs for postsecondary education, both on campuses and off, SUNY has dramatically increased its value to the regions in which its campuses are sited, to its students who will be able to move toward degree completion more expeditiously, and to the state upon which SUNY relies for direct support. In short, as a system, SUNY is closer today to fulfilling its historic mission: "To learn, to search, to serve."

ACKNOWLEDGMENTS

Our work has been inspired by the belief that SUNY has often failed to grab the hearts and minds of New Yorkers. We hope that this volume convinces the citizens and taxpayers of New York State that they have built an extraordinary institution, one that is critical to our future as an economy and civil society. Even we, professors in SUNY for over four decades, have been amazed by the scope and facilities that compose this system. We hope that you come away similarly impressed.

It has been a daunting task. No wonder there have been few attempts to communicate the complexity of state systems, especially of America's largest comprehensive university system, to broader audiences through pictorial histories. Despite their role as engines of the American experiment in mass higher education, the sagas of state university systems are largely invisible to the publics that support and depend upon them.

We found very few models. The nearest equivalent to this volume was the brainchild of Clark Kerr, the renowned president of the University of California system and author of the 1960 Master Plan that helped shape SUNY and other state systems. He commissioned famed photographer Ansel Adams to produce a volume intended to be part of the celebrations for the university's centennial in 1968. Adams and his coauthor Nancy Newhall duly completed a beautiful volume, *Fiat Lux: The University of California*, in 1967. But, as Kerr later commented, his term began and ended the same way—"fired with enthusiasm." His abrupt termination by recently elected Governor Ronald Reagan meant that the book was not promoted with enthusiasm. Consequently, it was largely forgotten, and Adams's precious prints were lost for more than four decades. Their rediscovery later inspired the production of a facsimile edition in 2012. This time the Regents enthusiastically distributed over ten thousand copies.

While we cannot compete with Ansel Adams's visual sensibilities, we do take pride in having depicted sixty-four units, rather than the mere nine that comprise the University of California. And while New York cannot match the grandeur of California's coastline, SUNY's campuses are placed within New York State's sometimes spectacular, often beautiful, and always varied natural environment.

SUNY has made one previous effort to tell its story to the public. *Sixty-four Campuses: The State University of New York to 1985* was a useful but modest production, limited to one small black-and-white picture and short text per campus. The modesty of the production reflected the financial straits of New York State and its university in that period. With the New York State economy and SUNY in far healthier condition, it is clearly time to tell the story more colorfully and fully, and we thank Chancellor Nancy L. Zimpher for initiating and supporting this effort to convey SUNY's achievements to a wider audience.

For those who wish to read further, either about the individual campuses, the SUNY system, or about other state university systems, we refer you to our extensive bibliography in *SUNY at Sixty*, which we edited with former interim chancellor John Clark. For works published since 2010 the campus websites are the best reference point. We draw your attention to volumes emanating from SUNY's annual conference, which has become a major event in American higher education, edited by Jason Lane and D. Bruce Johnstone and published by SUNY Press: *Universities and Colleges as Economic Drivers* (2012); *Higher Education Systems 3.0* (2013); *Building a Smarter University* (2014); and *Higher Education Reconsidered* (2015).

We have not worked in scholarly isolation. We have many debts to acknowledge. The first and most important is to Dr. Kimberly Schutte, former visiting professor at SUNY Brockport, whose research and writing gave the project momentum when we were otherwise occupied. Many of her words grace the text, and her name on the cover recognizes her critical role. The second is to Ricky Tomczak, a graduate of SUNY Brockport and currently a doctoral student at SUNY Stony Brook, who brought his interest in architecture and in the system that was educating him to bear on the campuses of western New York.

And telling the tale of a complex system with sixty-four units and nearly a half million students has required the assistance of well over a hundred colleagues on SUNY campuses who took time from busy schedules to answer our persistent requests for text and pictures.

We particularly want to thank those who wrote text that we could adapt to the parameters of the book and to our voice: Margaret Devereaux, Cayuga Community College; Gina Brightwell, Clinton Community College; Jennifer Micale, Broome Community College; Kimberly MacLeod, SUNY Delhi; Lenore Friend, Finger Lakes Community College; Mary Donohue, Fulton-Montgomery Community College; Donna Rae Sutherland, Genesee Community Collge; Anthony Hoppa, SUNY Geneseo; Bridgette Johnson, Jamestown Community College; Maryellen Keefe, Maritime College; Nancy Murillo, Orange County Community College; Douglas Skopp, SUNY Plattsburgh; and Jane M. Subramanian, SUNY Potsdam.

And we would like to thank all those from the campuses who submitted copies of text and photos:

Adirondack Community College: *Teresa Ronning, Library Division Chair, and Lucas Meyers, Communications Director*

University at Albany: *Geoff Williams and Greg Wiedeman, former and current Archivists*

Alfred State College: *Joseph Petrick, Technical Services Coordinator*

College of Ceramics at Alfred University: *Mark A. Smith, Director of Scholes Library, and Dr. Doreen Edwards, Acting Vice President for Statutory Affairs and Dean, School of Engineering*

University at Binghamton: *Yvonne J. Deligato, Binghamton University Archivist*

The College at Brockport: *Charles Cowling, College Archivist*

Broome Community College: *Jennifer Micale, Office of Marketing and Communications*

Buffalo State College: *Daniel DiLandro, Buffalo State Archivist and Special Collections Librarian*

University at Buffalo: *Amy Vilz, University Archivist, and James A. "Beau" Willis, former Vice President*

SUNY Canton: *Michelle L. Currier, Director, Southworth Library Learning Commons, and Rachel Santose, College Archivist*

Cayuga County Community College: *Margaret Devereaux, Library Director*

Clinton Community College: *Mary Ann Weiglhofer, Library Director, and Gina M. Schwizer Brightwell, Associate Director of College Relations*

SUNY Cobleskill: *Lois Goblet, Chief Advancement Officer*

Columbia-Greene Community College: *James R. Campion, President, and Allen Kovler, Director of Public Relations*

Corning Community College: *Amy Dibble, Librarian and Archivist*

Cortland College: *Henry J. Steck, SUNY Distinguished Service Professor, and Mike Besani, Public Relations*

SUNY Delhi: *Kimberly MacLeod, APR, Director of Communications and New Media*

Downstate Medical Center: *Cheryl M. Marriott, Coordinator of Archives and Special Collections, and Ellen Watson, Assistant VP for Institutional Advancement*

Dutchess Community College: *Judi Stokes and Jason Miller, Office of Community and Public Relations*

Empire State College: *David Henahan, Director of Communications*

SUNY College of Environmental Science and Forestry: *Wendy P. Osborne, Art Director, and Stephen P. Weiter, former Director of College Libraries*

Erie Community College: *Matthew Best, Senior College Librarian*

Farmingdale State College: *Karen Gelles, Librarian*

Fashion Institute of Technology: *Loretta Lawrence Keane, VP for Communications and External Relations, and Carol Leven, Assistant Vice President of Communications*

Finger Lakes Community College: *Lenore L. Friend, Director of Public Relations and Community Affairs*

SUNY Fredonia: *Michael Barone, Director of Marketing and Communications, and Lisa Eikenburg, Assistant Director Marketing and Communications*

Fulton-Montgomery Community College: *Professor Mary Donohue, Director of the Evans Library*

Genesee Community College: *Cindy Francis, Collection Development Librarian, and Donna Rae Sutherland and Lori Ivison Sutch, Marketing Communications*

SUNY Geneseo: *Liz Argentieri, Special Collections Librarian; Brian A. Bennett and Anthony Hoppa, College Communications; Keith Walters, Campus Photographer; and Becky Glass, Assistant to the President*

Herkimer County Community College: *Rebecca Ruffing, Director of Public Relations*

Hudson Valley Community College: *Brenda L. Hazard, Library Director, and Debby Gardner, Office of Communications and Marketing*

Jamestown Community College: *Bridget Johnson, Community Relations Coordinator*

Jefferson Community College: *Karen A. Carr, Assistant to the President, and Karen Freeman, Marketing and Public Relations*

Maritime College: *Professor Maryellen Keefe, OSU, Humanities Department; and Joseph Williams, Librarian*

Mohawk Valley Community College: *Matthew R. Snyder, Director Marketing and Communications*

Monroe Community College: *Mark McBride, Director of Library Services; Rosanna Yule, Assistant Director Marketing and Communications; and Eric Johannisson, Archives and Records Management*

Morrisville State College: *Sara Way, Assistant Vice President for Institutional Advancement*

Nassau Community College: *Professor Phyllis P. Kurland and Professor Linda Gorman, Archive Librarians*

SUNY New Paltz: *Shelly A. Wright, Chief of Staff and VP for Communication*

Niagara County Community College: *Gina L. Beam, Director of Public Relations, and Karen Ferington, Archive Librarian*

North Country Community College: *Brian O'Connor, Director of Library Services, and Meredith Chapman, Admissions*

Old Westbury: *Laura Anker, American Studies, and Michael Kinane, Assistant to the President for Advancement*

College at Oneonta: *Heather Beach, Archive Librarian*

Onondaga Community College: *Amy Kremenek, Vice President, Human Resources and External Relations*

College of Optometry: *Elaine Wells, Library Director*

Orange County Community College: *Nancy Murillo, Archives Librarian*

Oswego State: *Elizabeth Young, Coordinator of Archives and Special Collections; Tim Nekritz, Public Affairs; and Rose Throop, Publications Department*

Plattsburgh State: *Debra Kimok, Special Collections Librarian, and Douglas R. Skopp, SUNY Distinguished Teaching Professor of History Emeritus*

SUNY Potsdam: *Jane M. Subramanian, Archivist Emerita*

Purchase College: *Patrick Callahan, Director, Purchase College Library*

Rockland Community College: *Tzipora Reitman, Campus Communications; Jamie Kempton, Correspondent, Campus Communications; and Collette Fournier, Photographer, Campus Communications*

Schenectady County Community College: *Nancy Heller and Laura Welch, Archivists/Historians, and Heather Meaney, Public Relations Office*

Stony Brook University: *Kristen J. Nyitray, Head, Special Collections and University Archives and University Archivist, Frank Melville Jr. Memorial Library*

Suffolk County Community College: *Professor Kevin McCoy, Ammerman Library Technical Services*

Sullivan County Community College: *Karin Hilgersom, President*

SUNY Polytechnic Institute: *Barbara Grimes, Associate Librarian, and Jerry Gretzinger, Vice President for Strategic Communications and Public Relations*

Tompkins Cortland Community College: *Gregg Kiehl, Library Director*

Ulster County Community College: *President Donald C. Katt, and B. Robert Johnson, Director of Printing and Graphics*

Upstate Medical University: *Cara Howe, Curator*

Westchester Community College: *Patrick Hennessey, College Relations Director, and Edward Tatton III, Publications Assistant*

We sincerely hope that we have not overlooked anyone who materially contributed to this volume, though that is probably a vain wish in such a complex organizational task. And we know that there are numerous archivists, photographers, and others who have preserved the historical memories on the campuses whose names are unknown to us. Archives truly are the engine rooms of history.

Finally, we thank those at State University of New York Press with whom we have seemed to spend more time than our partners. To Donna Dixon and James Peltz, Co-Directors, we offer our heartfelt thanks for the constant support and quick answers to our questions. We thank Dana Foote for her painstaking attention in rooting out the errors in our text. And finally, our gratitude to Laurie Searl, who has virtually lived this book with us, for her acute visual sensibilities.

And on a personal note, thanks to our partners Tessa Harding and Diane O'Brien for their forbearance as we disappeared mentally and physically to the calls of the book for nearly three years. And our apologies to friends and relatives from whom we stole valuable time.

W. Bruce Leslie, Metfield, England
Kenneth P. O'Brien, Brockport, New York
July 2016

ILLUSTRATION CREDITS

All photos and illustrations courtesy of the State University of New York, with the exception of the following:

Page 1, Gary Gold Photography

Pages 11, 12, 90, 91 92, 151 (lower right), 152 (lower), 210 (upper), 234, 258, Library of Congress, Prints & Photographs Division.

Page 9, 33, 54, 89, 121, 149, 177, 209, 233, 257, iStock.

Pages 55, 92 (lower left) 122, 123, 150, 178 (lower), 179, 180, 234, 235 (lower) 236, 259, Wikimedia Commons/Public Domain.

Page 56, Fred Hsu/Wikimedia Commons/CC-BY-SA-3.0.

Page 151 (top left), Wknight94/Wikimedia Commons/CC-BY-SA-3.0.

Page 152 (top), George Robert Gilbert/Wikimedia Commons/CC-BY-SA-2.0.

Page 210, Kenneth C. Zirkel/Wikimedia Commons/CC-BY-SA-3.0.

Page 211 (top), Plutor/Wikimedia Commons/CC-BY-2.0.

Page 235 (top), Stephen Schweitzer/Wikimedia Commons/CC-BY-SA-3.0.

Page 294, Joseph Trumpler.

SUNY ADIRONDACK

UNIVERSITY AT ALBANY
State University of New York

 SUNY SULLIVAN

Plattsburgh
STATE UNIVERSITY OF NEW YORK

BINGHAMTON UNIVERSITY
STATE UNIVERSITY OF NEW YORK

SUNY ecc

New Paltz
STATE UNIVERSITY OF NEW YORK

 MARITIME COLLEGE
STATE UNIVERSITY OF NEW YORK
1874

 MARITIME COLLEGE
STATE UNIVERSITY OF NEW YORK

Suffolk
COUNTY COMMUNITY COLLEGE

SUNY FREDONIA
Where Success is a Tradition

 Cornell University

SUNY Cortland

 Potsdam
THE STATE UNIVERSITY OF NEW YORK
1816

NCC
NASSAU COMMUNITY COLLEGE

 corning community college
State University of New York

Hudson Valley Community College

 ONONDAGA COMMUNITY COLLEGE

 Delhi
STATE UNIVERSITY of NEW YORK

SUNY ONEONTA

SUNY CANTON

SUNY ORANGE

Alfred State
SUNY College of Technology

TOMPKINS CORTLAND COMMUNITY COLLEGE

 BUFFALO STATE
The State University of New York

MCC
MONROE COMMUNITY COLLEGE

BROOME
COMMUNITY COLLEGE

 NIAGARA COUNTY COMMUNITY COLLEGE
NCCC
STATE UNIVERSITY OF NEW YORK

 STATE UNIVERSITY OF NEW YORK
College of Optometry

 State University of New York
CLINTON Community College

SUNY POLYTECHNIC INSTITUTE

 Stony Brook University

THE SMART PLACE TO START